PEARSON
ReadyUp!™
INTERVENTION

PEARSON

Glenview, Illinois • Boston, Massachusetts • Chandler, Arizona • New York, New York

PEARSON

ISBN-13: 978-0-328-86980-0
ISBN-10: 0-328-86980-5

3 16

PART 1: FOUNDATIONAL SKILLS

PRINT CONCEPTS

RF.K.1.a Follow words from left to right, top to bottom, and page by page.

RF.K.1.b Recognize that spoken words are represented in written language by specific sequences of letters.

RF.K.1.c Understand that words are separated by spaces in print.

RF.K.1.d Recognize and name all upper- and lowercase letters of the alphabet.

PHONOLOGICAL AWARENESS

RF.K.2.a Recognize and produce rhyming words.

RF.K.2.b Count, pronounce, blend, and segment syllables in spoken words.

RF.K.2.c Blend and segment onsets and rimes of single-syllable spoken words.

PHONICS AND WORD RECOGNITION

RF.K.3.b Associate the long and short sounds with the common spellings (graphemes) for the five major vowels.

RF.K.3.c Read common high-frequency words by sight (e.g., the, of, to, you, she, my, is, are, do, does).

RF.K.3.d Distinguish between similarly spelled words by identifying the sounds of the letters that differ.

FLUENCY

RF.K.4 Read emergent-reader texts with purpose and understanding.

PART 2: READING, WRITING, AND LANGUAGE

READING LITERATURE

RL.K.1 With prompting and support, ask and answer questions about key details in a text.

RL.K.4 Ask and answer questions about unknown words in a text.

RL.K.2 With prompting and support, retell familiar stories, including key details.

RL.K.3 With prompting and support, identify characters, settings, and major events in a story.

RL.K.5 Recognize common types of texts (e.g., storybooks, poems).

RL.K.6 With prompting and support, name the author and illustrator of a story and define the role of each in telling the story.

RL.K.7 With prompting and support, describe the relationship between illustrations and the story in which they appear (e.g., what moment in a story an illustration depicts).

READING INFORMATIONAL TEXT

RI.K.1 *With prompting and support, ask and answer questions about key details in a text.*

RI.K.2 *With prompting and support, identify the main topic and retell key details of a text.*

RI.K.4 *With prompting and support, ask and answer questions about unknown words in a text.*

L.K.4 *Determine or clarify the meaning of unknown and multiple-meaning words and phrases based on kindergarten reading and content.*

RI.K.6 *Name the author and illustrator of a text and define the role of each in presenting the ideas or information in a text.*

RI.K.8 *With prompting and support, identify the reasons an author gives to support points in a text.*

RI.K.7 *With prompting and support, describe the relationship between illustrations and the text in which they appear (e.g., what person, place, thing, or idea in the text an illustration depicts).*

RI.K.9 *With prompting and support, identify basic similarities in and differences between two texts on the same topic (e.g., in illustrations, descriptions, or procedures).*

WRITING

W.K.1 Use a combination of drawing, dictating, and writing to compose opinion pieces in which they tell a reader the topic or the name of the book they are writing about and state an opinion or preference about the topic or book (e.g., My favorite book is . . .).

W.K.2 Use a combination of drawing, dictating, and writing to compose informative/ explanatory texts in which they name what they are writing about and supply some information about the topic.

W.K.3 Use a combination of drawing, dictating, and writing to narrate a single event or several loosely linked events, tell about the events in the order in which they occurred, and provide a reaction to what happened.

W.K.8 With guidance and support from adults, recall information from experiences or gather information from provided sources to answer a question.

W.K.5 With guidance and support from adults, respond to questions and suggestions from peers and add details to strengthen writing as needed.

LANGUAGE

L.K.1 Demonstrate command of the conventions of standard English grammar and usage when writing or speaking.

L.K.2 Demonstrate command of the conventions of standard English capitalization, punctuation, and spelling when writing.

L.K.5 With guidance and support from adults, explore word relationships and nuances in word meanings.

TABLE OF CONTENTS

ReadyUp! Intervention Program Overview

Targeted, Flexible Intervention

ReadyUp! Intervention is designed to help teachers target and address students' intervention needs, whether they require minor remediation or intensive instruction.

Targeted Intervention Every lesson is based on Common Core State Standards. Teachers can use the Table of Contents (p. iii) or Skills Trace (p. T10) to quickly find the lessons that correspond to particular grade-level standards or the broader skill concepts their students struggle to master. The program offers flexibility through multiple entry and exit points to accommodate students' differing intervention needs and rates of mastery.

Scaffolded Instruction Lessons are scaffolded in one of two ways, depending on the nature of the skills addressed.

- Discrete skills are scaffolded into small, manageable minilessons for thorough coverage and focused practice.
- Broader skills progress from easier minilessons to harder minilessons, offering a range of entry points for students as well as scaffolded practice to help them develop understanding and demonstrate proficiency.

Data-Driven Assessment Two levels of assessment checks—after discrete minilessons and after a series of related lessons—allow teachers to quickly monitor students' progress throughout the program.

Comprehensive Intervention Coverage in Two Parts

ReadyUp! Intervention offers lessons that cover the spectrum of students' intervention needs, from foundational skills to reading literature, reading informational text, writing, and language.

FOUNDATIONAL SKILLS

PART 1

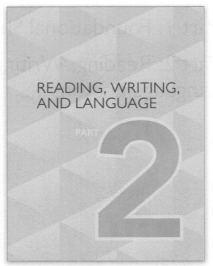

READING, WRITING, AND LANGUAGE

PART 2

Key Elements of Reading Intervention Lessons

Part 1: Foundational Skills Focus The first part of *ReadyUp! Intervention* focuses on the Common Core State Standards (CCSS) Foundational Skills and provides in-depth instruction, practice, and assessment in Print Concepts, Phonological Awareness, Phonics and Word Recognition, and Fluency (including comprehension, oral reading, and vocabulary).

Teacher Pages

Student Pages

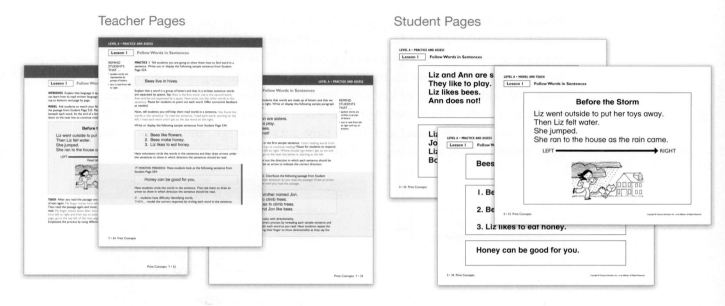

Part 2: Reading, Writing, and Language Focus The second part of *ReadyUp! Intervention* focuses on the Common Core State Standards for Reading Literature, Reading Informational Text, Writing, and Language.

Teacher Pages

Student Pages

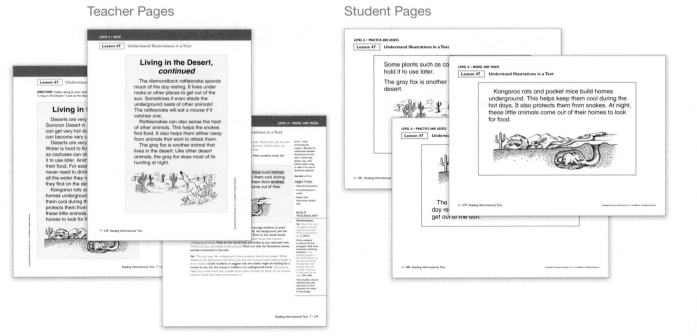

Lesson Overview

Teacher Pages

Format and Features Lessons follow an easy-to-use, consistent format, yet they are designed to be flexible. Each lesson offers multiple entry points, guided practice, independent practice, and progress monitoring to ensure mastery.

Model and Teach The first page of each lesson sets key objectives based on the Common Core State Standards. The Model and Teach page introduces the skill or concept through a reading context. The model, combined with intensive skill instruction across the subsequent lesson pages, reinforces students' understanding of key skills both in isolation *and* in context, helping students transfer skill knowledge to developing reading and writing proficiency. In other words, the Model and Teach page sets the stage, and the three pages of practice scaffold the teaching of the skills that have been introduced.

Introduce section identifies and defines the skill.

Model section and passage help teachers model the skill in context.

Teach section allows teachers to explain, expand on, and clarify the initial skill instruction.

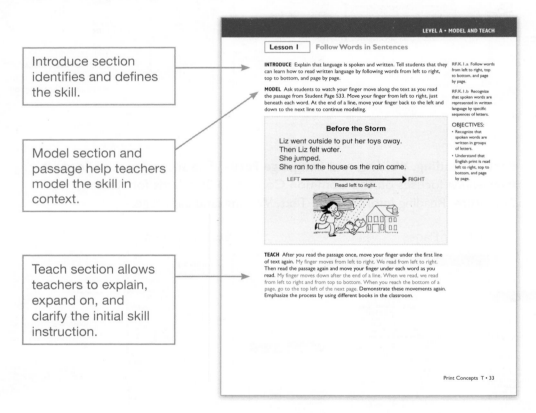

Practice and Assess Each lesson includes Practice and Assess pages that follow a gradual release of responsibility model to scaffold learning. Most lessons include three Practice and Assess pages that either increase in difficulty or teach different aspects of a complex skill. Routines, activities, and assessment (Monitor Progress and Independent Practice) are included at point of use within each lesson.

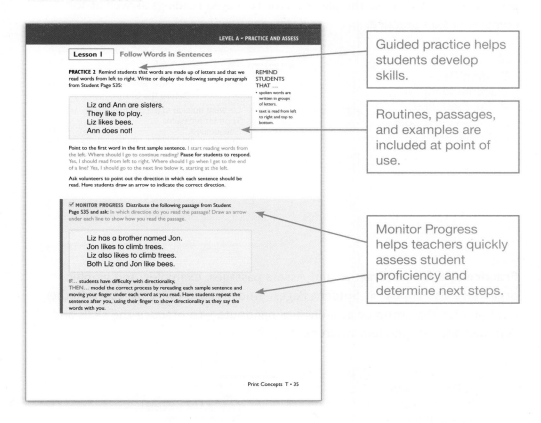

LEVEL A • PRACTICE AND ASSESS

Lesson 1 Follow Words in Sentences

PRACTICE 2 Remind students that words are made up of letters and that we read words from left to right. Write or display the following sample paragraph from Student Page S35:

> Liz and Ann are sisters.
> They like to play.
> Liz likes bees.
> Ann does not!

Point to the first word in the first sample sentence. I start reading words from the left. Where should I go to continue reading? **Pause for students to respond.** Yes, I should read from left to right. Where should I go when I get to the end of a line? Yes, I should go to the next line below it, starting at the left.

Ask volunteers to point out the direction in which each sentence should be read. Have students draw an arrow to indicate the correct direction.

✔ **MONITOR PROGRESS** Distribute the following passage from Student Page S35 and ask: In which direction do you read the passage? Draw an arrow under each line to show how you read the passage.

> Liz has a brother named Jon.
> Jon likes to climb trees.
> Liz also likes to climb trees.
> Both Liz and Jon like bees.

IF... students have difficulty with directionality,
THEN... model the correct process by rereading each sample sentence and moving your finger under each word as you read. Have students repeat the sentence after you, using their finger to show directionality as they say the words with you.

REMIND STUDENTS THAT ...
• spoken words are written in groups of letters.
• text is read from left to right and top to bottom.

Print Concepts T • 35

Guided practice helps students develop skills.

Routines, passages, and examples are included at point of use.

Monitor Progress helps teachers quickly assess student proficiency and determine next steps.

Student Pages

Projectable and Printable Pages The models, passages, examples, and graphic organizers on Teacher Lesson Pages are also included as student-facing pages. Student Pages can be projected digitally for group work. They can also be printed so students have their own copies for reading and writing.

Model and Teach Each Model and Teach passage also appears as a Student Page. Students can follow along as the teacher reads the passage aloud, noting how the focused skill is introduced in context. As students gain reading proficiency, they can use the passages for repeated readings as well as for comprehension practice.

Student Pages allow students to follow along, read, and annotate the model passage.

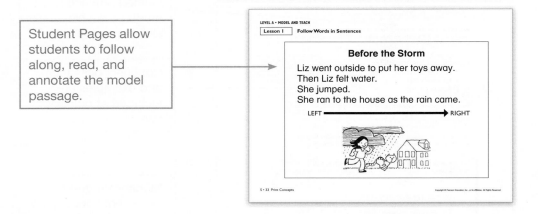

Practice and Assess Practice and Assess passages, examples, and graphic organizers also appear as Student Pages. Students use these pages—whether displayed for the group or as individual handouts—to practice the skills and demonstrate independent mastery.

Student Pages allow students to engage in the lesson through a variety of whole-group, small-group, and individual work that supports learning.

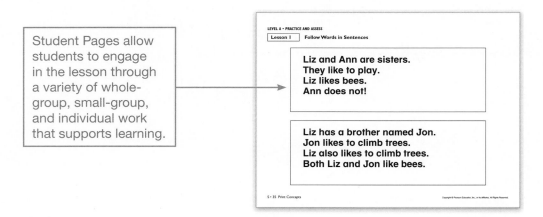

Read Passages and Build Vocabulary

Read Passages All Reading Literature and Reading Informational Text close reading lessons are preceded by a two-page reading passage. Teachers can read these passages aloud and give students copies to follow along or read and reread on their own. The Read passages offer a variety of brief texts on engaging, grade-appropriate literary, science and technology, and social studies topics, and they give students opportunities to apply close reading skills. Students are encouraged to annotate their copies of the passages as they analyze details and interact with the text and illustrations.

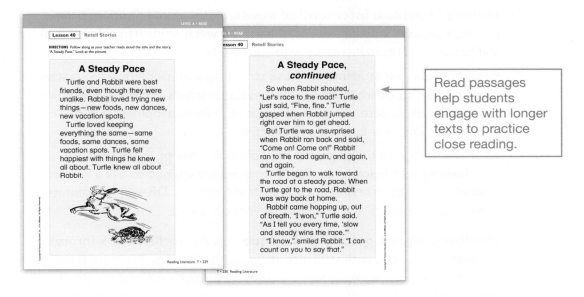

Read passages help students engage with longer texts to practice close reading.

Build Vocabulary In all Reading Literature and Reading Informational Text close reading lessons, the Model and Teach section includes a brief Build Vocabulary feature. The feature gives students targeted practice with strategies to help determine the meaning of words and phrases in context. After a Think Aloud, students demonstrate how to determine the meaning of a new word or phrase in context by applying the strategy on their own.

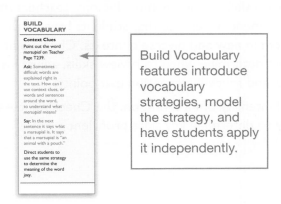

Build Vocabulary features introduce vocabulary strategies, model the strategy, and have students apply it independently.

Formative Assessment

Monitor Progress and Checkpoint Assessments Ongoing formative assessment guides intervention and ensures that struggling readers master the skills they need to learn without spending time on the skills they already know. Within the *ReadyUp! Intervention* program, formative assessment opportunities are quick, efficient, and data-driven. Formative assessment occurs within each Practice minilesson (Monitor Progress and Independent Practice) and after a series of related lessons within a strand (Checkpoint Assessments). For effective assessment, use these steps.

1. **Identify individual intervention needs.** Without intervention focused precisely on each student's needs, the gap between students performing at and below level often increases with each grade.

   • For the youngest students or those struggling with discrete skills, teachers may be able to clearly identify weaknesses. Teachers use the Checkpoint Assessments to determine precise gaps in skills development and to ensure that intervention is focused and effective.

   • For students with broad gaps in multiple skill areas or those who are performing well below grade level, teachers are advised to use a research-based diagnostic assessment tool, such as Pearson's DRA®2, to accurately determine students' full reading-intervention needs.

2. **Monitor progress quickly and frequently.** As teachers work through intervention lessons with students, they use the Monitor Progress activities to check students' progress and determine whether each student should advance or whether reeaching is needed. If students continuously struggle with the Monitor Progress and Independent Practice formative assessments, teachers can adjust the pace of the intervention (see p. T24).

3. **Check that students are retaining and developing knowledge.** Teachers use the Checkpoint Assessments to guide pacing and determine intervention entry and exit points.

   • As students develop skills across multiple lessons, teachers use the Checkpoint Assessments to ensure that students have retained the skills and can apply them in new and diverse contexts. Checkpoint Assessment data help teachers determine when to review skills, adjust instruction and pacing as needed, and gauge intervention exit points.

   • For any level and intensity of intervention, the Checkpoint Assessments offer a quick way to determine key skills proficiency.

Monitor Progress Monitor Progress assessment occurs after each minilesson. The final minilesson culminates in Independent Practice, in which students demonstrate what they have learned independently.

IF…/THEN… directives guide intervention based on Monitor Progress results.

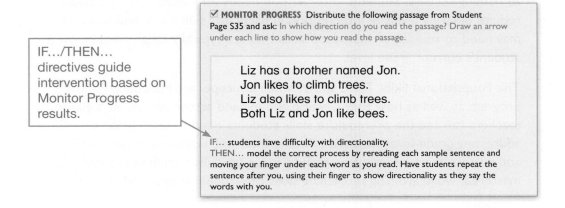

☑ **MONITOR PROGRESS** Distribute the following passage from Student Page S35 and ask: In which direction do you read the passage? Draw an arrow under each line to show how you read the passage.

> Liz has a brother named Jon.
> Jon likes to climb trees.
> Liz also likes to climb trees.
> Both Liz and Jon like bees.

IF… students have difficulty with directionality,
THEN… model the correct process by rereading each sample sentence and moving your finger under each word as you read. Have students repeat the sentence after you, using their finger to show directionality as they say the words with you.

Checkpoint Assessments Two-page Checkpoint Assessments occur after similar lessons within a strand. Assessment instructions, scoring, and remediation options are included with each Checkpoint Assessment.

Short, targeted assessments determine students' proficiency across multiple lessons of instruction.

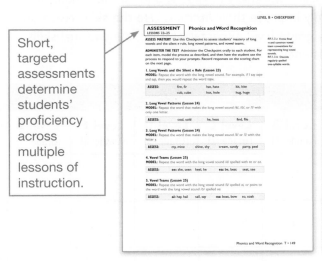

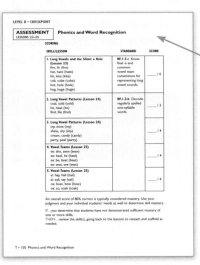

Scoring instructions help teachers assess students' mastery of skills and shape future instruction.

Skills Overview

Foundational Skills Trace

In Part 1, the *ReadyUp! Reading Intervention* program provides a clear sequence of discrete lessons that cover the full range of CCSS Foundational Skills critical to reading success. Students' intervention needs vary widely. Many students require differing levels of intervention in particular skill areas, and teachers may need to reteach or introduce skills that are typically taught well below a student's current grade level.

The Foundational Skills Trace shows when concepts are introduced in the program as well as how they develop and expand across grades. At a glance, teachers can see the prerequisite skills students need to learn prior to addressing grade-level standards. Teachers can then determine entry points and customize an intervention path to focus on skills a student has not yet mastered, while avoiding reteaching skills the student may already know.

The CCSS strands vary by grade level. Use a student's current grade-level proficiency to begin determining intervention needs. Then use the CCSS strands to determine main areas for foundational skills intervention, and identify skills and skill concepts requiring review or in-depth instruction. Students struggling with phonics and fluency may require intervention in basic Print Concepts and Phonological Awareness (Grade K and Grade 1 skills, in Levels A and B) to substantively improve their literacy. Use the skills trace on the next few pages to identify grade-level expectations for foundational skills and to gauge grade-level proficiency.

FOUNDATIONAL SKILLS STRAND	LEVEL					
	Level A (Grade K)	Level B (Grade 1)	Level C (Grade 2)	Level D (Grade 3)	Level E (Grade 4)	Level F (Grade 5)
Print Concepts	•	•				
Phonological Awareness	•	•				
Phonics and Word Recognition	•	•	•	•	•	•
Fluency	•	•	•	•	•	•

Focus on Decoding Follow each horizontal skill concept band to the left to determine prerequisite skills. For example, if a student struggles with Lesson 1, *Understand Sentences,* for Level B Print Concepts, begin intervention instruction with Level A Print Concepts, Lesson 2, or, if needed, with Level A, Lesson 1.

Levels A–B (Grades K–1)
Print Concepts and Phonological Awareness

STRAND AND TOPIC	LEVEL A (GRADE K)					LEVEL B (GRADE 1)				
Print Concepts										
Features of Print	L1 Follow Words in Sentences	L2 Understand Words and Sentences				L1 Understand Sentences				
Alphabetic Code	L3 Learn the Letters in the Alphabet 1	L4 Learn the Letters in the Alphabet 2								
Phonological Awareness										
Rhyme	L5 Identify Rhyme in Words	L6 Produce Rhyme in Words								
Syllables	L7 Blend and Count Syllables in Spoken Words	L8 Segment and Count Syllables in Spoken Words								
Onset and Rime	L9 Blend Onset and Rime	L10 Segment Onset and Rime								
Initial, Final, and Medial Sounds	L11 Identify Same and Different Initial Sounds	L12 Identify Same and Different Final Sounds	L13 Identify Same and Different Medial Sounds	L14 Isolate Initial, Final, and Medial Sounds		L8 Isolate Initial, Final, and Medial Sounds in Single-Syllable Words				
Adding, Substituting, and Changing Phonemes	L15 Add Initial Phonemes	L16 Add Final Phonemes	L17 Delete or Change Initial Phonemes	L18 Delete or Change Final Phonemes	L19 Change Medial Phonemes					
Blending and Segmenting	L20 Blend Two to Three Phonemes into Words					L9 Segment and Blend Sounds	L10 Blend and Segment Three- and Four-Phoneme Words	L11 Blend, Segment, and Count Five or More Phonemes	L12 *R*-Controlled Vowels	L13 Consonant Digraphs
Short Vowel Sounds						L2 Identify Short *a, i,* and *o*	L3 Identify Short *e* and *u*			
Long Vowel Sounds						L4 Identify Long *a, i,* and *o*	L5 Identify Long *e* and *u*	L6 Review Short and Long Vowel Sounds	L7 Distinguish Short and Long Vowel Sounds	
More Vowel Sounds						L14 Diphthongs and Variants	L15 Schwa /ə/ Sound			

All Print Concepts and Phonological Awareness skills are covered in Levels A and B (Grades K and 1).

Level A (Grade K)
Phonics and Word Recognition and Fluency

STRAND AND TOPIC	LEVEL A (GRADE K)				
Phonics and Word Recognition					
Consonants: Sounds and Graphemes	L21 Connect Sounds and Letters: Consonants 1	L22 Connect Sounds and Letters: Consonants 2	L23 Connect Sounds and Letters: Consonants 3	L24 Spelling: Soft Consonant Sounds	
Vowels: Sounds and Graphemes (Short Vowels)	L25 Short *a*	L26 Short *i*	L27 Short *o*	L28 Short *e*	L29 Short *u*
Vowels: Sounds and Graphemes (Long Vowels)	L30 Long *a, i,* and o	L31 Long *e* and *u*			
Vowels: Sounds and Graphemes (Vowel Teams and Patterns)					
High-Frequency Words	L32 High-Frequency Words 1	L33 High-Frequency Words 2	L34 High-Frequency Words 3	L35 Similarly Spelled Words	
Decoding (Segmenting and Blending)					
Syllable Patterns					
Prefixes, Suffixes, and Inflectional Endings					
Irregular Spellings					
Fluency					
Comprehension	L36 Activate Prior Knowledge	L37 Make Predictions About Text	L38 Understand Read-Aloud, Echo-Read, and Choral-Read Text		
Oral Reading (Accuracy and Rate)					
Oral Reading (Expression)					
Vocabulary (References)					
Vocabulary (Context Clues)					
Vocabulary (More Strategies)					

Level B (Grade 1)
Phonics and Word Recognition and Fluency

STRAND AND TOPIC	LEVEL B (GRADE 1)				
Phonics and Word Recognition					
Consonants: Sounds and Graphemes	L16 Common Consonant Digraphs 1 • /sh/ *sh* • /th/ *th* • /f/ *ph, gh*	L17 Common Consonant Digraphs 2 • /ch/ *ch* • /ch/ *tch* • /wh/ *wh*	L18 Common Consonant Digraphs 3 • /j/ *dge* • /ng/ *ng*, /ngk/ *nk* • /k/ *ck*	L19 Common Consonant Digraphs 4 • /n/ *kn* • /r/ *wr* • /m/ *mb*	
Vowels: Sounds and Graphemes (Short Vowels)					
Vowels: Sounds and Graphemes (Long Vowels)	L23 Long Vowels and the Silent *e* Rule	L24 Long Vowel Patterns • Long *e, o,* and *i* (Spelled *e, o, i*) • Long *i* (Spelled *y*) • Long *e* (Spelled *y*)	L25 Vowel Teams • Long *e* (Spelled *ee, ea*) • Long *a* (Spelled *ai*) • Long *o* (Spelled *oa*)		
Vowels: Sounds and Graphemes (Vowel Teams and Patterns)					
High-Frequency Words	L30 Irregular Spellings • Sound /d/ (Spelled *ld*) • Sound /k/ (Spelled *lk*) • Sound /w/ (Spelled *o*)				
Decoding (Segmenting and Blending)	L20 Decode Regularly Spelled VC and CVC Words	L21 Decode Words: Initial Blends • Initial *l* and *r* Blends • Initial *s* Blends • Three-Letter Initial *s* Blends	L22 Decode Words: Final Blends • *nd, nt, mp, ft* • *lt, ld, lp* • *sk, sp, st*		
Syllable Patterns	L26 Understand Syllables • Count Syllables • Closed Syllables • Open Syllables	L27 Syllable Patterns • VC/CV • V/CV • VC/V	L28 Syllable Patterns: *R*-Controlled Vowels		
Prefixes, Suffixes, and Inflectional Endings	L29 Inflectional Endings • *-s, -es* • *-ed* • *-ing*				
Irregular Spellings					
Fluency					
Comprehension	L31 Determine Genre and Purpose				
Oral Reading (Accuracy and Rate)	L32 Read Accurately	L33 Read with Appropriate Rate			
Oral Reading (Expression)	L34 Read with Appropriate Expression				
Vocabulary (References)	L35 Use a Dictionary and Glossary				
Vocabulary (Context Clues)	L36 Use Context Clues: Definition				
Vocabulary (More Strategies)					

Level C (Grade 2)
Phonics and Word Recognition and Fluency

STRAND AND TOPIC	LEVEL C (GRADE 2)				
Phonics and Word Recognition					
Consonants: Sounds and Graphemes					
Vowels: Sounds and Graphemes (Short Vowels)					
Vowels: Sounds and Graphemes (Long Vowels)	L1 Distinguish Short and Long Vowels	L2 More Vowel Teams I • Long *a* (Spelled *ay*) • Long *i* (Spelled *ie, igh*) • Long *o* (Spelled *ow*)			
Vowels: Sounds and Graphemes (Vowel Teams and Patterns)	L3 More Vowel Teams 2 • Short *e* (Spelled *ea*) • Sound /o͝o/ (Spelled *oo*) • Long *e* (Spelled *ie, ey*)	L4 Vowel Patterns with /o͞o/ • Sound /o͞o/ (Spelled *oo*) • Sound /o͞o/ (Spelled *ew*) • Sound /o͞o/ (Spelled *ue, ui*)	L5 Vowel Patterns with /aw/	L6 Vowel Diphthongs	
High-Frequency Words					
Decoding (Segmenting and Blending)					
Syllable Patterns	L7 Syllable Patterns • Syllable Types • C + *-le* • VCCCV	L8 Syllable Patterns: Long Vowels • CVVC • V/V • VVCV			
Prefixes, Suffixes, and Inflectional Endings	L9 Decode Words with Prefixes	L10 Decode Words with Suffixes			
Irregular Spellings	L11 Inconsistent Spellings • Schwa Sound /ə/ in First Syllable • Schwa Sound /ə/ in Second Syllable • /f/ *ff*, /l/ *ll*, /s/ *ss*	L12 Irregular Spellings • Spelling Pattern *ough* /uf/ • Spelling Patterns *gn* /n/ and *mn* /m/ • Spelling Patterns *st* /s/ and *rh* /r/			
Fluency					
Comprehension	L13 Make and Confirm Predictions				
Oral Reading (Accuracy and Rate)	L14 Read Accurately with Appropriate Rate	L15 Use Punctuation Cues for Appropriate Phrasing			
Oral Reading (Expression)	L16 Read with Appropriate Expression				
Vocabulary (References)					
Vocabulary (Context Clues)	L17 Use Context Clues: Synonyms and Antonyms				
Vocabulary (More Strategies)	L18 Understand Multiple-Meaning Words				

Level D (Grade 3)
Phonics and Word Recognition and Fluency

STRAND AND TOPIC	LEVEL D (GRADE 3)				
Phonics and Word Recognition					
Consonants: Sounds and Graphemes					
Vowels: Sounds and Graphemes (Short Vowels)					
Vowels: Sounds and Graphemes (Long Vowels)					
Vowels: Sounds and Graphemes (Vowel Teams and Patterns)					
High-Frequency Words					
Decoding (Segmenting and Blending)	L3 Decode Multisyllable Words	L4 Decode Compound Words • Compounds • More Compounds • Compounds with Longer Word Parts			
Syllable Patterns					
Prefixes, Suffixes, and Inflectional Endings	L1 Understand Prefixes and Suffixes • Isolate Prefixes • Isolate Suffixes • Determine Meaning of Affixes	L2 Decode Words with Latin Suffixes • -able • -er, -or, -ist • -ment, -ty, -ity			
Irregular Spellings	L5 Irregular Spellings: Endings • Ending -ed, -ing: Double Final Consonant • Endings -er, -est • Endings -ed, -ing: Drop Final e	L6 Plurals • Plural -s • Plural -es • Plural f or fe to v	L7 More Endings and Plurals • Ending -es: Spelling Change y to i • Ending -ed: Spelling Change y to i • Irregular Plurals	L8 Contractions • Contractions n't, 'm • Contractions 's, 'd • Contractions 're, 've, 'll	L9 Possessives and Abbreviations • Singular Possessives • Plural Possessives • Abbreviations
Fluency					
Comprehension	L10 Activate Prior Knowledge	L11 Ask and Answer Questions	L12 Retell and Summarize		
Oral Reading (Accuracy and Rate)	L13 Read Accurately with Appropriate Rate	L14 Use Punctuation Cues for Appropriate Phrasing			
Oral Reading (Expression)	L15 Read with Appropriate Expression				
Vocabulary (References)					
Vocabulary (Context Clues)	L16 Use Context Clues: Examples				
Vocabulary (More Strategies)	L17 Determine Meaning of Unfamiliar Words	L18 Understand Homographs			

Focus on Fluency and Comprehension Use each horizontal skill concept band to the left to determine prerequisite skills. Grade-level standards for students at Level E (Grade 4) and Level F (Grade 5) shift from decoding text to fluently reading and comprehending text. If students need intervention with print concepts, sound-letter correspondences, or basic phonics concepts, see references to skills in Levels A–D (Grades K–3) to guide instruction.

Level E (Grade 4)
Phonics and Word Recognition and Fluency

STRAND AND TOPIC	LEVEL E (GRADE 4)					
Phonics and Word Recognition						
Decoding	L1 Decode Compound Words	L2 Decode Words Using Roots				
Fluency						
Comprehension (Purpose and Understanding)	* See Part 2 (Reading, Writing, and Language)					
Comprehension (Literature)						
Comprehension (Informational Text)						
Comprehension (Vocabulary/ Meaning)						
Oral Reading (Accuracy and Rate)	L3 Accuracy and Rate					
Oral Reading (Appropriate Phrasing/ Punctuation Cues)	L4 Appropriate Phrasing and Punctuation Cues					
Oral Reading (Expression and Intonation)	L5 Expression and Intonation					
Overall Fluency						
Vocabulary (Context Clues)	L6 Use Context Clues 1	L7 Use Context Clues 2	L8 Use Context Clues 3	L9 Understand Multiple-Meaning Words		
Vocabulary (Word Relationships)	L10 Understand Synonyms	L11 Understand Antonyms				
Vocabulary (Greek and Latin Affixes and Roots)						
Vocabulary (Affixes and Roots)	L12 Understand Prefixes un-, dis-, mis-	L13 Understand Prefixes pre-, re-	L14 Understand Suffixes -ful, -less			
Vocabulary (References)						

Level F (Grade 5)
Phonics and Word Recognition and Fluency

STRAND AND TOPIC	LEVEL F (GRADE 5)					
Phonics and Word Recognition						
Decoding	L3 Decode Words Using Greek and Latin Roots	L4 Decode Multisyllabic Words				
Fluency						
Comprehension (Purpose and Understanding)	* See Part 2 (Reading, Writing, and Language)					
Comprehension (Literature)						
Comprehension (Informational Text)						
Comprehension (Vocabulary/ Meaning)						
Oral Reading (Accuracy and Rate)	L3 Accuracy and Rate					
Oral Reading (Appropriate Phrasing/ Punctuation Cues)	L4 Appropriate Phrasing and Punctuation Cues					
Oral Reading (Expression and Intonation)	L5 Expression and Intonation					
Overall Fluency	L6 Fluency 1	L7 Fluency 2				
Vocabulary (Context Clues)						
Vocabulary (Word Relationships)						
Vocabulary (Greek and Latin Affixes and Roots)	L8 Understand Greek and Latin Prefixes	L9 Understand Greek and Latin Suffixes	L10 Understand Greek and Latin Roots			
Vocabulary (Affixes and Roots)	L11 Understand Suffixes -ly, -al	L12 Understand Suffixes -able, -ive; -ous, -ish	L13 Understand Suffixes -ness, -ion			
Vocabulary (References)	L14 Use a Dictionary, Glossary, and Thesaurus					

Reading, Writing, and Language Skills Trace

In *ReadyUp! Intervention,* Part 1: Foundational Skills lessons focus on the fundamental elements of decoding. In Part 2: Reading, Writing, and Language, intervention lessons focus on a deeper analysis of both literary and informational texts and on writing and language. The Part 2 skills are intended to be taught initially alongside and then as a continuation of the reading foundational skills as students move from basic decoding toward deeper understanding of text.

Reading Literature and Informational Texts As students master decoding, they move toward an increasingly sophisticated skill level in reading analysis, writing, and language development. These skills move in a continuum across the grade levels in CCSS, and *ReadyUp!* follows that depth and breadth from level to level. Use the Skills Trace on the following pages to identify prerequisite skills for each reading standard within a strand and to adjust intervention to meet students' current needs and goals.

Writing Intervention lessons for writing target the skills and concepts that offer the greatest payoff for struggling students. Students focus on the basics of understanding writing tasks and processes, including research and technology. Each Practice and Assess page within the lessons tailors the instruction to one of the three main modes (opinion, informative/explanatory, or narrative), so students understand how to apply the skills across writing genres. Use the Skills Trace to target key topics for writing intervention or remediation as well as to gauge students' progress.

Language Intervention lessons for language development similarly target skills and concepts that prove hardest to master and/or are most crucial for struggling students. Students can immediately transfer these targeted skills to other real-life writing tasks both in and out of school.

Vocabulary The CCSS address both vocabulary acquisition and use as students determine word meanings, acquire new words, and use these new words in their own speaking and writing. In *ReadyUp! Intervention,* students acquire vocabulary skills through in-depth, stand-alone lessons throughout the strands. In addition, students apply vocabulary strategies as they access frequent point-of-use Build Vocabulary features in the Part 2 Reading lessons.

Reading Literature Skills Trace

STRAND AND TOPIC		LESSONS BY LEVEL						
		LEVEL A (GRADE K)	LEVEL B (GRADE 1)	LEVEL C (GRADE 2)	LEVEL D (GRADE 3)	LEVEL E (GRADE 4)	LEVEL F (GRADE 5)	LEVEL G (GRADE 6)
Key Ideas and Details	RL.1	L39 Ask and Answer Questions	L37 Ask and Answer Questions About a Story	L19 Ask and Answer Questions About a Text	L19 Ask and Answer Questions About a Text	L15 Make Inferences	L15 Draw Conclusions	L1 Cite Text Evidence
	RL.2	L40 Retell Stories	L38 Retell Stories	L20 Recount Stories	L20 Determine Central Message or Moral	L16 Determine Theme	L16 Determine Theme	L2 Determine Theme
	RL.3		L39 Describe Characters, Settings, and Major Events	L21 Describe Characters	L21 Describe Characters	L17 Understand Character L18 Understand Plot L19 Understand Setting	L17 Compare and Contrast Characters, Setting, and Events	L3 Understand Development in a Narrative
Craft and Structure	RL.4		L40 Identify the Meaning of Words	L22 Describe the Meaning of Words and Phrases	L22 Distinguish Between Literal and Nonliteral Language	L20 Recognize Idioms, Adages, Proverbs, and Allusions	L18 Interpret Figurative Language	L4 Determine Connotation, Denotation, and Tone
	RL.5	L41 Recognize Types of Texts		L23 Learn Story Structure	L23 Describe Structure in Literature	L21 Compare and Contrast Structure and Point of View	L19 Analyze Structure in Literature	L5 Analyze Narrative Structure
	RL.6	L42 Identify the Role of Storytellers	L41 Analyze Characters' Experiences	L24 Compare Characters' Points of View	L24 Distinguish Between Points of View		L20 Describe Point of View	L6 Explain Point of View
Integration of Knowledge and Ideas	RL.7	L43 Understand Illustrations in a Story		L25 Use Information from Illustrations	L25 Interpret Illustrations		L21 Analyze Visual Elements in Literature	L7 Compare and Contrast Experiences of a Text
	RL.9			L26 Compare and Contrast Two Versions of a Story	L26 Compare and Contrast in Literature	L22 Compare and Contrast Literature	L22 Compare and Contrast Literature	L8 Compare and Contrast Literature

Reading Informational Text Skills Trace

STRAND AND TOPIC		LESSONS BY LEVEL						
		LEVEL A (GRADE K)	**LEVEL B** (GRADE 1)	**LEVEL C** (GRADE 2)	**LEVEL D** (GRADE 3)	**LEVEL E** (GRADE 4)	**LEVEL F** (GRADE 5)	**LEVEL G** (GRADE 6)
Key Ideas and Details	RI.1 RI.2	L44 Identify Main Topic and Key Details	L42 Identify Main Topic and Key Details	L27 Identify Main Ideas	L27 Find the Main Idea	L23 Determine the Main Idea and Details	L23 Determine Multiple Main Ideas	L9 Determine Central Ideas
	RI.3		L43 Connect Information in a Text	L28 Describe Relationships Between Ideas	L28 Describe the Relationship Between Ideas	L24 Explain Ideas from Informational Texts	L24 Understand Cause-Effect Relationships	L10 Analyze Development of Ideas
							L25 Understand Compare-Contrast Relationships	
Craft and Structure	RI.4	L45 Define Unfamiliar Words		L29 Understand Academic and Domain-Specific Words	L29 Understand Academic and Domain-Specific Words	L25 Learn Academic and Domain-Specific Words	L26 Understand Domain-Specific Vocabulary	L11 Determine the Meaning of Words and Phrases
	RI.5			L30 Use Text Features	L30 Use Text Features	L26 Describe Text Structure	L27 Compare Structure in Two Texts	L12 Analyze Structure
	RI.6	L46 Examine the Presentation of Information		L31 Identify Main Purpose	L31 Understand Point of View	L27 Compare and Contrast Accounts	L28 Analyze Multiple Accounts	L13 Determine Author's Point of View and Purpose
Integration of Knowledge and Ideas	RI.7	L47 Understand Illustrations in a Text	L44 Understand Illustrations	L32 Examine Images in a Text	L32 Use Illustrations to Understand a Text	L28 Interpret Visual, Oral, and Quantitative Information		L14 Integrate Information
	RI.8		L45 Determine Reasons	L33 Describe Points and Supporting Reasons	L33 Describe Logical Connections Between Sentences and Paragraphs	L29 Analyze Author's Reasons and Evidence	L29 Analyze Author's Reasons and Evidence	L15 Analyze Author's Reasons and Evidence
	RI.9	L48 Compare Texts	L46 Compare Two Texts	L34 Compare Two Texts	L34 Compare Two Texts	L30 Compare and Contrast Two Texts	L30 Draw Evidence and Integrate Information	L16 Compare and Contrast Texts

Writing Skills Trace

STRAND AND TOPIC		LESSONS BY LEVEL						
		LEVEL A (GRADE K)	LEVEL B (GRADE 1)	LEVEL C (GRADE 2)	LEVEL D (GRADE 3)	LEVEL E (GRADE 4)	LEVEL F (GRADE 5)	LEVEL G (GRADE 6)
Plan and Develop Writing	W.4 W.5	L49 Ask and Answer Questions About a Prompt	L47 Use a Prompt to Identify a Writing Topic		L35 Analyze a Prompt	L31 Analyze a Writing Prompt	L31 Plan Response to a Prompt	L17 Analyze and Plan Before Writing
			L35 Write Clear Sentences		L36 Plan and Draft a Piece of Writing	L32 Create Coherent Paragraphs	L32 Use Clear Organization	L18 Produce Clear, Coherent Writing
Research	W.6 W.7 W.8	L50 Use a Topic to Recall and Gather Information	L48 Recall and Gather Information About a Topic	L36 Collaborate on Planning and Developing Writing		L33 Research a Topic	L33 Paraphrase Sources	L19 Quote and Paraphrase from Sources
				L37 Gather Information on a Topic	L37 Research a Writing Assignment			L20 Use Technology in Writing
Strengthen and Revise Writing	W.5	L51 Add Details to Writing	L49 Add Specific Details to Support Ideas				L34 Strengthen Opening and Concluding Statements	L21 Revise and Rewrite Drafts
				L38 Revise and Focus Paragraphs	L38 Revise Organization in a Piece of Writing	L34 Link Ideas with Transitions	L35 Revise, Edit, and Rewrite	
				L39 Edit and Publish Writing	L39 Revise Language in a Piece of Writing	L35 Revise Sentences for Clarity and Precision		

Detailed instruction on and practice with main writing modes
(W.1, W.2, and W.3) are covered within most lessons.

Language Skills Trace

STRAND AND TOPIC		LESSONS BY LEVEL						
		LEVEL A (GRADE K)	LEVEL B (GRADE 1)	LEVEL C (GRADE 2)	LEVEL D (GRADE 3)	LEVEL E (GRADE 4)	LEVEL F (GRADE 5)	LEVEL G (GRADE 6)
Grammar and Usage	L.1	L52 Understand Nouns, Verbs, and Prepositions	L50 Use Subject-Verb Agreement	L40 Understand Nouns, Verbs, and Agreement	L40 Understand Subject-Verb and Pronoun-Antecedent Agreement	L36 Use Progressive Tense Verbs and Modals	L36 Use Correct Verb Tense	L22 Use Pronouns Correctly
					L41 Understand Coordinating and Subordinating Conjunctions	L37 Use Frequently Confused Words Correctly		
Capitalization, Punctuation and Spelling	L.2	L53 Capitalize and Punctuate Sentences	L51 Produce and Expand Sentences	L41 Use Contractions and Possessives		L38 Punctuate Quotations and Direct Speech	L37 Use Commas Correctly	
			L52 Understand Spelling Patterns		L42 Use Conventional Spellings and Suffixes			
Language and Craft	L.3			L42 Use Formal and Informal English			L38 Expand, Combine, and Reduce Sentences for Style and Effect	L23 Vary Sentence Patterns for Meaning Style, and Effect
Word Relationships	L.5	L54 Sort Words into Categories						L24 Use Word Relationships

Intervention and Your Students

ReadyUp! Intervention includes the common threads of effective reading intervention programs: a focus on planning, pacing, and adapting to students' needs; supportive activities to build language, fluency, and home-school connections; and a current research base on proven intervention philosophy and practice.

Planning

ReadyUp! Intervention offers a consistent lesson format to make instruction, practice, and assessment during intervention clear and easy to use. Student models, activities, routines, and assessments are provided at point of use and follow a gradual-release model. The pace of the lessons is naturally dependent on the needs of each student. The chart below provides a suggested pacing for lessons, many of which might typically take about one week.

Weekly Lesson Plan

DAY 1	MODEL AND TEACH	**INTRODUCE** ("I do")	• Introduce general concept or skill to students.
		MODEL ("I do")	• Identify the skill in context, through an annotated reading model. • Reinforce that the foundational skills are intrinsic to overall reading fluency. • Model fluency through regular read-alouds. • Give repeated practice with decodable, developmentally appropriate text.
		TEACH ("I do")	• Explain the skill in context. • Teach the skill explicitly.
DAY 2	PRACTICE AND ASSESS	**PRACTICE 1** ("We do")	• Guide practice of the most basic aspects of the skill through reteaching and routines. • Display or distribute Student Pages to give students guided practice.
		MONITOR PROGRESS ("We do")	• Assess students' progress. • Review or reteach as needed.
DAY 3		**PRACTICE 2** ("We do")	• Guide practice of intermediate aspects of the skill through reteaching and routines. • Display or distribute Student Pages to give students guided practice.
		MONITOR PROGRESS ("We do")	• Assess students' progress. • Review or reteach as needed.
DAY 4		**PRACTICE 3** ("We do")	• Guide practice of the most difficult aspects of the skill through reteaching and routines. • Display or distribute Student Pages to give students guided practice.
		INDEPENDENT PRACTICE ("You do")	• Assess students' independent progress. • Review or reteach as needed. • Move on to next lesson.

Pacing

ReadyUp! Intervention is intended to be used in addition to the core curriculum and may be used in a variety of ways. The lesson format is consistent but adaptive and easy to implement. It can be flexibly used both for students needing brief, targeted intervention for particular skills and for students requiring broader and more intensive intervention across strands and even across multiple grade levels. Teachers can focus on intervention lessons that complement and reinforce grade-level instruction taught in their core curriculum. Alternatively, they may focus on reviewing (or introducing) prerequisite skills from earlier grades needed for students to approach and achieve grade-level reading expectations.

Customizing Intervention Models Teachers can adapt the program in ways that best fit the intervention needs of their students, adjusting for the percentage of students in class requiring intervention and the resources available in their classroom, school, and district. The models below offer several ways to use *ReadyUp! Intervention*.

Intervention Models
- **One-on-one intervention**
- **Small groups (outside of class)**
- **Small groups (in class)**

Level of Intervention Needed (LOW → HIGH)			
HIGH	One-on-One Extensive Intervention (classroom teacher)		One-on-One Intervention (literacy specialists/aides)
		Small Groups (groups organized by intervention needs of students)	
LOW	Small Groups (in class to reteach/review core instruction)		Small Groups (before or after class to reteach/review core instruction)
	Number of Students Requiring Intervention LOW ⟶ HIGH		

Adapting to Students' Needs

ReadyUp! Intervention follows a consistent format, but the sequence and number of lessons in the program are not prescriptive. Intervention should be quick and efficient, targeted to the skills and concepts that are proving barriers to grade-level reading proficiency. If a straightforward concept is introduced and quickly mastered in a session or two, teachers should move on. On the other hand, some lessons may require several sessions for instruction, modeling, and to practice skills before students will show mastery. The number of sessions, their duration, and the intervention model used should be tailored to students' needs. For example, students needing intensive intervention may require 30-minute daily sessions for instruction, practice and progress monitoring. For students needing minimal intervention, two to three 30-minute small-group sessions may be enough to teach the concept and provide sufficient guided practice and assessment.

Customizing Intervention As students' proficiency improves, teachers may wish to have students focus on only the second or third minilesson after concepts are taught and modeled. The goal is to make intervention as quick and efficient as possible. Pacing should be adapted as students' skill level increases.

Intensive Intervention

- 30-minute sessions of daily instruction one-on-one or in small groups

Moderate Intervention

- 30-minute sessions, 2–3 times/week, one-on-one or in small groups

Minimal Intervention

- 30-minute sessions, 2–3 times/week, stations in class
- 30-minute sessions, 2–3 times/week, in small groups, to preteach or reteach

IF... students continue to struggle, THEN... adjust pacing by

1. determining gaps in knowledge and teaching prerequisite skills.
2. increasing number of sessions per week.
3. decreasing the number of students in sessions.

IF... students improve quickly, THEN... adjust pacing by

1. using the Checkpoint Assessments to gauge student mastery, teaching entire lessons only if needed.
2. decreasing the number of sessions per week.
3. increasing the number of students in sessions.

Building Language

A sound knowledge of how language works is critical to reading and writing. Familiarizing students with word-building activities can help them recognize and pronounce words, decode words in text, and improve spelling and writing.

Word-Building Activities Word building helps students develop an understanding of the alphabetic principle and reinforces a generative understanding of words and language as students create and manipulate words. Word-building practice has been shown to help students shift from partial alphabet decoding to full alphabetic decoding,[1] which in turn leads to improvements in word recognition.[2]

Word building involves creating simple cards or tiles to build words. The teacher instructs students to form a particular word using the cards. The teacher then has students add, delete, or replace a letter, such as changing the initial *t* in *tap* to an *m*, forming the new word, *map*. Students focus on changing the initial, final, and medial letters (or phonemes, such as *ch*). After each word is "built," the teacher and students read the word aloud, with the teacher offering corrective feedback as needed. As students' phonological awareness and phonics knowledge increases, they are able to build increasingly sophisticated words, as well as sort words by their features, expanding their understanding from letters and phonemes to words and their morphemes, affixes, and inflected endings. The process helps students transfer knowledge between decoding (reading) and encoding (spelling and writing) to reinforce understanding in both areas. For additional word-building activities and ideas for the classroom, see Patricia Cunningham's series, *Making Words*.

t	a	p
m	a	p
m	o	p
p	o	p
p	o	t
p	i	t
	i	t

Elkonin Boxes and letter tiles help students create words and manipulate them to create new words.

---

1. Ehri, Linnea C. 2005. "Learning to Read Words: Theory, Findings, and Issues." *Scientific Studies of Reading* 9 (2): 167–188.

2. McCandliss, Bruce, Isabel Beck, Rebecca Sandak, and Charles Perfetti. 2003. "Focusing Attention on Decoding for Children with Poor Reading Skills: Design and Preliminary Tests of the World Building Intervention." *Scientific Studies of Reading* 7: 75–104.

Building Fluency

Reading fluency is inextricably linked to reading comprehension. As students develop fluency, or automaticity with decoding, they are able to focus more attention on comprehension, or understanding the meaning of a text. Repeated readings of the same text help students develop automaticity, and this technique is emphasized throughout *ReadyUp! Intervention*. As teachers gauge students' fluency, they should keep in mind that comprehension is the true goal of automaticity in decoding and proficiency in oral reading.

Mastering Full Alphabet Decoding To develop fluency, students must first develop full alphabetic knowledge and be proficient in full alphabet decoding. Students who use only the first and last parts of a word to identify it are using partial alphabetic decoding. Students who only partially decode may seem to read fluently and quickly at first, but they will struggle as texts become more complex and include more unfamiliar words (and fewer visual cues). Students who partially decode should be encouraged to slow down and fully decode each word, focusing on improving accuracy as opposed to rate. As students achieve full alphabetic decoding, their rate will improve as well.

Miscue Analysis Once students are capable of independently reading passages, teachers can use miscue analysis to diagnose students' reading proficiency. To perform a miscue analysis, give the student an unfamiliar passage to read aloud. As the student reads, mark the following types of errors on your own copy of the passage. Log students' miscues to determine areas in which they need additional review and support.

Miscue	Explanation	Example	Analysis
correction	Student corrects error without prompting.	I even saw a fox! was/saw	Self correcting is a good strategy, but check that the student is not reading too quickly.
omission	Student leaves out a word(s).	I saw a (bat) fly and a kangaroo jump.	Check that the student is not reading too quickly. Omission may also signal that sight-word recognition is weak.
insertion	Student inserts a word(s) that isn't in the text.	We went to the zoo. too I saw a bat fly and a kangaroo jump.	The student may be reading too quickly. Check that insertions do not detract from meaning.

Miscue	Explanation	Example	Analysis
repetition	Student repeats a word or section of text.	I saw a bat fly and a kangaroo jump.	Repetition of a word or phrase often means the student is struggling to comprehend meaning.
reversal	Student reverses order of the print (e.g., saying "of" instead of "for").	I heard a duck quack.	Check for reversals that change the meaning. The student may need to slow down.
substitution	Student reads a different word from the one in the text.	want We went to the zoo.	The student may not understand the word. Check whether the substituted word is logical or simply a guess. Focus on full alphabet decoding.

How to Measure Fluency Reading passages are differentiated to cover a range of reading levels within a classroom.

LEVEL/GRADE	MINILESSON	WCPM
A (Grade K)	N/A	N/A
B (Grade 1)	1	Choral read
B (Grade 1)	2	20–35
B (Grade 1)	3	35–50
C (Grade 2)	1	50–65
C (Grade 2)	2	65–80
C (Grade 2)	3	80–95
D (Grade 3)	1	70–85
D (Grade 3)	2	85–100
D (Grade 3)	3	100–115
E (Grades 4)	1	95–105
E (Grades 4)	2	105–115
E (Grades 4)	3	115–125
F (Grade 5)	1	110–120
F (Grade 5)	2	120–130
F (Grade 5)	3	130–140

Adapted from Hasbrouck, Jan, and Gerald Tindal. 2005. "Oral Reading Fluency: 90 Years of Measurement." Web. 3 August 2015. http://eric.ed.gov/?id=ED531458.

Teachers can use the following routine with students individually or in student pairs. It is important to emphasize that learning to read fluently takes practice and that doing repeated readings and keeping track of reading times helps students see how their reading improves with practice. The goal of fluency practice is not to read fast, but to read accurately, at an appropriate rate, and with expression. Automaticity with print enables students to devote more mental energy to comprehension.

1. Introduce Timed Repeated Readings Tell students that today they will read a passage multiple times. Each time they read, they (or you) will keep track of how many words they read correctly in one minute. Say that you will time their reading for one minute. They will underline any words they don't know as they read. When the time is up, students will draw a line after the last word they read.

2. Measure Fluency After one minute, tell students that it is time to figure out how many words they read correctly. Show them how to use the numbers at the right of the passage to identify the total number of words they read. Then have them count the words they underlined. To figure out how many words they read correctly, tell students to take the total number of words they read and subtract the number of underlined words. For example, if their total is 65 words and they underlined 5 words, they will subtract 5 from 65. That means they read 60 words correct per minute (60 WCPM). Have students read the same selection three times and record their best score on their charts.

3. Track Progress Use the chart below to track fluency and especially to show students how repeated readings and practice in general improves their scores.

Fluency Progress Chart

Name _____

	1	2	3	4	5	6	7	8	9	10	11	12	13	14	15	16	17	18	19	20	21	22	23	24	25	26	27	28	29	30
115																														
110																														
105																														
100																														
95																														
90																														
85																														
80																														
75																														
70																														
65																														
60																														
55																														
50																														
45																														
40																														
35																														
30																														
25																														
20																														

Building a Home-School Connection

Successful intervention is dependent on regular communication between teachers and students' parents or guardians. Sharing learning goals and expectations as well as any potential concerns is critical. Through clear, consistent, and regular communication, teachers can outline how they are working with students in class and what additional intervention instruction will address gaps in learning. They can share which techniques are most effective with each student and offer suggestions for how to expand learning gains to engage students outside the classroom. When teachers share clear expectations and regular progress updates, parents and guardians can better reinforce their student's learning while also offering their own questions and observations to guide further instruction. Shared knowledge is empowering—it gives parents and guardians more leverage as advocates for and contributors to their student's learning, both in recognizing and addressing concerns and in developing curious, enthusiastic, and motivated learners.

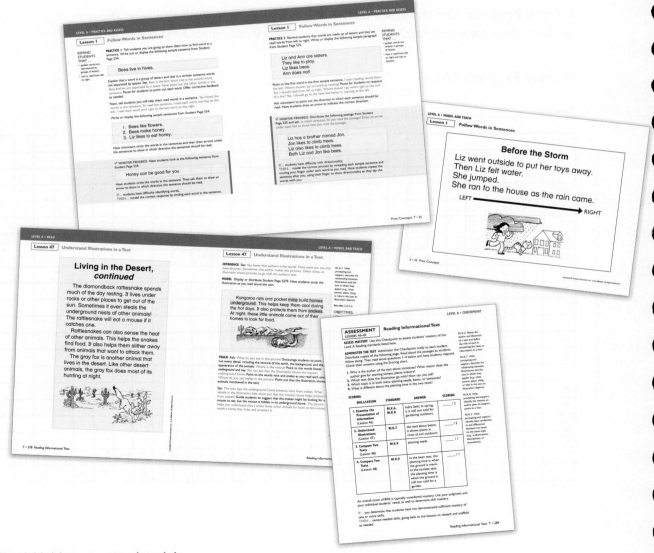

Understanding the Research Base

Effective, targeted intervention is research based in best-practices instruction. The more teachers understand the reasons for particular skills and strategies, the more effective they can be in facilitating student mastery of critical learning goals.

Developing a Research-Based Approach According to the Common Core State Standards, "no set of grade-specific standards can fully reflect the great variety in abilities, needs, learning rates, and achievement levels of students in any given classroom." Instead of being an isolated measure of grade-level proficiency, standards should be used as markers along the path to college and career readiness. The way students learn to read and develop critical thinking skills depends on many different factors, including age, primary language, cultural heritage, and experiences (*FirstSchool* 2014). To address the needs of all students, a curriculum must be flexible. The skill sequence should be progressive but integrated, with each grade's skills building on previous grade-level instruction. The sequence for each grade makes connections and prerequisites among skills clear, within and across grades, to make scaffolding and targeted intervention appropriately flexible and efficient.

To facilitate skills mastery, research supports a gradual release of responsibility. Teachers model first, and then they guide practice. Eventually students work in groups and then independently (Frey and Fisher 2011). This approach matches the common "I do it," "We do it," "You do it together," and "You do it alone" model for lessons (Fisher and Frey 2014).

Teaching Skills in Context Engaging and motivating context allows for effective reading instruction (Shanahan et al. 2010). When a skill is presented in context, students know exactly why they need to practice that particular skill and how that skill fits into general reading proficiency. Context, therefore, gives students a real-world example of the skill in practice and motivates students to engage in the lesson. All lessons in the program include a model passage or stimulus to anchor the lesson. This modeling reinforces the fact that literacy skills are in service to mastery of real-world texts and tasks.

Using Formative Assessment to Guide Intervention Instruction Teachers use assessment to set goals for students, monitor progress toward those goals, give feedback on that progress, and adjust teaching as needed (Allal 2010). By observing how students respond to this ongoing formative assessment, teachers can adjust or focus activities in each lesson. Research shows that effective formative assessment strives to answer the questions *Where am I going? Where am I now?* and *Where to next?* (Frey and Fisher 2011). By answering these questions, students know exactly why they are being assessed, what skills they need to address to improve, and what skills they will need for future classroom work.

Understanding the Research Base: Bibliography

Allal, Linda. 2010. "Assessment and the Regulation of Learning." Penelope Peterson, Eva Baker, and Barry McGaw (Eds.), *International Encyclopedia of Education Vol. 3* (3rd ed.), 348–352. Oxford: Elsevier.

California Department of Education. 2014. *ELA/ELD Framework.* Sacramento, California: California Department of Education. Ch. 1, 33–34; Ch. 3, 39–40; Ch. 4; Ch. 5; Ch. 12, 16.

FirstSchool: Transforming PreK–3rd Grade for African American, Latino, and Low-Income Children. Ed. Ritchie, Sharon, and Laura Gutmann. 2014. New York: Teachers College Press.

Fisher, Douglas, and Nancy Frey. 2014. *Better Learning Through Structured Teaching: A Framework for the Gradual Release of Responsibility (Second Ed).* Alexandria, VA: ASCD.

Frey, Nancy, and Douglas Fisher. 2011. *The Formative Assessment Action Plan: Practical Steps to More Successful Teaching and Learning.* Alexandria, VA: ASCD.

Hudson, Roxanne. 2011. "Fluency Problems: When, Why, and How to Intervene." Rollanda E. O'Connor and Patricia F. Vadasy (Eds.), *Handbook of Reading Interventions,* 169–197. New York: Guilford.

National Association for the Education of Young Children. 2009. *Developmentally Appropriate Practice in Early Childhood Programs Serving Children from Birth Through Age 8.* Washington, D.C.: National Association for the Education of Young Children. 5-6.

National Governors Association Center for Best Practices and Council of Chief State School Officers. 2010. *Common Core State Standards for English Language Arts and Literacy in History/Social Studies, Science, and Technical Subjects.* Washington, DC: Authors. 6.

Shanahan, Timothy, K. Callison, C. Carriere, N. K. Duke, P. D. Pearson, C. Schatschneider, and J. Torgesen. 2010. *Improving Reading Comprehension in Kindergarten Through 3rd Grade: A Practice Guide* (NCEE 2010-4038). Washington, DC: National Center for Education Evaluation and Regional Assistance, Institute of Education Sciences, U.S. Department of Education.

FOUNDATIONAL SKILLS

PART

1

Lesson 1	Follow Words in Sentences

INTRODUCE Explain that language is spoken and written. Tell students that they can learn how to read written language by following words from left to right, top to bottom, and page by page.

MODEL Ask students to watch your finger move along the text as you read the passage from Student Page S33. Move your finger from left to right, just beneath each word. At the end of a line, move your finger back to the left and down to the next line to continue modeling.

Before the Storm

Liz went outside to put her toys away.
Then Liz felt water.
She jumped.
She ran to the house as the rain came.

LEFT ⟶ RIGHT
Read left to right.

TEACH After you read the passage once, move your finger under the first line of text again. My finger moves from left to right. We read from left to right. Then read the passage again and move your finger under each word as you read. My finger moves down after the end of a line. When we read, we read from left to right and from top to bottom. When you reach the bottom of a page, go to the top left of the next page. Demonstrate these movements again. Emphasize the process by using different books in the classroom.

RF.K.1.a Follow words from left to right, top to bottom, and page by page.

RF.K.1.b Recognize that spoken words are represented in written language by specific sequences of letters.

OBJECTIVES:
- Recognize that spoken words are written in groups of letters.
- Understand that English print is read left to right, top to bottom, and page by page.

| Lesson 1 | Follow Words in Sentences |

- spoken words are represented by groups of letters.
- text is read from left to right.

PRACTICE 1 Tell students you are going to show them how to find word in a sentence. Write out or display the following sample sentence from Student Page S34:

> # Bees live in hives.

Explain that a word is a group of letters and that in a written sentence words are separated by spaces. Say: *Bees* is the first word. *Live* is the second word. *Bees* and *live* are separated by a space. Now point out the other words in this sentence. Pause for students to point out each word. Offer corrective feedback as needed.

Next, tell students you will help them read words in a sentence. You found the words in the sentence. To read the sentence, I read each word, starting on the left. I read each word until I get to the last word on the right.

Write or display the following sample sentences from Student Page S34:

> 1. Bees like flowers.
> 2. Bees make honey.
> 3. Liz likes to eat honey.

Have volunteers circle the words in the sentences and then draw arrows under the sentences to show in which direction the sentences should be read.

☑ **MONITOR PROGRESS** Have students look at the following sentence from Student Page S34:

> # Honey can be good for you.

Have students circle the words in the sentence. Then ask them to draw an arrow to show in which direction the sentence should be read.

IF... students have difficulty identifying words,
THEN... model the correct response by circling each word in the sentence.

Lesson 1	Follow Words in Sentences

PRACTICE 2 Remind students that words are made up of letters and that we read words from left to right. Write or display the following sample paragraph from Student Page S35:

> Liz and Ann are sisters.
> They like to play.
> Liz likes bees.
> Ann does not!

Point to the first word in the first sample sentence. I start reading words from the left. Where should I go to continue reading? **Pause for students to respond.** Yes, I should read from left to right. Where should I go when I get to the end of a line? Yes, I should go to the next line below it, starting at the left.

Ask volunteers to point out the direction in which each sentence should be read. Have students draw an arrow to indicate the correct direction.

☑ **MONITOR PROGRESS** Distribute the following passage from Student Page S35 and ask: In which direction do you read the passage? Draw an arrow under each line to show how you read the passage.

> Liz has a brother named Jon.
> Jon likes to climb trees.
> Liz also likes to climb trees.
> Both Liz and Jon like bees.

IF… students have difficulty with directionality,
THEN… model the correct process by rereading each sample sentence and moving your finger under each word as you read. Have students repeat the sentence after you, using their finger to show directionality as they say the words with you.

REMIND STUDENTS THAT …

• spoken words are written in groups of letters.

• text is read from left to right and top to bottom.

Lesson 1 | ## Follow Words in Sentences

REMIND
STUDENTS
THAT …

- spoken words are written in print by groups of letters.
- words are read from left to right, top to bottom, and page by page.

PRACTICE 3 Tell students they will learn how to read written words. Display the following passage from Student Page S36:

The Monster

One day, Jon was in the woods.
He saw a big egg.
He took it home.
A baby monster came out!
Jon told his mother.
They put it in a basket.

Read aloud the title and author of the story. Where should I start reading this story? Pause for students to respond. Yes, I should read starting from the left, at the top of the text. I will read the words from left to right. **Read the passage to the end of the first line, underlining each word with your finger.** Where do I read next? Pause for students to respond. Yes, I should read the next line down, starting from the left. **Continue reading aloud to the end of the passage, modeling directionality with your finger as you read.**

Open a classroom book and have a student volunteer demonstrate directionality by moving a finger across the page. Have the student model how to read a line, page, and book by pointing to the text.

☑ **INDEPENDENT PRACTICE** Have individuals choose a classroom book and open to the first page with words. Then ask the following questions: Where should you start reading? Where should you go after you get to the end of the first line? Where should you go after you get to the end of the first page?

IF… students have difficulty determining basic print concepts,
THEN… model the correct process by moving your finger under the text, emphasizing your movements from left to right and top to bottom.

Before the Storm

Liz went outside to put her toys away.

Then Liz felt water.

She jumped.

She ran to the house as the rain came.

LEFT → RIGHT

Bees live in hives.

1. Bees like flowers.

2. Bees make honey.

3. Liz likes to eat honey.

Honey can be good for you.

Lesson 1   Follow Words in Sentences

Liz and Ann are sisters.
They like to play.
Liz likes bees.
Ann does not!

Liz has a brother named Jon.
Jon likes to climb trees.
Liz also likes to climb trees.
Both Liz and Jon like bees.

The Monster

One day, Jon was in the woods.

He saw a big egg.

He took it home.

A baby monster came out!

Jon told his mother.

They put it in a basket.

| Lesson 2 | Understand Words and Sentences |

INTRODUCE Remind students that they have looked at words on the pages of books. Hold up a book that is open to a page with a short sentence. Words are groups of letters. Point to the individual words, from left to right. We read words from left to right. We read words together to understand what is written. Sweep your hand from left to right as you read the words.

MODEL Display or share copies of the passage "A Winning Team" from Student Page S37. Read the first line aloud. Repeat the sentence, pausing after each word. A sentence is a group of words. The words are separated by spaces. This sentence has three words. Point to each word. The words are made of letters.

RF.K.1.c Understand that words are separated by spaces in print.

OBJECTIVES:

• Understand that sentences are made of words.

• Understand that words are made of letters.

• Segment and count words in spoken sentences.

A Winning Team

Kim runs fast.
So does Sam.
I run fast too.
We are on a team.
Our team races.
We win a lot.

TEACH A sentence says something or asks a question. These sentences tell about a team. Point to the first sentence and say: Let's count the words in this sentence. Raise a finger, starting with the thumb, as you say the sentence. *Kim runs fast.* I raised one finger for *Kim*, one finger for *runs*, and one finger for *fast*. Repeat the sentence, pointing to one finger for each word. How many words does this sentence have? Yes, the sentence has three words. Follow the same procedure with the remaining sentences. Ask students to tell you how many words are in the sentence, and affirm correct answers.

Lesson 2 | Understand Words and Sentences

REMIND
STUDENTS
THAT ...
- words are groups of letters that are separated by spaces.

PRACTICE 1 Tell students that you are going to show them how to find written words. Say: *We run fast.* How many words did you hear? I will say the sentence again: *We run fast.* Repeat the sentence and hold up a finger, starting with the thumb, for each word. There are three words in this sentence: We (pause and point to your thumb) run (pause and point to the next finger) fast (point to the third finger).

Display or write out the sentence from Student Page S38. Point to *We*. We is the first word. It has two letters. There is a space after the last letter. Repeat with *run* (run is the next word; it has three letters; there is a space after the last letter) and *fast* (fast is another word; it has four letters).

> ## We run fast.

Display or share the following sentences from Student Page S38. Have volunteers circle the individual words in each sentence. When they are done, point to each sentence and ask: How many words do we see in this sentence? Affirm correct answers.

> ## Two teams race.
> ## Our team wins.
> ## We run home.

☑ **MONITOR PROGRESS** Have students circle each word in the following sentence from Student Page S38. Have them count the words and tell you how many words are in the sentence.

> ## Sam and Kim go home.

IF... students have difficulty isolating words,
THEN... point to the spaces between words and say: A space comes before a new word. Then, model counting the words.

Lesson 2 | Understand Words and Sentences

PRACTICE 2 Tell students you are going to help them find words in sentences and that later they will count the words.

Display the sentence from Student Page S39. Let's start by listening for words in sentences. We'll raise one finger for each word that we hear. Raise your thumb first.

Listen closely: *Sam runs*. We raise a thumb for *Sam* and we raise the next finger for *runs*. Now let's see how the sentence looks on a page. **Repeat the sentence as you display it or write it on the board.**

REMIND STUDENTS THAT …
• words are separated by spaces in print.

> Sam runs.

Read the sentence, raising your thumb for *Sam* and the next finger for *runs*. Point to your thumb, say: *Sam*, and then point to the printed word *Sam*. Point to your finger, say: *runs*, and then point to the written word *runs*. How many words do you see? **(2)**

Then write or display the following sample sentences from Student Page S39.

> Kim runs past Sam.
> Sam yells.
> Kim runs faster.
> Kim gets home first.

Have students point to the separate words in each sentence and tell you how many words there are.

☑ **MONITOR PROGRESS** Distribute the following sentences from Student Page S39 and ask: Which sentences have two words? **Have students point to sentences with two words. Repeat for the sentences with three words and four words.**

> Kim ate lunch.
> Sam rested.
> Sam slept.
> Sam woke up hungry.

IF… students miscount words in sentences,
THEN… **point to the first sentence.** I can use the number of spaces to help me count the words. *Kim, space, ate, space, lunch. Kim ate lunch.* There are three words in this sentence. **Repeat as needed.**

| Lesson 2 | Understand Words and Sentences |

REMIND
STUDENTS
THAT ...

• they can count the words in a printed sentence.

PRACTICE 3 Help students learn the segmenting procedure. Begin with a spoken sentence from Student Page S40. I will say a sentence. Listen carefully for the different words: *Our school has teams.* Now watch my hand as I say the sentence again. I will raise a finger for each word, starting with my thumb. Raise a finger for each word as you repeat the sentence. How many words did I say? Yes, I said four words.

Our school has teams.
Teams work hard.
I am on two teams.

Display the sample sentences from Student Page S40. Remind students that words are separated by spaces in printed text. Point to the first sentence and say: You know that this sentence has four words. How many words do the other sentences have? Point to each sentence and invite students to respond. After completing the list once, ask for volunteers to point to the sentence with three words, the sentence with four words, and the sentence with five words.

☑ **INDEPENDENT PRACTICE** Show students the sentence list from Student Page S40. Have them silently count the words in each sentence.

Kim and Sam and I are on a team.
Bo is also on our team.
We race other teams.
When we win, we are happy.
When we lose, we cheer for the other team.

IF... students count too many or too few words,
THEN... model counting orally while pointing to each word in the sentence.

A Winning Team

Kim runs fast.
So does Sam.
I run fast too.
We are on a team.
Our team races.
We win a lot.

We run fast.

Two teams race.
Our team wins.
We run home.

Sam and Kim go home.

Lesson 2   Understand Words and Sentences

Sam runs.

Kim runs past Sam.
Sam yells.
Kim runs faster.
Kim gets home first.

Kim ate lunch.
Sam rested.
Sam slept.
Sam woke up hungry.

Our school has teams.

Teams work hard.

I am on two teams.

Kim and Sam and I are on a team.

Bo is also on our team.

We race other teams.

When we win, we are happy.

When we lose, we cheer for the other
team.

ASSESSMENT
LESSONS 1–2

Print Concepts

ASSESS MASTERY Use this Checkpoint to assess students' mastery of how to follow words in sentences and identify the number of words in a sentence.

ADMINISTER THE TEST Administer the Checkpoint orally to each student. Give each student a copy of the next page. Instruct students as follows.

1. Follow Words in Sentences (Lesson 1)
I will ask you about words in sentences. Look at the sentence and show me the way to read it. For example, you can move your hand to show me how to read the sentence.

ASSESS:	Cats are fun pets.

2. Understand Words and Sentences (Lesson 2)
Look at the sentence and tell me how many words you see. You may count the words silently or out loud.

ASSESS:	The big dog sat.

SCORING

SKILL/LESSON	SCORE
1. Follow Words in Sentences (Lesson 1) Cats are fun pets. ———▶	Y N
2. Understand Words and Sentences (Lesson 2) The big dog sat. (4 words)	____ / 4

An overall score of 80% correct is typically considered mastery. Use your judgment and your individual students' needs as well to determine skill mastery.

IF… students score below the benchmark,
THEN… review those discrete skills, going back to the lessons to reteach and scaffold as needed.

RF.K.1.a Follow words from left to right, top to bottom, and page by page.

RF.K.1.b Recognize that spoken words are represented in written language by specific sequences of letters.

RF.K.1.c Understand that words are separated by spaces in print.

ASSESSMENT
LESSONS 1–2

Print Concepts

Cats are fun pets.

The big dog sat.

| Lesson 3 | Learn the Letters in the Alphabet I |

INTRODUCE Explain that every word is made of letters. Letters are used to spell sounds. Letters can be written as uppercase or lowercase. In this lesson, we'll learn how to look for and write letters. Sing the alphabet song with students.

MODEL Display the passage "At the Zoo" or share copies of Student Page S43 with students. Read it aloud. Say: The words in this passage use every letter in the alphabet.

RF.K.1.d Recognize and name all upper- and lowercase letters of the alphabet.

OBJECTIVES:

• Recognize all letters.

• Identify letters in words.

• Print all letters.

At the Zoo

We went to the zoo.
I saw a bat fly and a kangaroo jump.
I heard a duck quack.
I even saw a fox!

TEACH Display a large alphabet chart with both upper- and lowercase letters. Say the name of each letter, and then help students locate all the lowercase letters in the passage. For example, say: This is a lowercase letter *a*. Do you see *a* in the passage? Circle the letters as you identify them. *At* starts with *a*. The *a* in *At* is uppercase. *A* sounds like /a/. Point to the letter. What is the name of this letter? *A*.

Lesson 3 | Learn the Letters in the Alphabet 1

REMIND STUDENTS THAT ...

- they can recognize the letters *a* and *b*.
- they can identify the letters *a* and *b* in words.
- they can print the letters *a* and *b*.

PRACTICE 1: Recognize Letters *a* and *b* Display or distribute the letter cards from Student Page S44. Follow the routine to teach each letter. You may wish to cut the letters out to create separate picture cards.

Routine

1. Display the letter. Model how to write upper- and lowercase *a* on the board. For example, say: This is uppercase A. This is lowercase *a*.

2. Name the letter. What is the name of this letter? Yes; *a*.

3. Identify the letter. Point to the apple card. What is this? Pause for responses. Yes, an apple. What letter does *apple* start with? Have students circle the letter and say it aloud. Yes, it's the letter *a*. *Apple* starts with *a*.

4. Write the letter. Model writing lowercase *a*. Have students print lowercase *a* several times. Then model writing uppercase A and have students print it several times.

5. Extend practice. Extend practice by having students write the letter *a* on several sticky notes and then attach them to any objects in the room that begin with *a*.

Aa	Bb
apple	ball

Repeat the routine for the remaining letter.

☑ **MONITOR PROGRESS** Display the sentence from Student Page S44. Have individuals identify all instances of each letter taught. Check that students can print each letter independently.

> A girl named Barbara has the bat.

IF... students misidentify or confuse any letters,
THEN... review key steps in the routine, and provide additional practice.

Lesson 3	Learn the Letters in the Alphabet I

PRACTICE 2: Recognize Letters c and d Display or distribute the letter cards from Student Page S45. Follow the routine to teach each letter. You may wish to cut the letters out to create separate picture cards.

Routine

1. Display the letter.   Model how to write upper- and lowercase *c* on the board. For example, say: This is uppercase *C*. This is lowercase *c*.

2. Name the letter.   What is the name of this letter? Yes; *c*.

3. Identify the letter.   Point to the cat card. What is this? Pause for responses. Yes, a cat. What letter does *cat* start with? Have students circle the letter and say it aloud. Yes, it's the letter *c*. *Cat* starts with *c*.

4. Write the letter.   Model writing lowercase *c*. Have students print lowercase *c* several times. Then model writing uppercase *C* and have students print it several times.

5. Extend practice.   Have students find examples of the letter *c* in words around the room, including students' names, signs, and objects.

REMIND STUDENTS THAT …
• they can recognize the letters *c* and *d*.
• they can identify the letters *c* and *d* in words.
• they can print the letters *c* and *d*.

Cc	Dd
cat	dog

Repeat the routine for the remaining letter. Call attention to letters that are easily confused, such as *b* and *d*. Give students extra practice distinguishing and writing these letters.

☑ **MONITOR PROGRESS** Display the sentence from Student Page S45. Have individuals identify all instances of each letter taught. Check that students can print each letter independently.

> The ice made Doug cold.

IF… students struggle to write particular letters,
THEN… model again how to write the letter and give students additional practice writing both the letter and new words containing it.

Lesson 3 — Learn the Letters in the Alphabet I

REMIND STUDENTS THAT …

- they can recognize the letters e and f.
- they can identify the letters e and f in words.
- they can print the letters e and f.

PRACTICE 3: Recognize Letters e and f Display or distribute the letter cards from Student Page S46. Follow the routine to teach each letter. You may wish to cut the letters out to create separate picture cards.

Routine

1. Display the letter.	Model how to write upper- and lowercase e on the board. For example, say: This is uppercase E. This is lowercase e.
2. Name the letter.	What is the name of this letter? Yes; e.
3. Identify the letter.	Point to the egg card. What is this? Pause for responses. Yes, an egg. What letter does egg start with? Have students circle the letter and say it aloud. Yes, it's the letter e. Egg starts with e.
4. Write the letter.	Model writing lowercase e. Have students print lowercase e several times. Then model writing uppercase E and have students print it several times.
5. Extend practice.	Have students choose a classroom book and then find and copy two words that begin with or include the letter e.

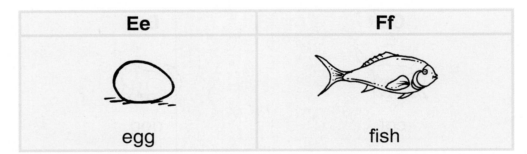

Ee	Ff
egg	fish

Repeat the routine for the remaining letter. Call attention to letters that are easily confused, such as E and F. Give students extra practice distinguishing and writing these letters.

☑ **MONITOR PROGRESS** Display the sentence from Student Page S46. Have individuals identify all instances of each letter taught. Check that students can print each letter independently.

> Every fly likes fresh food.

IF… students misidentify or confuse any letters,
THEN… review key steps in the routine, and have students practice writing additional words with those letters.

Lesson 3 | Learn the Letters in the Alphabet 1

PRACTICE 4: Recognize Letters *g* and *h* Display or distribute the letter cards from Student Page S47. Follow the routine to teach each letter. You may wish to cut the letters out to create separate picture cards.

Routine

1. Display the letter. Model how to write upper- and lowercase *g* on the board. For example, say: This is uppercase G. This is lowercase g.

2. Name the letter. What is the name of this letter? Yes; *g*.

3. Identify the letter. Point to the guitar card. What is this? Pause for responses. Yes, a guitar. What letter does *guitar* start with? Have students circle the letter and say it aloud. Yes, it's the letter *g*. *Guitar* starts with *g*.

4. Write the letter. Model writing lowercase *g*. Have students print lowercase *g* several times. Then model writing uppercase *G* and have students print it several times.

5. Extend practice. Have students make their own picture cards by drawing a letter on each card and then finding or drawing a picture of something that begins with the letter.

REMIND STUDENTS THAT ...

- they can recognize the letters *g* and *h*.
- they can identify the letters *g* and *h* in words.
- they can print the letters *g* and *h*.

Gg	Hh
guitar	hat

Repeat the routine for the remaining letter. Call attention to letters that students may find difficult, such as *C* and *G*. Give students extra practice distinguishing and writing these letters.

☑ **MONITOR PROGRESS** Display the sentence from Student Page S47. Have individuals identify all instances of each letter taught. Check that students can print each letter independently.

> ## That is great, Hugh!

IF... students struggle to identify particular letters,
THEN... model again how to identify the letters in several words and give students additional writing practice.

Lesson 3 — Learn the Letters in the Alphabet 1

REMIND STUDENTS THAT ...

- they can recognize the letters *i* and *j*.
- they can identify the letters *i* and *j* in words.
- they can print the letters *i* and *j*.

PRACTICE 5: Recognize Letters *i* and *j* Display or distribute the letter cards from Student Page S48. Follow the routine to teach each letter. You may wish to cut the letters out to create separate picture cards.

Routine

1. Display the letter. Model how to write upper- and lowercase *i* on the board. For example, say: This is uppercase *I*. This is lowercase *i*.

2. Name the letter. What is the name of this letter? Yes; *i*.

3. Identify the letter. Point to the igloo card. What is this? Pause for responses. Yes, it is an igloo. What letter does *igloo* start with? Have students circle the letter and say it aloud. Yes, it's the letter *i*. *Igloo* starts with *i*.

4. Write the letter. Model writing lowercase *i*. Have students print lowercase *i* several times. Then model writing uppercase *I* and have students print it several times.

5. Extend practice. Have students create an alphabet book, using a marker to write and decorate each letter on its own page. Later, have them open to a page and trace the letter with a finger.

Ii	Jj
igloo	jar

Repeat the routine for the remaining letter. Note that lowercase *i* and *j* are easily confused. Give students ample practice distinguishing and writing these letters.

☑ **MONITOR PROGRESS** Display the sentence from Student Page S48. Have individuals identify all instances of each letter taught. Check that students can print each letter independently.

> I told Ji I was just too tired.

IF... students misidentify or confuse any letters,
THEN... review key steps in the routine, and have students practice writing additional words with those letters.

Lesson 3 Learn the Letters in the Alphabet 1

PRACTICE 6: Recognize Letters *k* and *l* Display or distribute the letter cards from Student Page S49. Follow the routine to teach each letter. You may wish to cut the letters out to create separate picture cards.

Routine

1. Display the letter. Model how to write upper- and lowercase *k* on the board. For example, say: This is uppercase *K*. This is lowercase *k*.

2. Name the letter. What is the name of this letter? Yes; *k*.

3. Identify the letter. Point to the key card. What is this? Pause for responses. Yes, a key. What letter does *key* start with? Have students circle the letter and say it aloud. Yes, it's the letter *k*. *Key* starts with *k*.

4. Write the letter. Model writing lowercase *k*. Have students print lowercase *k* several times. Then model writing uppercase *K* and have students print it several times.

5. Extend practice. Have students choose a classroom book and then find and copy two words that include the letter *k*.

Kk	Ll
key	lion

Repeat the routine for the remaining letter. Call attention to letters that are easily confused, such as lowercase *i* and uppercase *l*. Give students extra practice distinguishing and writing these letters.

☑ **MONITOR PROGRESS** Display the sentence from Student Page S49. Have individuals identify all instances of each letter taught. Check that students can print each letter independently.

> King Luis lost his kite.

IF... students misidentify or confuse any letters,
THEN... review key steps in the routine, and have students practice writing additional words with those letters.

REMIND STUDENTS THAT …

- they can recognize the letters *k* and *l*.
- they can identify the letters *k* and *l* in words.
- they can print the letters *k* and *l*.

| Lesson 3 | Learn the Letters in the Alphabet 1 |

- they can recognize the letters *m* and *n*.
- they can identify the letters *m* and *n* in words.
- they can print the letters *m* and *n*.

PRACTICE 7: Recognize Letters *m* and *n* Display or distribute the letter cards from Student Page S50. Follow the routine to teach each letter. You may wish to cut the letters out to create separate picture cards.

Routine

1. Display the letter. Model how to write upper- and lowercase *m* on the board. For example, say: This is uppercase *M*. This is lowercase *m*.

2. Name the letter. What is the name of this letter? Yes; *m*.

3. Identify the letter. Point to the monkey card. What is this? Pause for responses. Yes, a monkey. What letter does *monkey* start with? Have students circle the letter and say it aloud. Yes, it's the letter *m*. *Monkey* starts with *m*.

4. Write the letter. Model writing lowercase *m*. Have students print lowercase *m* several times. Then model writing uppercase *M* and have students print it several times.

5. Extend practice. Have students write the letter *m* on a clean sheet of paper. Ask them to think of words that begin with the sound /m/. As they name each word, ask them to draw a picture of the word.

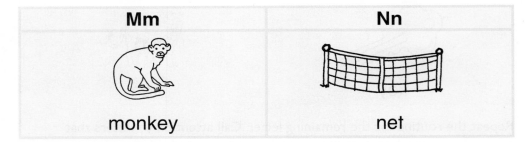

Mm	Nn
monkey	net

Repeat the routine for the remaining letter. Note that students may find it difficult to distinguish lowercase *m* and *n*. Give students ample practice distinguishing and writing these letters.

☑ **MONITOR PROGRESS** Display the sentence from Student Page S50. Have individuals identify all instances of each letter taught. Check that students can print each letter independently.

> Miss Lin makes banana nut muffins.

IF... students struggle to identify particular letters,
THEN... model again how to identify the letters in several words and give students additional writing practice.

Lesson 3   Learn the Letters in the Alphabet I

At the Zoo

We went to the zoo.
I saw a bat fly and a kangaroo jump.
I heard a duck quack.
I even saw a fox!

Learn the Letters in the Alphabet I

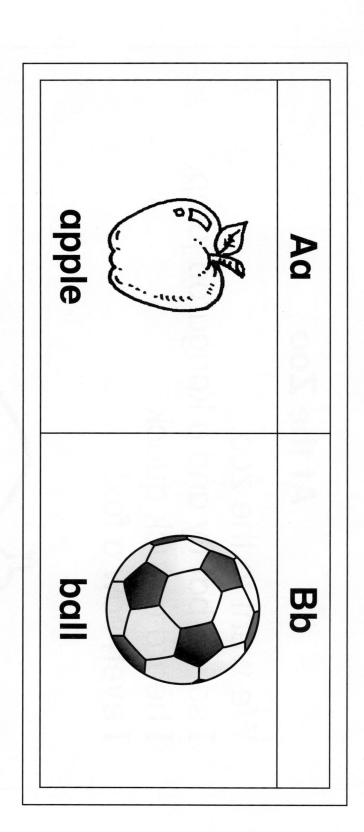

Aa

apple

Bb

ball

A girl named Barbara has the bat.

Learn the Letters in the Alphabet 1

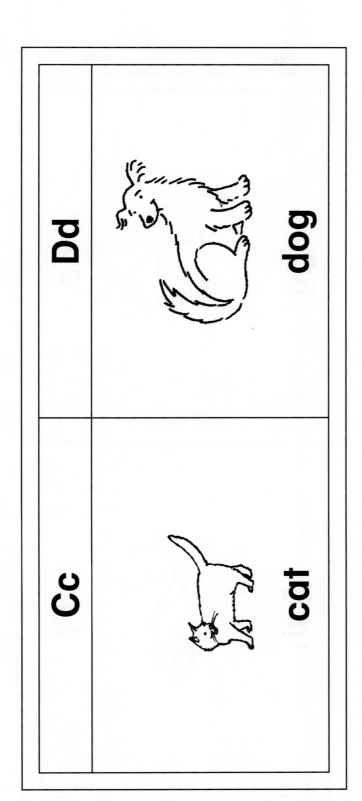

Cc	Dd
cat	dog

The ice made Doug cold.

Learn the Letters in the Alphabet I

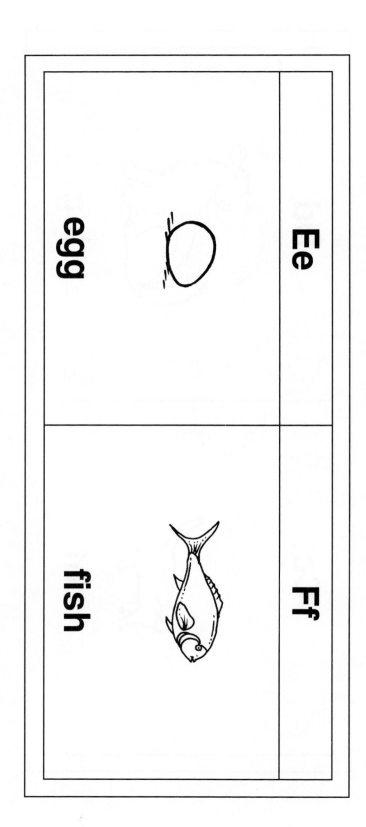

Ee	Ff
egg	fish

Every fly likes fresh food.

Lesson 3   Learn the Letters in the Alphabet I

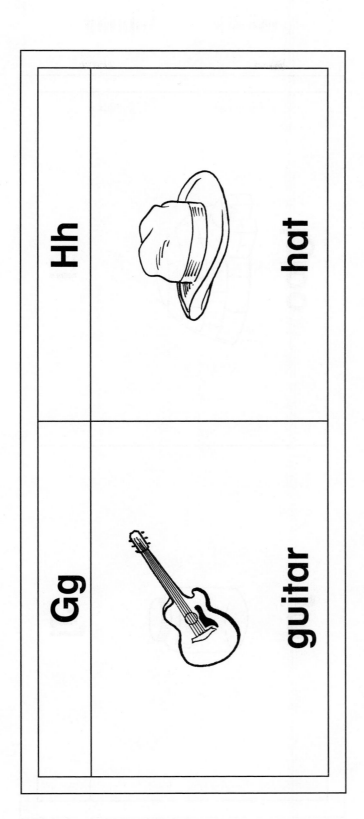

Gg	Hh
guitar	hat

That is great, Hugh!

Lesson 3   Learn the Letters in the Alphabet I

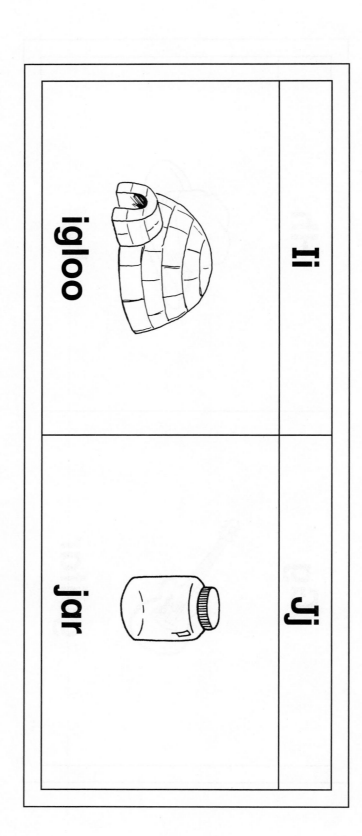

| Ii | Jj |
| igloo | jar |

I told Ji I was just too tired.

Lesson 3   Learn the Letters in the Alphabet I

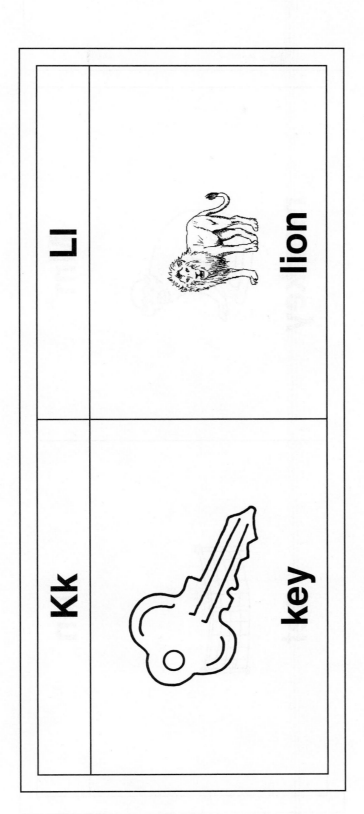

Kk	Ll
key	lion

King Luis lost his kite.

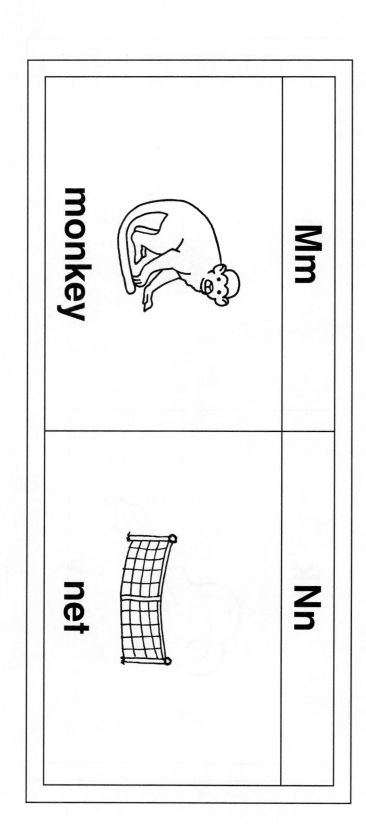

Mm	Nn
monkey	net

Miss Lin makes banana nut muffins.

Lesson 4	Learn the Letters in the Alphabet 2

INTRODUCE Explain that every word is made of letters. Letters are used to spell sounds. Letters can be written as uppercase or lowercase. In this lesson, we'll learn how to look for and write letters. Sing the alphabet song with students.

MODEL Display the following passage "Indoors" or share copies of Student Page S51. Read it aloud. Say: The words in this passage use every letter in the alphabet.

RF.K.1.d Recognize and name all upper- and lowercase letters of the alphabet.

OBJECTIVES:
• Recognize all letters.
• Identify letters in words.
• Print all letters.

Indoors

We fly through the rain.
Quick, indoors!
Remove our boots.
Unzip the wet parkas.
Change into pajamas.
How exciting!

TEACH Display a large alphabet chart with both upper- and lowercase letters. Say the name of each letter, and then help students locate all the letters in the passage. For example, say: This is a capital letter R. This is a lowercase letter r. Do you see Rs in the passage? Circle the letters as you identify them. Remove starts with r. R sounds like /r/. Point to the letter. What is the name of this letter? R.

Lesson 4 | Learn the Letters in the Alphabet 2

REMIND
STUDENTS
THAT …

- they can recognize the letters *o* and *p*.
- they can identify the letters *o* and *p* in words.
- they can print the letters *o* and *p*.

PRACTICE 1: Recognize Letters *o* and *p* Display or distribute the letter cards from Student Page S52. Follow the routine to teach each letter. You may wish to cut the letters out to create separate picture cards.

Routine

1. Display the letter.	Model how to write upper- and lowercase *o* on the board. For example, say: This is uppercase *O*. This is lowercase *o*.
2. Name the letter.	What is the name of this letter? Yes; *o*.
3. Identify the letter.	Point to the otter card. What is this? Pause for responses. Yes, an otter. What letter does *otter* start with? Have students circle the letter and say it aloud. Yes, it's the letter *o*. *Otter* starts with *o*.
4. Write the letter.	Model writing lowercase *o*. Have students print lowercase *o* several times. Then model writing uppercase *O* and have students print it several times.
5. Extend practice.	Extend practice by having students find examples of the letter *o* in words around the room, including students' names, signs, and objects.

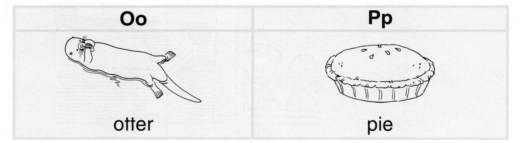

Oo	Pp
otter	pie

Repeat the routine for the remaining letter. Call attention to letters that are easily confused, such as *b* and *p*. Give students extra practice distinguishing and writing these letters.

☑ **MONITOR PROGRESS** Display the sentence from Student Page S52. Have individuals identify all instances of each letter taught. Check that students can print each letter independently.

> Open the present now, Pat.

IF… students misidentify or confuse any letters,
THEN… review key steps in the routine, and provide additional practice.

Lesson 4 | Learn the Letters in the Alphabet 2

PRACTICE 2: Recognize Letters *q* and *r* Display or distribute the letter cards from Student Page S53. Follow the routine to teach each letter. You may wish to cut the letters out to create separate picture cards.

Routine

1. Display the letter. Model how to write upper- and lowercase *q* on the board. For example, say: This is uppercase Q. This is lowercase q.

2. Name the letter. What is the name of this letter? Yes; q.

3. Identify the letter. Point to the queen card. What is this? Pause for responses. Yes, a queen. What letter does *queen* start with? Have students circle the letter and say it aloud. Yes, it's the letter q. Queen starts with q.

4. Write the letter. Model writing lowercase *q*. Have students print lowercase *q* several times. Then model writing uppercase *Q* and have students print it several times.

5. Extend practice. Have students make picture cards. Have them draw the letter *Q* on a card. Say several words that begin with *q* (*quilt, quarter*) and have students draw one of the words on their card. Then help them write the word on the card.

REMIND STUDENTS THAT …
- they can recognize the letters *q* and *r*.
- they can identify the letters *q* and *r* in words.
- they can print the letters *q* and *r*.

Qq	Rr
queen	rock

Repeat the routine for the remaining letter. Call attention to letters that students may find difficult, such as *p* and *q*. Give students extra practice distinguishing and writing these letters.

☑ **MONITOR PROGRESS** Display the sentence from Student Page S53. Have individuals identify all instances of each letter taught. Check that students can print each letter independently.

> Red quilts are quite warm.

IF… students struggle to write particular letters,
THEN… model again and give students additional practice writing the letter and new words containing it.

Lesson 4 | Learn the Letters in the Alphabet 2

REMIND
STUDENTS
THAT …

• they can recognize
the letters *s* and *t*.

• they can identify
the letters *s* and *t* in
words.

• they can print the
letters *s* and *t*.

PRACTICE 3: Recognize Letters *s* and *t* Display or distribute the letter cards from Student Page S54. Follow the routine to teach each letter. You may wish to cut the letters out to create separate picture cards.

Routine

1. Display the letter. Model how to write upper- and lowercase *s* on the board. For example, say: This is uppercase S. This is lowercase s.

2. Name the letter. What is the name of this letter? Yes; s.

3. Identify the letter. Point to the sun card. What is this? Pause for responses. Yes, the sun. What letter does *sun* start with? Have students circle the letter and say it aloud. Yes, it's the letter s. *Sun* starts with s.

4. Write the letter. Model writing lowercase s. Have students print lowercase s several times. Then model writing uppercase S and have students print it several times.

5. Extend practice. Have students find examples of the letter s in words around the room, including students' names, signs, and objects.

Ss	Tt
sun	tiger

Repeat the routine for the remaining letter. Call attention to letters that are easily confused, such as *t* and *f*. Give students extra practice distinguishing and writing these letters.

☑ **MONITOR PROGRESS** Display the sentence from Student Page S54. Have individuals identify all instances of each letter taught. Check that students can print each letter independently.

Sis eats toast.

IF… students misidentify or confuse any letters,
THEN… review key steps in the routine, and have students practice writing additional words with those letters.

Lesson 4 | Learn the Letters in the Alphabet 2

PRACTICE 4: Recognize Letters *u* and *v* Display or distribute the letter cards from Student Page S55. Follow the routine to teach each letter. You may wish to cut the letters out to create separate picture cards.

Routine

1. Display the letter. Model how to write upper- and lowercase *u* on the board. For example, say: This is uppercase *U*. This is lowercase *u*.

2. Name the letter. What is the name of this letter? Yes; *u*.

3. Identify the letter. Point to the umbrella card. What is this? Pause for responses. Yes, an umbrella. What letter does *umbrella* start with? Have students circle the letter and say it aloud. Yes, it's the letter *u*. Umbrella starts with *u*.

4. Write the letter. Model writing lowercase *u*. Have students print lowercase *u* several times. Then model writing uppercase *U* and have students print it several times.

5. Extend practice. Have students choose a classroom book and then find and copy two words that begin with or include *u*.

REMIND STUDENTS THAT …
• they can recognize the letters *u* and *v*.
• they can identify the letters *u* and *v* in words.
• they can print the letters *u* and *v*.

Uu	Vv
umbrella	volcano

Repeat the routine for the remaining letter. Call attention to letters that are easily confused, such as *u, v,* and *w*. Give students extra practice distinguishing and writing these letters.

☑ **MONITOR PROGRESS** Display the sentence from Student Page S55. Have individuals identify all instances of each letter taught. Check that students can print each letter independently.

> Use a very quiet voice to whisper.

IF… students struggle to identify particular letters,
THEN… model again how to identify the letters in several words and give students additional writing practice.

Lesson 4 | Learn the Letters in the Alphabet 2

REMIND STUDENTS THAT ...

• they can recognize the letters *w* and *x*.

• they can identify the letters *w* and *x* in words.

• they can print the letters *w* and *x*.

PRACTICE 5: Recognize Letters *w* and *x* Display or distribute the letter cards from Student Page S56. Follow the routine to teach each letter. You may wish to cut the letters out to create separate picture cards.

Routine

1. Display the letter. Model how to write upper- and lowercase *w* on the board. For example, say: This is uppercase W. This is lowercase *w*.

2. Name the letter. What is the name of this letter? Yes; *w*.

3. Identify the letter. Point to the worm card. What is this? Pause for responses. Yes, a worm. What letter does *worm* start with? Have students circle the letter and say it aloud. Yes, it's the letter *w*. *Worm* starts with *w*.

4. Write the letter. Model writing lowercase *w*. Have students print lowercase *w* several times. Then model writing uppercase *W* and have students print it several times.

5. Extend practice. Have students write the letter *w* on several sticky notes and then attach them to any objects in the room that begin with or contain *w*.

Ww	Xx
worm	x-ray

Repeat the routine for the remaining letter. Explain that not many words begin with *x*, but *x* can be found inside words such as *exciting* and at the end of words such as *box*. Give students ample practice distinguishing and writing these letters.

☑ **MONITOR PROGRESS** Display the sentence from Student Page S56. Have individuals identify all instances of each letter taught. Check that students can print each letter independently.

> We drink extra water when we exercise.

IF... students misidentify or confuse any letters,
THEN... review key steps in the routine, and have students practice writing additional words with those letters.

Lesson 4 — Learn the Letters in the Alphabet 2

PRACTICE 6: Recognize Letters y and z Display or distribute the letter cards from Student Page S57. Follow the routine to teach each letter. You may wish to cut the letters out to create separate picture cards.

Routine

1. Display the letter. Model how to write upper- and lowercase y on the board. For example, say: This is uppercase Y. This is lowercase y.

2. Name the letter. What is the name of this letter? Yes; y.

3. Identify the letter. Point to the yo-yo card. What is this? Pause for responses. Yes, a yo-yo. What letter does yo-yo start with? Have students circle the letter and say it aloud. Yes, it's the letter y. Yo-yo starts with y.

4. Write the letter. Model writing lowercase y. Have students print lowercase y several times. Then model writing uppercase Y and have students print it several times.

5. Extend practice. Have students find examples of the letter y in words around the room, including students' names, signs, and objects as well as in books.

Yy	Zz
yo-yo	zebra

Repeat the routine for the remaining letter. Call attention to letters that students might find difficult, such as lowercase z and s. Give students extra practice distinguishing and writing these letters.

☑ **MONITOR PROGRESS** Display the sentence from Student Page S57. Have individuals identify all instances of each letter taught. Check that students can print each letter independently.

> Did you see the zebra at the zoo yet?

IF… students misidentify or confuse any letters,
THEN… review key steps in the routine, and have students practice writing additional words with those letters.

Lesson 4 | Learn the Letters in the Alphabet 2

REMIND STUDENTS THAT …

- they can recognize the letters in the alphabet.
- they can identify letters in words.
- they can print each letter.

PRACTICE 7: Review Follow the routine to review any letter. You may wish to cut out letters to create new picture cards.

Routine

1. Display the letter.   Model how to write upper- and lowercase letters on the board. For example, say: This is uppercase *M*. This is lowercase *m*.

2. Name the letter.   Point to the letter. What is the name of this letter? Yes; *m*. The name of this letter is *m*.

3. Identify the letter.   Point to a card or an object with a name beginning with *m*. What is this? Pause for responses. Yes, a mouth. The beginning sound is /m/. What letter does *mouth* start with? Have students say the name of the letter aloud. Yes, it's the letter *m*. *Mouth* starts with *m*.

4. Write the letter.   Model writing upper- and lowercase *m*. Have students print both letters several times.

5. Extend practice.   Have students continue developing their own alphabet books. Turn to the page with the letter. Ask for examples of words that begin with that letter. Have students draw pictures of new words that begin with the letter, and then help students write the words.

For additional practice, have students print each letter and write words that begin with that letter.

☑ **INDEPENDENT PRACTICE** Display the illustration from Student Pages S58. Have individuals identify the letter being reviewed. Check that students can print the upper- and lowercase letters independently.

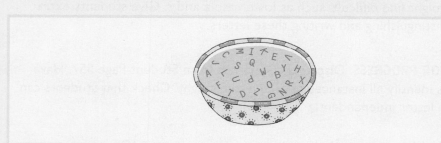

IF… students struggle to identify or reproduce particular letters,
THEN… model again how to identify the letters and give students additional writing practice.

Indoors

We fly through the rain.

Quick, indoors!

Remove our boots.

Unzip the wet parkas.

Change into pajamas.

How exciting!

Lesson 4   Learn the Letters in the Alphabet 2

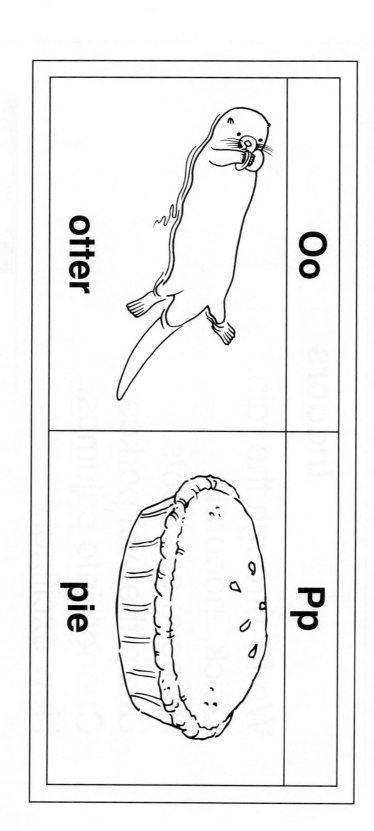

Oo	Pp
otter	pie

Open the present now, Pat.

Lesson 4   **Learn the Letters in the Alphabet 2**

Qq	Rr
queen	rock

Red quilts are quite warm.

Lesson 4   Learn the Letters in the Alphabet 2

Ss	Tt
sun	tiger

Sis eats toast.

Lesson 4   Learn the Letters in the Alphabet 2

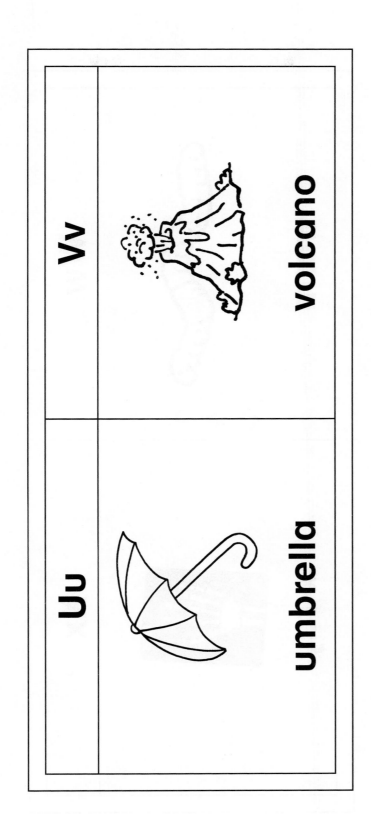

Uu	Vv
umbrella	volcano

Use a very quiet voice to whisper.

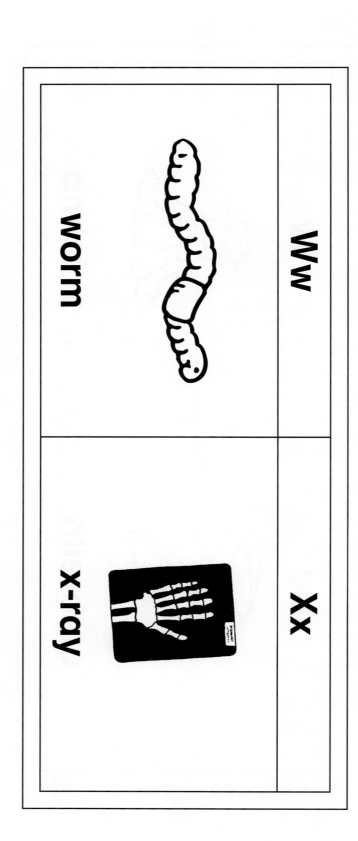

Ww	Xx
worm	x-ray

We drink extra water when we exercise.

Lesson 4

Learn the Letters in the Alphabet 2

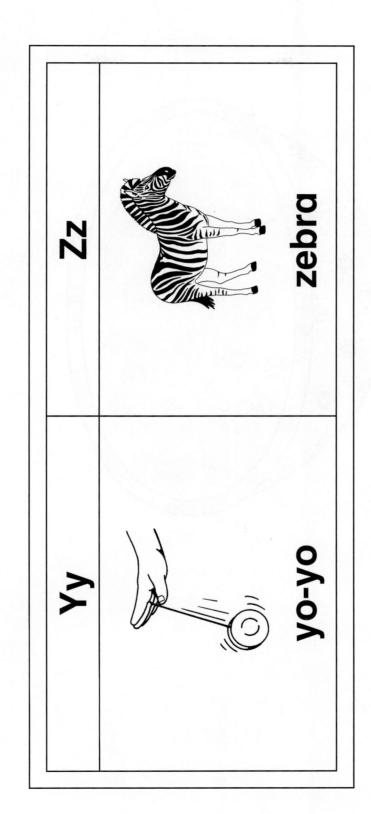

Yy	Zz
yo-yo	zebra

Did you see the zebra at the zoo yet?

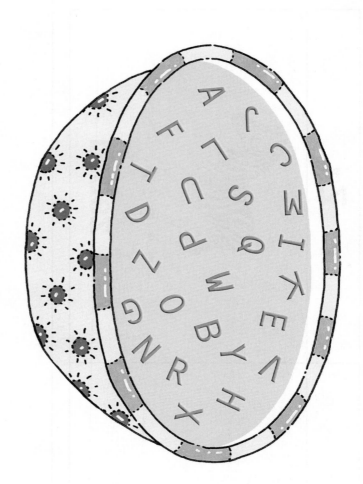

ASSESSMENT
LESSONS 3–4

Print Concepts

ASSESS MASTERY Use this Checkpoint to assess students' mastery of upper- and lowercase letters of the alphabet.

ADMINISTER THE TEST Administer the Checkpoint orally to each student. For each student, make two copies of the next page. Give each student a copy and use the other copy for marking the student's responses.

MODEL: Point to g. What letter is this? That's right; this is g. Now you name as many of these letters as you can. Start here **(point to E)** and go across the page. When you finish one line, go to the next line, and read across the page. If you come to a letter you don't know, I'll name it for you.

RF.K.1.d Recognize and name all upper- and lowercase letters of the alphabet.

SCORING

SKILL/LESSON	SCORE
1. Learn the Letters of the Alphabet 1 and 2 (Lessons 3–4)	_____ / 51

An overall score of 80% correct is typically considered mastery. Use your judgment and your individual students' needs as well to determine skill mastery.

IF… students score below the benchmark,
THEN… review the missed letters, going back to the lessons to reteach and scaffold as needed.

ASSESSMENT
LESSONS 3–4

Print Concepts

g	E	v	a	J	o	q	L	R	b	h
s	I	G	c	K	p	t	d	V	S	
e	n	f	H	r	m	T	g	Q	M	z
u	A	l	Y	j	F	P	B	k	Z	x
N	O	y	W	U	D	w	C	X		

Lesson 5 | Identify Rhyme in Words

INTRODUCE Explain that when the ending parts of words sound alike, the words rhyme. Tell students that they will listen to some words and decide which ones rhyme.

MODEL Reinforce the concept of rhyme. Words that rhyme sound the same, such as *bike* and *like*. Other words that sound like those are *Mike* and *trike*. The words rhyme because their ending parts sound the same. Display or write the following lines from Student Page S61.

RF.K.2.a Recognize and produce rhyming words.

OBJECTIVES:
• Determine if spoken pairs of words rhyme.
• Identify which spoken words rhyme.

New Wheels

Mike rides a trike.
What would Mike like?
Mike would like a bike.

TEACH I'm going to say two words. If they rhyme, I will clap my hands. If they do not rhyme, I will not clap my hands. *Rose, pill* (do not clap). *Run, fun* (clap).

Now you try. Read aloud the following single-syllable word pairs: *top, drop; hit, sit; nose, ear; fall, call; nice, neat; date, late; try, fly.*

If students respond incorrectly, say: Listen carefully. Do the ending parts have the same sound? Repeat the pair. Affirm correct responses: Yes, those words rhyme.

Use triplets to distinguish rhyming words from non-rhyming words. Say three words. Tell students two of the words rhyme and one does not.

Slowly say: *pat, rip, sat.* Repeat the words. Pay attention to how each word ends. *Pat.* The word *pat* ends with /at/. Say it with me: /at/. *Rip.* The word *rip* ends with /ip/. That's not the same as /at/, so those two words do not rhyme. *Sat.* The word *sat* ends with /at/. That's the same ending sound as in *pat. Pat* and *Sat* rhyme.

Lesson 5 | Identify Rhyme in Words

REMIND STUDENTS THAT ...

- words that rhyme have the same ending sound.

PRACTICE 1 Tell students they will practice finding words that rhyme. I'm going to say two words. If they rhyme, clap your hands. If they do not rhyme, do not clap. Let's do one pair of words together. *Fin, pin* (clap).

Now you try. Display and read aloud the single-syllable word pairs from Student Page S62.

got cot (clap)	pit put	cow now (clap)	bed bad

If students respond incorrectly, say: Listen carefully. Do the ending parts have the same sound? Repeat the pair. Affirm correct responses: Yes, those words rhyme.

Read aloud the rhyming pairs from Student Page S62. Have students repeat the words aloud, emphasizing the rhyming sounds.

did, hid mile, pile	fat, rat roar, soar	how, wow

☑ **MONITOR PROGRESS** Read the following word pairs aloud to students: *fair, pair; dark, bark; oil, boil; rap, good; send, fan.* After each pair ask: Do these words rhyme? Affirm correct responses.

IF... students cannot identify rhyming words,
THEN... model hearing rhyme by saying two rhyming words, emphasizing the ending in each one.

Lesson 5 | Identify Rhyme in Words

PRACTICE 2 Ask students to listen to these words: *hot, lot, can.* Say: *hot.* Say the ending /ot/, then have students say it with you. Repeat with *lot.* Then say: *can.* Say its ending: /an/. Have students repeat the ending. Ask: Which words have the same ending? Pause to let students respond. Yes, *hot* and *lot* have the same ending. *Hot* and *lot* rhyme.

Then say each set of words from Student Page S63 and ask students to name the rhyming words. After doing the oral exercise, you may wish to display Student Page S63 and point out the word endings to reinforce the final sounds and rhymes.

REMIND STUDENTS THAT ...
- words that rhyme have the same ending sound.
- words that do not have the same ending sound do not rhyme.

pat	cat	joke
pig	sit	woke
wig	mat	wake

Next, say the following word sets aloud, and have students name the rhyming words.

<u>weak</u>, watch, <u>beak</u>	<u>crab</u>, <u>grab</u>, cup
plan, <u>plane</u>, <u>gain</u>	<u>fin</u>, fat, <u>pin</u>
grin, <u>mug</u>, <u>jug</u>	

☑ **MONITOR PROGRESS** Say each set of words below and have students name the rhyming words.

tip, <u>gate</u>, <u>wait</u>
<u>book</u>, <u>look</u>, back
<u>bad</u>, bid, <u>mad</u>

IF... students cannot identify the rhyming words in a set,
THEN... say each word in the set and have students repeat the words after you. Ask: Which words end with the same sound? Repeat the words emphasizing the ending of each to help students identify the words that rhyme.

Lesson 5	Identify Rhyme in Words

REMIND STUDENTS THAT ...

- words that rhyme have the same ending sound.
- words that do not have the same ending sound do not rhyme.
- rhyming words can have one or more than one syllable.

PRACTICE 3 Tell students that short words can rhyme, and longer words can rhyme as well. Let's start with short words. Here are some short words that rhyme: *lap, tap, map*. All of those words end with the sound /ap/.

Now listen to these longer words: *Pocket, happy, rocket*. The word *pocket* ends with /ok it/. Say it with me: /ok it/. The word *happy* ends with /ap ē/. That is not the same as /ok it/, so those two words don't rhyme. *Pocket, rocket*. The word *rocket* ends with /ok it/ like *pocket*. *Pocket* and *rocket* rhyme.

Here are other longer words: *tower, shower, flicker*. Which two words end with /ow er/? Let's say the words together: *tower, shower*.

Next, display and say each set of words from Student Page S64, and have students name the rhyming words.

pile	rider	pickle
line	wider	label
fine	later	tickle

Say each set of words aloud, and have students name the rhyming words.

ring, <u>kick</u>, <u>quick</u>	<u>stumble</u>, bother, <u>crumble</u>
<u>might</u>, <u>fight</u>, spot	<u>cool</u>, <u>pool</u>, rail
<u>sunny</u>, rabbit, <u>funny</u>	phone, <u>yarn</u>, <u>barn</u>

☑ **INDEPENDENT PRACTICE** Say each set of words aloud, and have students name the rhyming words.

<u>bread</u>, drip, <u>said</u>	<u>simple</u>, <u>dimple</u>, ticket
drag, <u>snug</u>, <u>plug</u>	<u>sneezy</u>, snazzy, <u>breezy</u>

IF... students cannot identify two-syllable rhyming words in a set, THEN... say each word in the set and have students repeat the words after you. Guide students to identify the ending sounds in each word. Which endings are the same? Pause for students to respond. The words with the same ending sounds rhyme.

New Wheels

Mike rides a trike.
What would Mike like?
Mike would like a bike.

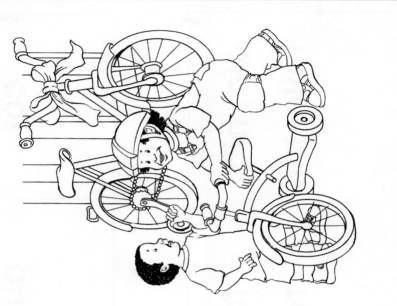

Teacher: This Student Page is intended as an *optional extension* of the lesson. After teaching the phonological awareness lesson orally, you can distribute or display this page to connect the phonological awareness skills (sounds) to phonics skills (sound-spelling).

S • 61 Phonological Awareness

Lesson 5 Identify Rhyme in Words

got cot	pit put	cow now	bed bad

did, hid   fat, rat

mile, pile   roar, soar   how, wow

Teacher: This Student Page is intended as an *optional extension* of the lesson. After teaching the phonological awareness lesson orally, you can distribute or display this page to connect the phonological awareness skills (sounds) to phonics skills (sound-spelling).

Lesson 5 | Identify Rhyme in Words

pat	cat
pig	sit
wig	mat
joke	
woke	
wake	

Teacher: This Student Page is intended as an *optional extension* of the lesson. After teaching the phonological awareness lesson orally, you can distribute or display this page to connect the phonological awareness skills (sounds) to phonics skills (sound-spelling).

Lesson 5   Identify Rhyme in Words

pile	rider	pickle
line	wider	label
fine	later	tickle

Teacher: This Student Page is intended as an *optional extension* of the lesson. After teaching the phonological awareness lesson orally, you can distribute or display this page to connect the phonological awareness skills (sounds) to phonics skills (sound-spelling).

Lesson 6 | Produce Rhyme in Words

INTRODUCE Remind students that rhyming words have ending parts that sound the same. Today I'm going to say some words, and then we're going to think of new words that rhyme with the ones I say.

MODEL Display or distribute the passage "My Friend Pat" from Student Page S65. Then, read the passage, emphasizing the ending sounds.

RF.K.2.a Recognize and produce rhyming words.

OBJECTIVE:
- Produce a spoken word to rhyme with another spoken word.

My Friend Pat

My friend Pat
has more than one hat.
One hat has a bat.
One hat has a cat.
One hat has a very fat rat.
That is one ugly hat!

Use the passage as you review the concept of rhyme with students. I want to find a word that rhymes with *cat*. Say *cat* aloud several times, slowly at first, and then at a normal rate. The word *cat* ends with /at/. Say /at/ several times. What other words do I know that end the same way? I know—*bat*. The word *bat* rhymes with *cat*: /k//at/, /b//at/. Repeat with the words *fit* and *hit*.

TEACH Use simple segmenting to reinforce the concept that rhyme involves the ending parts of words. A lot of the words we know have beginning sounds and ending sounds. Listen closely: *Shake*. *Shake* has the beginning sound /sh/ and the ending sound /āk/. To make a rhyming word, we need another word that ends with /āk/. How about *take*? *cake*? *break*? All of those words have the ending sound /āk/. All of the words rhyme with *shake*. Invite students to add other words that rhyme. Examples include *bake, fake, Jake, lake, make,* and *rake*. Allow students to offer nonsense words that rhyme as well.

| Lesson 6 | Produce Rhyme in Words |

REMIND STUDENTS THAT …

- words that rhyme have the same ending.
- words that do not have the same ending do not rhyme.

PRACTICE 1 Invite students to help you think of rhyming words. I'll say a word, and we'll all figure out words that rhyme with it. Say *tip*. Have students repeat the word. Say the ending with me: /ip/. What's another word that ends the same way? Pause to let students tell you a word. Yes, (*dip, drip, lip, sip, trip*) rhymes with *tip*.

Follow this procedure to guide practice, using the words from Student Page S66. Accept nonsense words as well as real words that rhyme.

> **sat** (bat, cat, fat, hat, mat, rat, pat)
> **hug** (rug, jug, mug, bug, dug, tug, plug, chug)
> **fan** (man, ran, van, Jan, Dan, can, pan)
> **bed** (fed, led, head, said, red, Ned, Ted)
> **fox** (box, locks, socks, rocks, knocks)

Then give students the following words from Student Page S66 and have them produce rhyming words for each. Accept nonsense words as well as real words that rhyme.

> **run** (fun, one, son, bun, done, none)
> **pin** (fin, win, chin, bin, tin)
> **get** (bet, pet, set, jet, wet, vet)
> **bag** (drag, lag, nag, rag, sag, tag, wag)

☑ **MONITOR PROGRESS** Give students the following words from Student Page S66 and have them produce at least two rhyming words for each.

> **sip** (drip, slip, rip, dip, clip, hip, trip, tip, nip)
> **hop** (bop, cop, chop, drop, shop, mop, pop, top)

IF… students say words with similar beginning sounds instead of similar endings, **THEN…** say the word again, emphasizing the ending, and model a correct response.

Lesson 6	Produce Rhyme in Words

PRACTICE 2 Invite students to help you think of rhyming words. Listen closely: *light.* Have students repeat the word slowly. Say the ending with me: /īt/. What's one other word that ends the same way? Pause to let students tell you a word. Yes, (*bite, sight, fight, might, night, right, white, tight, kite*) rhymes with *light.* **Ask** for more rhyming words until students have produced four or five. Follow this procedure to guide practice, using the following words from Student Page S67. Accept nonsense words as well as real words that rhyme.

REMIND STUDENTS THAT ...
• words that rhyme have the same ending.
• words that do not have the same ending do not rhyme.

dog (log, fog, blog, hog, frog)
club (rub, tub, sub, cub, dub)
sheet (beat, feet, heat, meat, neat, seat)
trick (sick, click, thick, brick, tick, pick, quick)

Display and read aloud the following words from Student Page S67, and have students produce rhyming words for each. Accept nonsense words as well as real words that rhyme.

book (cook, look, took, shook, nook, hook, rook)
school (rule, cool, pool, tool, fool)
sit (bit, fit, spit, mitt, hit, pit, quit)
read (bead, feed, lead, need, seed)

☑ **MONITOR PROGRESS** Read aloud the following words from Student Page S67, and have students produce at least two rhyming words for each.

rap (cap, map, lap, tap, nap, app)
face (ace, lace, race, place, chase, erase, pace)

IF... students cannot produce rhyming words,
THEN... say each word slowly. Help students segment the sounds in the word and guide them to identify the ending sound in the word. Then ask: What other words do you know that have the same ending sound? Offer one example to help students produce rhyming words.

Lesson 6 | Produce Rhyme in Words

REMIND
STUDENTS
THAT …

• words that rhyme
have the same ending.

• long words can
rhyme.

PRACTICE 3 Explain that words of all sizes can rhyme. Some words with just one sound can rhyme. **Point to your eye and say:** *Eye.* This word has just one sound. What words rhyme with *eye?* **Let students respond.** Yes, (*buy, fly, why, my, try*) rhymes with *eye.*

What about longer words? If their ending sounds match, they rhyme. Listen: *berry.* The ending sound is /er ē/. What words rhyme with *berry?* **Have students respond.** Yes, (*fairy, merry, cherry, hairy, scary*) rhymes with *berry.*

What if I want a word that rhymes with *agrees? Agrees* ends with /ēz/. **Say /ēz/** several times. What other words end this way? How about *sneeze?* The words *agrees* and *sneeze* both end in /ēz/. They rhyme. So do *bees, knees,* and *chimpanzees!* Follow this procedure to guide practice, using the words below from Student Page S68.

> **funny** (honey, money, sunny, runny, bunny)
> **better** (wetter, sweater, letter, setter)

Next, say each word below from Student Page S68 and have students repeat the word. Ask for a rhyming word: What word rhymes with _____?

> **many** (any, penny, Jenny)
> **dinner** (winner, thinner, spinner, inner)

☑ **INDEPENDENT PRACTICE** Read aloud the following words from Student Page S68, and have students produce at least two rhyming words for each. Accept nonsense words as well as real words that rhyme.

> **sticker** (quicker, thicker, flicker, kicker, sicker)
> **bend** (friend, end, send, spend, lend, depend)

IF… students cannot produce rhyming words with more than one syllable, THEN… model a correct response by saying *mister* and *twister*, emphasizing the ending part in each one. Guide students to suggest other words that end with the /is ter/ sound, such as *sister.* Encourage students to use this process to produce rhyming words.

Lesson 6 | **Produce Rhyme in Words**

My Friend Pat

My friend Pat
has more than one hat.
One hat has a bat.
One hat has a cat.
One hat has a very fat rat.
That is one ugly hat!

Teacher: This Student Page is intended as an *optional extension* of the lesson. After teaching the phonological awareness lesson orally, you can distribute or display this page to connect the phonological awareness skills (sounds) to phonics skills (sound-spelling).

Lesson 6   **Produce Rhyme in Words**

sat	
hug	bed
fan	fox

run	
pin	get
	bag

sip
hop

Teacher: This Student Page is intended as an *optional extension* of the lesson. After teaching the phonological awareness lesson orally, you can distribute or display this page to connect the phonological awareness skills (sounds) to phonics skills (sound-spelling).

Lesson 6   Produce Rhyme in Words

dog
club

sheet
trick

book
school

sit
read

rap
face

Teacher: This Student Page is intended as an *optional extension* of the lesson. After teaching the phonological awareness lesson orally, you can distribute or display this page to connect the phonological awareness skills (sounds) to phonics skills (sound-spelling).

Lesson 6   Produce Rhyme in Words

funny
better

many
dinner

sticker
bend

Teacher: This Student Page is intended as an *optional extension* of the lesson. After teaching the phonological awareness lesson orally, you can distribute or display this page to connect the phonological awareness skills (sounds) to phonics skills (sound-spelling).

Lesson 7 — Blend and Count Syllables in Spoken Words

INTRODUCE Remind students that some words are short and some are long. You know that sentences are made of parts called words. Words are made of parts too. The parts of words are called *syllables*. Today we will put syllables together to make words.

MODEL Explain that short words have one syllable and some longer words have more than one syllable. Listen as I say the syllables that make a word. As you say each syllable, clap your hands: *mu* (clap) *sic* (clap). Now I will put the syllables together to make the word. I will say them quickly without stopping: *music.*

How many syllables are in the word *music*? Remember, I clapped my hands for the syllables: *mu* (clap) *sic* (clap). *Music* has two syllables. Now let's count on our fingers. Watch: *mu* (raise your thumb) *sic* (raise your index finger on the same hand). Repeat and have students count with you.

Follow the same procedure to model blending and then counting the syllables of *rain* and *bow* (*rainbow*) and *af* and *ter* (*after*). After the oral exercise, you may wish to distribute or display Student Page S69.

mu sic   rain bow   af ter

TEACH Wave your hand around the room and say: *classroom.* There are two syllables in *classroom*: *class* (hold up your thumb) *room* (hold up the index finger). When we put the syllables together, we make a word: *classroom.* Repeat with *playground, classmates,* and *daylight.*

Reinforce hearing and counting syllables. Slowly say *sunset* as you raise two fingers. Listen and count with me: *sun•set.* Repeat with *animal,* raising three fingers: *an•i•mal.*

RF.K.2.b Count, pronounce, blend, and segment syllables in spoken words.

OBJECTIVES:
- Pronounce and count syllables in spoken words.
- Blend spoken words into compound words.
- Blend syllables into spoken words.

Lesson 7 | Blend and Count Syllables in Spoken Words

REMIND STUDENTS THAT …

• words are made of parts called syllables.

• saying a word slowly makes it easy to hear the syllables.

PRACTICE 1 Remind students that some words have just one syllable. Other words have two or more syllables.

Let's try some words. First, I will say the syllables. Next, you say the syllables with me. Then, we'll make a word by saying the syllables together.

Say *pic* and *ture*, clapping after you say each syllable. Now say the syllables with me and clap after each one. *Pic* (clap) *ture* (clap). Let's say the syllables without clapping. Speak the syllables distinctly. As you speak, raise your thumb for the first syllable and another finger for the second syllable. Have students repeat what you do. Now, let's say the syllables together in a word: *picture*. Repeat the word: *picture*.

Follow the same procedure with the words *zig•zag* and *cor•ner*.

Say the syllables of the first set of three words on Student Page S70, and have students repeat the syllables with you. Then ask students to say the syllables together as a word. If students falter, model saying the word and have them repeat it with you several times.

air port	run way	rain y

☑ **MONITOR PROGRESS** Say the syllables of each word below and ask students how many syllables they hear. Then have students say the syllables together as a word.

pen cil	bee hive	gar den	cheer ful

IF… students make an error,
THEN… model the correct response by saying the syllables separately, holding up a finger for each syllable and then blending the syllables to say the word.

Lesson 7	**Blend and Count Syllables in Spoken Words**

PRACTICE 2 Explain that you are going to practice making words that have two or more syllables. We will make words with two or more syllables from shorter words. Here are two short words: *cup* (pause) *cake*. Now I will say the words together to make one word: *cupcake*. Do you know what a cupcake is? Allow students to respond.

Let's try some words together. We will take two short words and make them into one word. Distinctly say the words in each of the following word pairs from Student Page S71. Have students repeat each pair and then combine them into a single word.

cat fish	blue bird	sting ray

Say each of the following pairs of words from Student Page S71. Have students repeat each word distinctly. Then have students combine each pair of words into a single word.

bed room	night light	fire fly

☑ **MONITOR PROGRESS** Say each of the following sets of words from Student Page S71. Have students repeat each set of words distinctly and then combine them into a single word.

gold fish	sun beam	fire place

IF... students make errors in blending syllables,
THEN... model the correct response by saying the syllables together and having students repeat after you.

| Lesson 7 | Blend and Count Syllables in Spoken Words |

- words are made of parts called syllables.
- to make a word, we say syllables together without stopping.

PRACTICE 3 Review hearing and counting syllables. Let's count the syllables, or parts, in the word *sidewalk.* Say the word slowly, and count the parts on your fingers: *side* (raise your thumb) *walk* (raise the next finger). There are two syllables in *sidewalk, side* and *walk.* When we put the syllables together, we get *sidewalk.*

Now we will put together some other syllables to make words. Here are two syllables: *kit•chen.* Can you tell what word they make? **Have students respond.** That's right; the word is *kitchen.*

Display and say the following syllables from Student Page S72. Have students repeat the syllables distinctly, and then have them say the word.

bath robe	bathrobe
morn ing	morning
count er	counter
toast er	toaster
mi cro wave	microwave

Have students listen closely as you say each of these sets of distinct syllables from Student Page S72. Have them repeat the syllables separately and then blend the syllables into a word. Allow students to begin slowly and make several attempts to say each word normally.

sham poo	tooth brush	tel e phone
jack et	um brel la	ad ven ture

☑ **INDEPENDENT PRACTICE** Say the following syllables from Student Page S72 and have students repeat after you. After each set, have them say the syllables together as one word. Allow them to begin slowly and speed up to make the word.

nap kin	din ner	in doors	di no saur

IF... students make an error in blending syllables,
THEN... say the word, say the syllables separately, and then blend the syllables back into the word.

Lesson 7 | **Blend and Count Syllables in Spoken Words**

mu sic

rain bow

af ter

Teacher: This Student Page is intended as an *optional extension* of the lesson. After teaching the phonological awareness lesson orally, you can distribute or display this page to connect the phonological awareness skills (sounds) to phonics skills (sound-spelling).

Lesson 7 Blend and Count Syllables in Spoken Words

air port   run way   rain y

pen cil   bee hive   gar den   cheer ful

Teacher: This Student Page is intended as an *optional extension* of the lesson. After teaching the phonological awareness lesson orally, you can distribute or display this page to connect the phonological awareness skills (sounds) to phonics skills (sound-spelling).

Lesson 7 | **Blend and Count Syllables in Spoken Words**

cat fish	blue bird	sting ray

bed room	night light	fire fly

gold fish	sun beam	fire place

Teacher: This Student Page is intended as an *optional extension* of the lesson. After teaching the phonological awareness lesson orally, you can distribute or display this page to connect the phonological awareness skills (sounds) to phonics skills (sound-spelling).

S • 71 Phonological Awareness

Lesson 7   Blend and Count Syllables in Spoken Words

bath robe
morn ing
count er
toast er
mi cro wave

sham poo   tooth brush   tel e phone
jack et   um brel la   ad ven ture

nap kin   din ner   in doors   di no saur

Teacher: This Student Page is intended as an *optional extension* of the lesson. After teaching the phonological awareness lesson orally, you can distribute or display this page to connect the phonological awareness skills (sounds) to phonics skills (sound-spelling).

Lesson 8 | Segment and Count Syllables in Spoken Words

INTRODUCE Remind students that some words have more than one part. Listen as I say a word: *dinosaur*. Can you hear the parts in *dinosaur*? Let me say the parts more slowly: *di•no•saur*. There are three parts, or syllables, in *dinosaur*.

MODEL Refer to Student Page S73. I'm going to say a word: *number*. I'll say the word again as I use my fingers to count each syllable I hear. Say *num•ber* again slowly, holding up your thumb for *num* and your index finger for *ber*.

Use your other hand to point to your raised fingers as you repeat the syllables. Say: *one, two* to count your fingers. Count with me: one, two. I hear two syllables. The syllables are *num•ber*.

RF.K.2.b Count, pronounce, blend, and segment syllables in spoken words.

OBJECTIVES:
- Count syllables in spoken words.
- Segment spoken compound words.
- Segment spoken words into syllables.

num ber
sleep y
bed time
sev en

TEACH Follow the modeling procedure to segment the remaining words on Student Page S73. Let's do some other words together. First, we'll say a word: *sleepy*. Say the word with me: *sleepy*. Next, we will say the syllables and count them. *Sleep* (hold up your thumb and have students imitate you) *y* (hold up your index finger and have students imitate you). How many syllables did we count? Use your other hand to point to your raised fingers and count. Have students imitate you. That's right. We counted two syllables. Continue with the words *bedtime* (*bed•time*) and *seven* (*sev•en*).

| Lesson 8 | Segment and Count Syllables in Spoken Words |

REMIND STUDENTS THAT …

• words may have two or more syllables, or parts.

• they know how to count syllables.

PRACTICE 1 Explain that hearing the separate syllables in words is called segmenting. You have counted syllables in words. Some words are just one syllable. An example is *cow*. Some words have more syllables. An example is *cowboy*. How many parts can we hear in *cowboy*? Let's count them.

Raise your thumb as you say: *cow*. Raise your index finger as you say: *boy*. Point to each finger and say: Count with me. One, two. There are two syllables in *cowboy*.

Have students segment each of the following words from Student Page S74.

> **bunny** (bun•ny)   **piglet** (pig•let)
> **baby** (ba•by)   **duckling** (duck•ling)
> **puppy** (pup•py)   **butterfly** (but•ter•fly)
> **kitten** (kit•ten)   **caterpillar** (cat•er•pil•lar)

Say each of the following words from Student Page S74 and have students repeat each one with you. Then have them count the syllables in the words using the process outlined above.

> **family** (fam•i•ly, 3 syllables)
> **picnic** (pic•nic, 2 syllables)
> **outdoors** (out•doors, 2 syllables)
> **catnap** (cat•nap, 2 syllables)

☑ **MONITOR PROGRESS** Display and read the following words from Student Page S74. Have students segment the words and count the syllables.

> **robot** (ro•bot, 2 syllables)
> **helper** (help•er, 2 syllables)
> **wonder** (won•der, 2 syllables)
> **afternoon** (af•ter•noon, 3 syllables)

IF… students have difficulty identifying the correct number of syllables in a word,
THEN… review how to count the number of syllables on one hand, and provide some familiar multisyllabic words to help students practice.

Lesson 8 | Segment and Count Syllables in Spoken Words

PRACTICE 2 Remind students that they know some words that are made of smaller words. *Our school has classrooms. The word* classroom *has two syllables. Each syllable is its own word. Can you hear the two syllables? Let me say them:* class (pause) room. *Say the syllables with me:* class (pause) room. *If we say these words together quickly, it is like saying syllables together quickly. It makes a word:* classroom.

Let's take apart some words together. These words have two syllables. Each syllable is a short word. The first word is armchair. *What are the two syllables?* Let students respond. *That's right. The two syllables are* arm *and* chair. *Say them with me:* arm (pause) chair.

Repeat the process with the words *eyelash, handshake, wristwatch,* and *footstep.*

Read aloud the following compound words from Student Page S75. After reading each word, ask students to tell you the two syllables, or short words, that make it up.

outside (out•side)	shoelace (shoe•lace)
haircut (hair•cut)	football (foot•ball)
doghouse (dog•house)	doorway (door•way)

☑ **MONITOR PROGRESS** Read aloud each of the following compound words from Student Page S75. Have students segment each word.

ballpark (ball•park)
homework (home•work)
campfire (camp•fire)

IF... students have difficulty segmenting syllables,
THEN... model segmenting the word and have students repeat the syllables after you. Provide additional practice with familiar compound words.

REMIND STUDENTS THAT ...

• syllables are the separate word parts they can hear.

• many longer words are made of syllables that are really two short words.

Lesson 8 | Segment and Count Syllables in Spoken Words

REMIND STUDENTS THAT …

• words may have two or more syllables, or parts.

• segmenting words lets them count the syllables.

PRACTICE 3 Tell students they will listen to words and decide which syllables they contain. For example, I can say the word *winter*. I am going to say it slowly so you can hear the parts: *win* (pause) *ter*. The word *winter* contains the syllables *win* and *ter*. Say them with me: *win* (pause) *ter*.

Some words have more syllables. Say this word with me: *sharpener*. **Have students say the word.** Now let's say it very slowly so that we can hear the syllables. Repeat after me: *sharp* (pause) *en* (pause) *er*. There are three syllables: *sharp* (pause) *en* (pause) and *er*.

Repeat the process with the following words from Student Page S76.

window (win•dow)	hamster (ham•ster)
thunderstorm (thun•der•storm)	insect (in•sect)
pencil (pen•cil)	mystery (mys•ter•y)
hamburger (ham•bur•ger)	garden (gar•den)

☑ **INDEPENDENT PRACTICE** Read the following words from Student Page S76 and have students repeat each word with you. Then ask students to say the word slowly so you can hear the syllables, or parts.

> birthday (birth•day)
> monkey (mon•key)
> sleepover (sleep•o•ver)
> doctor (doc•tor)
> elephant (el•e•phant)

IF… students are unable to segment syllables,
THEN… model the correct response by saying the word in distinct syllables as you raise a finger to count each one. Have students repeat after you. If needed, help students brainstorm familiar multisyllabic words for additional practice.

Lesson 8   **Segment and Count Syllables in Spoken Words**

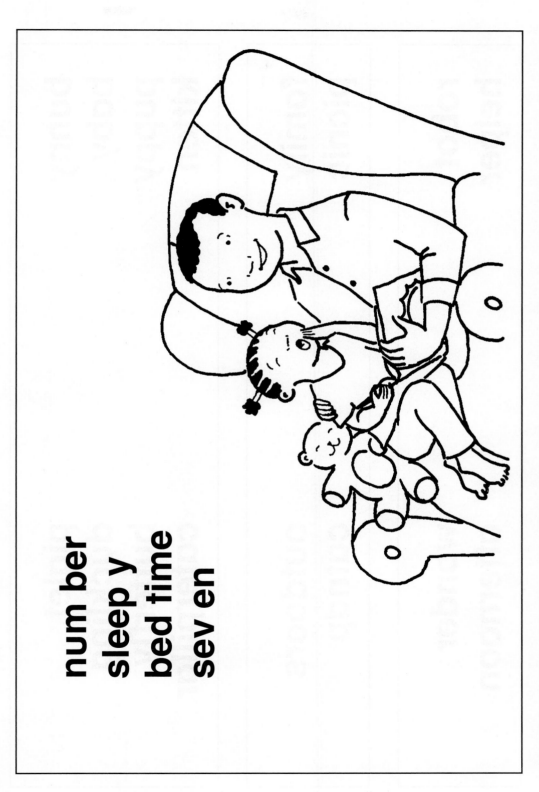

num ber

sleep y

bed time

sev en

Teacher: This Student Page is intended as an *optional extension* of the lesson. After teaching the phonological awareness lesson orally, you can distribute or display this page to connect the phonological awareness skills (sounds) to phonics skills (sound-spelling).

Lesson 8   Segment and Count Syllables in Spoken Words

bunny
baby
puppy
kitten

piglet
duckling
butterfly
caterpillar

family
picnic

outdoors
catnap

robot
helper

wonder
afternoon

Teacher: This Student Page is intended as an *optional extension* of the lesson. After teaching the phonological awareness lesson orally, you can distribute or display this page to connect the phonological awareness skills (sounds) to phonics skills (sound-spelling).

Lesson 8   Segment and Count Syllables in Spoken Words

outside
haircut
doghouse

shoelace
football
doorway

ballpark
homework
campfire

Teacher: This Student Page is intended as an *optional extension* of the lesson. After teaching the phonological awareness lesson orally, you can distribute or display this page to connect the phonological awareness skills (sounds) to phonics skills (sound-spelling).

Lesson 8   Segment and Count Syllables in Spoken Words

window   hamster

thunderstorm   insect

pencil   mystery

hamburger   garden

---

birthday

monkey

sleepover

doctor

elephant

Teacher: This Student Page is intended as an *optional* extension of the lesson. After teaching the phonological awareness lesson orally, you can distribute or display this page to connect the phonological awareness skills (sounds) to phonics skills (sound-spelling).

ASSESSMENT
LESSONS 5–8

Phonological Awareness

ASSESS MASTERY Use this Checkpoint to assess students' mastery of rhyming words and syllables in spoken words.

ADMINISTER THE TEST Administer the Checkpoint orally to each student. For each item, model the process as described, and then have the student use the process to respond to your prompts. Record responses on the scoring chart on the next page.

RF.K.2.a Recognize and produce rhyming words.

RF.K.2.b Count, pronounce, blend, and segment syllables in spoken words.

1. Identify Rhyme in Words (Lesson 5)
MODEL: I am going to read three words. Then you tell me which two words rhyme. For example, I could say *pan, can,* and *pin. Pan* and *can* are words that rhyme. The word *pin* does not rhyme with *pan* and *can*.

ASSESS:	lip, dip, cup	try, hot, fly	bubble, litter, sitter

2. Produce Rhyme in Words (Lesson 6)
MODEL: I am going to ask you for rhyming words. I will say a word. Then you will say a word that rhymes. It can be a real word or a made-up word. For example, I could say *cat. Hat* is a word that rhymes with *cat*.

ASSESS:	sit	dot	pet	bed	can	cow

3. Blend and Count Syllables in Spoken Words (Lesson 7)
MODEL: I will say some syllables. Then you blend them together to say the word. For example, the word *picnic* has two syllables, *pic•nic*. To say the word, we blend the syllables together without stopping: *picnic*.

ASSESS:	high•way	nev•er	re•cess	mu•sic

4. Segment and Count Syllables in Spoken Words (Lesson 8)
MODEL: I will say a word. I will ask you to say each syllable of the word and count the syllables on your fingers. For example, the word *feather* has two syllables. I hold up a finger for each syllable: *feath•er*. There are two fingers, for two syllables.

ASSESS:	haircut	family	sandwich	quarter

ASSESSMENT
LESSONS 5–8

Phonological Awareness

SCORING

SKILL/LESSON	STANDARD	SCORE
I. Identify Rhyme in Words (Lesson 5) lip, dip try, fly litter, sitter	**RF.K.2.a** Recognize and produce rhyming words.	_____ / 3
2. Produce Rhyme in Words (Lesson 6) sit dot pet bed can cow		_____ / 6
3. Blend and Count Syllables in Spoken Words (Lesson 7) highway never recess music	**RF.K.2.b** Count, pronounce, blend, and segment syllables in spoken words.	_____ / 4
4. Segment and Count Syllables in Spoken Words (Lesson 8) 2 3 2 2		_____ / 4

An overall score of 80% correct is typically considered mastery. Use your judgment and your individual students' needs as well to determine skill mastery.

IF… students score below the benchmark,
THEN… review those discrete skills, going back to the lessons to reteach and scaffold as needed.

Lesson 9 | Blend Onset and Rime

INTRODUCE Say the word *get* using onset and rime: /g/ (pause) /et/. What word did you hear? Did it sound right? Let me say the sounds together: *get.* Did that sound better? Today we will practice hearing the sounds in words. We will also blend sounds to make words.

MODEL Remind students that rhyming words have the same ending sound (rime). Display or share copies of Student Page S79. Read it aloud. Then say: Watch my face as I say some of these words. **Point to** *let, wet, pet, net,* **and** *yet* **as you say the words:** *let, wet, pet, net, yet.* These words have the same ending sound, or rime: /et/. They have different beginning sounds, or onsets. Listen. Repeat each word as onset and rime: /l/ (pause) /et/, and so on. Elongate each onset for emphasis. I can hear the onset and the rime in each word. I blend them together to make a whole word.

RF.K.2.c Blend and segment onsets and rimes of single-syllable words.

OBJECTIVES:
- Detect the initial sound (onset) in spoken words.
- Identify the initial sound (onset) in spoken words.
- Blend onset and rime to make a whole word.

Stop!

Do not let that wet pet jump out of the net yet!

TEACH Point to your face and say: This is my face. Listen to the sounds in the word: *face.* What sound do you hear at the beginning of the word? Make the sound for me. **After students respond, slowly say the onset and then the rime:** /f/ (pause) /ās/. Now I will make the word by putting together the onset and the rime. I will say them together without stopping: *face.* The word is *face.* Say it with me: *face.*

Lesson 9 | Blend Onset and Rime

REMIND
STUDENTS
THAT ...

- words are made of beginning sounds (onsets) and ending sounds (rimes).
- they can blend onsets and rimes to make whole words.

PRACTICE I Help students hear and reproduce onsets. Model, using the following routine.

Routine

1. Model. Say a word, isolating and elongating the onset. Listen: *lap*. /lap/; /l/ is the onset.

2. Practice together. Say *lap* with me: *lap*. Say the onset in *lap*: /l/. Yes, /l/ is the onset in *lap*.

3. Extend practice. Now try it on your own. Say *lap* (pause to have students respond). Say the onset in *lap* (have students respond). Yes, /l/ is the onset in *lap*.

Follow the routine using the following words from Student Page S80.

nap	rip
fog	vet
cut	

Continue by blending. Have students say the distinct sounds of each word and then blend the sounds into a whole word: /n/ /ap/, *nap*, and so on.

Finally, use the list of words to check that students hear onsets correctly. Do you hear the sound /n/ at the beginning of the word *nap*? (yes) Do you hear the sound /n/ at the beginning of the word *cap*? (no) Continue with /f/ *fog* and *dog*, /k/ *cut* and *hut*, /r/ *rip* and *dip*, and /v/ *vet* and *met*.

☑ **MONITOR PROGRESS** Have students distinguish sounds with you and then blend them on their own. Repeat after me: /s/ /ĭx/. Now blend the sounds into a word. Have students blend. Continue with the words *bake* (/b//āk/), *sip* (/s//ĭp/), *mud* (/m//ud/), and *laugh* (/l//af/).

IF... students make an error when blending onset and rime,
THEN... model the correct response by blending the onset and rime slowly and having students echo you. Repeat with additional words until they develop proficiency.

Lesson 9 | Blend Onset and Rime

PRACTICE 2 Have students identify initial sounds (onsets) and then blend onset and rime. Listen closely as I say a word. Then tell me what the onset is. Let's do one together. Here is the word: *red*. What is the onset? Pause for students to respond. Yes, the onset is /r/. Now listen to this word: *save*. What is the onset? Pause for students to respond. Yes, the onset is /s/.

Display the following words from Student Page S81 and read each one aloud. Repeat each word several times and ask: What is the onset?

fun	peek	roll
hop	neck	sing
line	help	van
mine	jump	wow

Provide these words: *bang, cap, day, fish, good, joke, map, nap,* and *run*. For each word, ask: What sound do you hear at the beginning of the word *[bang]*? Then have students blend onset and rime for each word. I will say the sounds in a word. You blend the sounds. Say them together, without stopping, to make a word. Ready? Let's start. Here are the sounds: /b//ang/ Students should blend the onset and rime to make the word *bang*. Continue with the remaining eight words.

☑ **MONITOR PROGRESS** Say each of the following words. Say each word and ask: What sound do you hear at the beginning of the word? After students respond, you may wish to extend the activity by showing Student Page S81 and pointing out the beginning sounds of the words.

cup	zoo	tub
jet	sit	pal
bite	five	roll

IF... students make an error,
THEN... have students watch your mouth as you repeat the word slowly, and then have them imitate the initial sound you made.

REMIND STUDENTS THAT ...
- words are made of beginning sounds (onsets) and ending sounds (rimes).
- they can hear onsets and rimes in words.
- they can blend onsets and rimes to make whole words.

Lesson 9 | Blend Onset and Rime

- words are made of different sounds.
- blending all of the sounds together makes a whole word.

PRACTICE 3 Listen as I say some different sounds: /f//i//sh/. Do you hear a word when I say the sounds? Let me say them again: /f//i//sh/. Now I will say them again without stopping: *fish*. The word is *fish*. When I blend the sounds quickly, the word is *fish*.

Remember that onsets are beginning sounds and rimes are ending sounds. I will say some onsets and rimes. **Point to a light in the room.** Listen to the onset and the rime: /l//īt/. Now you make the word by blending the sounds together quickly. **Pause for students to blend the word.** That's right! The word is *light*.

Continue the activity with the following words from Student Page S82. When possible, point to an object as you say the onset and the rime.

shoe	wall
roof	book
man	shelf
paint	rug

Continue with sets of words that rhyme. I will say the sounds in a word. Listen carefully. When I finish, you say the word. /l//īk/ (like). Continue with *bike, mike, tyke,* and *hike.* Then repeat the process with the following sets of words: *curl, girl, hurl,* and *pearl*; *red, head, said,* and *fed*; *jar, far, car,* and *tar*.

☑ **INDEPENDENT PRACTICE** Have students watch your face and listen closely as you say the onset-rime combinations below. After you say each set twice, have students blend the sounds into a whole word.

/n//īs/	/r//īs/	/m//īs/
/l//ās/	/f//ās/	/r//ās/
/p//an/	/j//ak/	/s//ip/

IF... students make an error,
THEN... return to the word later during practice. Model the correct response by blending onset and rime, and have students echo you.

Lesson 9 — Blend Onset and Rime

Stop!

Do not let
that wet pet
jump out of
the net yet!

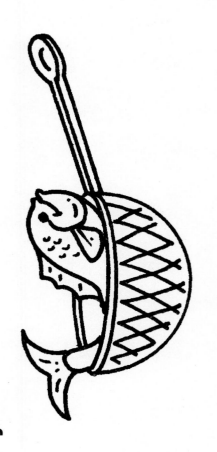

Teacher: This Student Page is intended as an *optional extension* of the lesson. After teaching the phonological awareness lesson orally, you can distribute or display this page to connect the phonological awareness skills (sounds) to phonics skills (sound-spelling).

Lesson 9   Blend Onset and Rime

nap   rip

fog

cut   vet

Teacher: This Student Page is intended as an *optional extension* of the lesson. After teaching the phonological awareness lesson orally, you can distribute or display this page to connect the phonological awareness skills (sounds) to phonics skills (sound-spelling).

Lesson 9   **Blend Onset and Rime**

fun	peek	roll
hop	neck	sing
line	help	van
mine	jump	wow

cup	zoo	tub
jet	sit	pal
bite	five	roll

Teacher: This Student Page is intended as an *optional extension* of the lesson. After teaching the phonological awareness lesson orally, you can distribute or display this page to connect the phonological awareness skills (sounds) to phonics skills (sound-spelling).

Lesson 9   Blend Onset and Rime

shoe   wall

roof   book

man   shelf

paint   rug

Teacher: This Student Page is intended as an *optional extension* of the lesson. After teaching the phonological awareness lesson orally, you can distribute or display this page to connect the phonological awareness skills (sounds) to phonics skills (sound-spelling).

Lesson 10 | Segment Onset and Rime

INTRODUCE Remind students that they have learned to break words apart into syllables and that they know how to blend onset and rime to make a word. Remember that an onset is the beginning sound in a word, and a rime is the ending sound in a word. Today we will break words into their onsets and rimes. For example, we know the word *sun*. It has the onset /s/. **Hold up one finger.** It has the rime /un/. **Hold up a second finger.** The sounds are /s/ and /un/. We heard two parts in the word.

MODEL Hold up a pen and ask: What is this? Yes, this is a pen. Listen to the word: *pen*. I will break the word *pen* into its onset and rime. **Model how to say the onset and rime slowly, pausing between the two:** /p/ (pause) /en/. The onset is /p/, and the rime is /en/. **Repeat this procedure with the words** *map* **and** *zip*.

Present the following words from Student Page S83 and read the lines aloud from left to right.

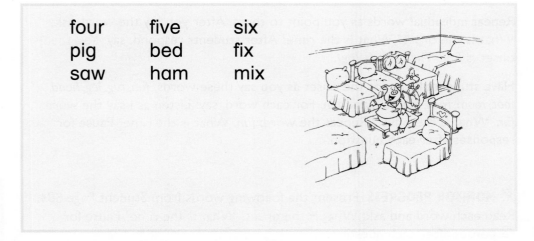

four	five	six
pig	bed	fix
saw	ham	mix

TEACH Point to each word as you segment it into onset and rime. I will break the word *four* into its onset and rime. Listen: /f//or/. This time, I will tap my hand on the desk as I say the onset again: /f/ **(tap)**. I'll slide my hand as I say the rime again: /or/ **(slide)**. Say the sounds with me: /f//or/.

Repeat the procedure with the remaining words. Tap as you say the onset. Slide your hand as you say the rime. Have students repeat the onset and rime with you.

RF.K.2.c Blend and segment onsets and rimes of single-syllable words.

OBJECTIVE:

• Segment the sounds of spoken words into onset and rime.

Lesson 10 | Segment Onset and Rime

REMIND STUDENTS THAT …

- every word has a beginning sound (onset).
- they can break, or segment, a word into its beginning sound (onset) and ending sound (rime).

PRACTICE 1 Present the following words from Student Page S84. Have students listen for the onset as you say the words in each line. For example, point to the first line and say: Listen as I say these words: *mug, mad, mop.* What sound do you hear at the beginning of each word? Pause for responses. Yes, the beginning sound is /m/. Continue with the remaining lines.

mug	mad	mop
cup	cot	call
lip	lose	like
zoom	zap	zing
net	nut	nip
tap	top	tell

Repeat individual words as you point to them. After you say the word, ask: What is the onset? What is the rime? After students respond, say: Yes, the onset is /m/. The rime is /ug/.

Have students listen for the onset as you say these words: *fun, rug, leg, head, foot, room, mail, pail, sad,* and *ten.* For each word, say: Listen as I say the word: *fun.* What is the onset? Repeat the word: *fun.* What is the rime? Pause for responses after each question.

☑ **MONITOR PROGRESS** Present the following words from Student Page S84. Read each word and ask: What is the onset? What is the rime? Pause for responses after each question.

feet	bug	tag	sell
pot	jump	cake	rag

IF… students struggle to separate the sounds,
THEN… model segmenting by tapping your hand as you say the onset and sliding your hand as you say the rime. Have students repeat the sounds and gestures with you.

| **Lesson 10** | **Segment Onset and Rime** |

PRACTICE 2 Tell students that they will listen to the sounds in words. I will say a word. Then you will say it with me, one time normally and one time slowly. When we say the word slowly, we can hear its onset and its rime. Then we will say the onset by itself and the rime by itself.

Here is the word: *pat.* Say it with me normally, then slowly. **Say the word *pat* twice with students, first at a normal pace, then slowly.** The onset is /p/. Say it with me: /p/. The rime is /at/. Let's say it together: /at/. **Repeat the process with the words *top, dig, back,* and *good.***

Say each of the following words from Student Page S85 slowly, drawing out the vowels and emphasizing the final consonant. For each word, ask: What is the onset? **Pause for responses. Repeat the word as many times as necessary for students to isolate the onset. Once they have succeeded, repeat the word and ask:** What is the rime? **Affirm correct responses by saying:** Yes, the onset is /k/. The rime is /ap/. **Correct errors as needed.**

cap	day	fur	get
big	pot	sip	van

☑ **MONITOR PROGRESS** Work with words that students have already segmented successfully. Say the word (for example, *top*). Have students repeat the word slowly. Ask: What is the onset? What is the rime? **Pause for responses after each question.**

IF... students cannot segment onset and rime,
THEN... model segmenting a familiar CVC word correctly, and have students echo you. Provide other CVC words for practice as needed.

REMIND STUDENTS THAT ...

- every word has a beginning sound (onset).

- they can break, or segment, a word into its beginning sound (onset) and ending sound (rime).

Lesson 10 | Segment Onset and Rime

REMIND STUDENTS THAT ...

- they can break, or segment, a word into parts with different sounds.

PRACTICE 3 Present the following words from Student Page S86. Prompt students to listen for the onset and rime as you say each word. Model with the word *hen*. Listen as I say the word: *hen*. What is the onset? Pause for responses. Repeat the word *hen* and ask: What is the rime? Pause for responses. I will say the word *hen* one more time. You will say both the onset and the rime. Repeat the word *hen* and have students say /h//en/. Continue the activity for the remaining words.

hen	cow	pig	lamb
kid	goat	goose	dog
pup	ram	bat	peep

Point to any of these objects that are visible in the classroom: *door, desk, shelf, book, pen, board, wall, map, chair, boot,* and *shoe*. Name each object as you point to it, and ask: What is the onset in the word *door*? What is the rime? Pause for responses after each question.

☑ **INDEPENDENT PRACTICE** Say *cup, knife, pot, jam,* and *soup*. Have students identify the onset in each word. Repeat each word and have students segment it into onset and rime.

IF... students cannot isolate the onset or rime in a word,
THEN... say the onset, tap your fingers on the desk, and then say the rime. Repeat the process and have students pantomime you. Use this method with other CVC words to give students additional practice.

Lesson 10   Segment Onset and Rime

four   five   six
pig   bed   fix
saw   ham   mix

Teacher: This Student Page is intended as an *optional extension* of the lesson. After teaching the phonological awareness lesson orally, you can distribute or display this page to connect the phonological awareness skills (sounds) to phonics skills (sound-spelling).

S • 83 Phonological Awareness

mug	mad	mop
cup	cot	call
lip	lose	like
zoom	zap	zing
net	nut	nip
tap	top	tell

| feet | bug | tag | sell |
| pot | jump | cake | rag |

Teacher: This Student Page is intended as an *optional extension* of the lesson. After teaching the phonological awareness lesson orally, you can distribute or display this page to connect the phonological awareness skills (sounds) to phonics skills (sound-spelling).

Lesson 10   Segment Onset and Rime

cap	day	fur	get
big	pot	sip	van

Teacher: This Student Page is intended as an *optional extension* of the lesson. After teaching the phonological awareness lesson orally, you can distribute or display this page to connect the phonological awareness skills (sounds) to phonics skills (sound-spelling).

Lesson 10   Segment Onset and Rime

hen	cow	pig	lamb
kid	goat	goose	dog
pup	ram	bat	peep

Teacher: This Student Page is intended as an *optional extension* of the lesson. After teaching the phonological awareness lesson orally, you can distribute or display this page to connect the phonological awareness skills (sounds) to phonics skills (sound-spelling).

ASSESSMENT
LESSONS 9–10

Phonological Awareness

ASSESS MASTERY Use this Checkpoint to assess students' mastery of blending and segmenting onsets and rimes of single-syllable words.

ADMINISTER THE TEST Administer the Checkpoint orally to each student. For each item, model the process as described, and then have the student use the process to respond to your prompts. Record responses on the scoring chart on the next page.

RF.K.2.c Blend and segment onsets and rimes of single-syllable spoken words.

1. Blend Onset and Rime (Lesson 9)
MODEL: Every word has an onset, or initial sound. I will say the onset and the rime, or ending, in a word. Then you will say the two parts together without stopping to say the word. For example, I could say /m//ud/. Then you blend the sounds together to say *mud*.

ASSESS:	/s//ink/	/f//ās/	/p//ark/	/w//et/

2. Segment Onset and Rime (Lesson 10)
MODEL: I will say a word. You will listen and then tell me the onset, or initial sound, and the rest of the word, or rime. For example, I could say *coat*. Then you would say /k/ and /ōt/, /k//ōt/.

ASSESS:	toy	big	pup	shoe	laugh

ASSESSMENT
LESSONS 9–10

Phonological Awareness

SCORING

SKILL/LESSON	SCORE
1. Blend Onset and Rime (Lesson 9) sink face park wet	_____ / 4
2. Segment Onset and Rime (Lesson 10) /t//oi/ /b//ig/ /p//up/ /sh//o͞o/ /l//af/	_____ / 5

An overall score of 80% correct is typically considered mastery. Use your judgment and your individual students' needs as well to determine skill mastery.

IF... students score below the benchmark,
THEN... review those discrete skills, going back to the lessons to reteach and scaffold as needed.

| **Lesson 11** | Identify Same and Different Initial Sounds |

INTRODUCE Explain that students will learn how to determine whether words begin with the same sounds.

MODEL Display or share copies of the passage "Katy and Ted" from Student Page S89, and read it aloud.

Katy and Ted

Katy had a pet rock.
She named the rock Ted.
Katy made a grass bed for Ted.
She put the bed in a red pan.
She set the bed in the sun.
Ted did not mind.
He liked the warm sun.

same beginning sound (/p/)

different beginning sound (/b/ and /s/)

RF.K.2.d Isolate and pronounce the initial, medial vowel, and final sounds (phonemes) in three-phoneme (consonant-vowel-consonant, or CVC) words. (This does not include CVCs ending with /l/, /r/, or /ks/.)

OBJECTIVES:

• Identify and pronounce the initial sound in CVC words.

• Compare and distinguish among initial sounds.

• Produce words with the same initial sounds.

TEACH Listen to these words: *pet, pan*. As I say them again, I'm going to listen carefully to their beginning sounds. **Emphasize the beginning sounds as you blend the words. Repeat the words again, drawing out the beginning sounds. Make sure to pronounce the short consonant /p/ (not /puh/).** I hear /p/ at the beginning of *pet*. Repeat the word *pet* with me. **Listen to make sure students pronounce the word correctly.** Do you hear /p/ at the beginning of the word *pan*? **Pause for students to respond.** Yes, both words have the same beginning sound (/p/).

Repeat the model activity with the words *sun* and *bed* from the passage. Point out that the words have different sounds. I hear /s/ at the beginning of *sun*, but I hear /b/ at the beginning of *bed*.

Lesson 11 | Identify Same and Different Initial Sounds

REMIND STUDENTS THAT ...

- they can identify and pronounce continuous initial sounds in words.
- they can compare and distinguish among continuous initial sounds.

PRACTICE 1 Use the following routine to make sure students can identify and pronounce initial sounds.

Routine

1. Model.   Say the word. Listen to the word: *sat.* /s//at/. Isolate and elongate the initial sound as you pronounce it. I hear /s/ first: /s//at/.

2. Practice together.   Say it with me: *sat.* /s//at/. What is the first sound? Yes, /s/ is the first sound.

3. Extend practice.   Have students identify and pronounce the initial sound with other CVC words. First practice with words with continuous initial consonant sounds that are easiest to identify (*l, r, s, m*).

Next, model how to identify same and different initial sounds. Say the words *mat* and *mine* with me: *mat, mine.* What is the first sound you hear in *mat*? (/m/) What is the first sound you hear in *mine*? (/m/) Do the words have the same or different beginning sounds? (**same**)

Have students follow the same procedure using the word pairs below, which also appear on Student Page S90.

bat, fin (different)	not, nap (same)
fat, fog (same)	net, cut (different)
van, vet (same)	fit, wet (different)

☑ **MONITOR PROGRESS** Have students listen to the following sets of words from Student Page S90. For each set, ask: What is the first sound you hear in the first word? Do you hear the same sound in the second word?

met, mop	rat, bad	sit, so

IF... students make an error,
THEN... have them watch your mouth as you repeat the word pair for clues to whether the beginning sounds are the same.

Lesson 11 | Identify Same and Different Initial Sounds

PRACTICE 2 Use the following routine to help students identify and pronounce the initial sound in a word.

REMIND STUDENTS THAT ...
- they can identify and pronounce the initial sound in words.
- they can compare and distinguish among initial sounds.

Routine

1. Model.	Say the word. Listen to the word: *let. /l//et/.* Isolate and elongate the initial sound as you pronounce it. *I hear /l/ first: /l//et/.*
2. Practice together.	Say it with me: *let. /l//et/.* What is the first sound? Yes, /l/ is the first sound.
3. Extend practice.	Have students identify and pronounce the initial sound with other CVC words. If students can identify continuous initial consonant sounds *l, r, s,* and *m,* have them practice with the short initial consonant sounds *b, d,* and *t.*

Next, have students play a game to practice identifying same and different initial sounds. Model how to play the game. Listen as I say two words: *top, toe.* Raise your hand if these words begin with the same sound. Raise your hand. Repeat the process with the words *cot* and *map.* Do not raise your hand. These words begin with different sounds, so we don't raise our hands.

Continue the game with the following word pairs, which also appear on Student Page S91.

take, tip (hands)	win, vote (no hands)
mop, man (hands)	cat, dog (no hands)
cup, pup (no hands)	gas, go (hands)

☑ **MONITOR PROGRESS** Have students listen to the following set of words from Student Page S91. Then ask: What sound do you hear at the beginning of each word? Which words have the same beginning sound? Have students pronounce the words again, if needed.

led	lip	sip	lap

IF... students have difficulty identifying words that have the same initial sound, THEN... have them say each word slowly, paying close attention to the positioning of their lips and tongue as they initiate the word. Have them note which words involve the same positioning of the lips and tongue.

Lesson 11	Identify Same and Different Initial Sounds

REMIND STUDENTS THAT …

- they can identify and pronounce the initial sound in words.
- they can compare and distinguish among initial sounds.
- they can produce words with the same initial sounds.

PRACTICE 3 Use the following routine to help students identify and pronounce the initial sound in a word.

Routine

1. Model. Say the word. Listen to the word: *put.* Isolate the initial sound as you pronounce it. I hear /p/ first: /p//ut/.

2. Practice together. Say it with me: *put.* /p//ut/. What is the first sound? Yes, /p/ is the first sound.

3. Extend practice. Have students identify and pronounce the initial sound with other CVC words. Have them practice with the short initial consonant sounds *h, p,* and *w.*

Next, have students play a game to name words that begin with the same sound. I will start the game by naming something I could shop for. I went shopping, and I bought a *rug.* Later, I went shopping and bought a *ring.* What else could we shop for that begins with the /r/ sound? Pause for responses. We could buy a *rope* and a *rake.*

Continue the game using the following words from Student Page S92.

cake /k/ (cap, key, kite)	hat /h/ (hose, hen, ham)
van /v/ (vase, vine, vat)	pan /p/ (pin, pot, pie)
bed /b/ (bat, boat, bass)	tub /t/ (tea, toy, top)

☑ **INDEPENDENT PRACTICE** Ask: What is the first sound you hear in the word *hip*? What other words begin with the /h/ sound?

IF… students have difficulty identifying the initial /h/ sound,
THEN… model the correct pronunciation of the /h/ sound and words beginning with /h/ as students pay close attention to the positioning of your mouth. Then have them pantomime your actions until they can correctly identify the sound.

Lesson 11   **Identify Same and Different Initial Sounds**

Katy and Ted

Katy had a pet rock.

She named the rock Ted.

Katy made a grass bed for Ted.

She put the bed in a red pan.

She set the bed in the sun.

Ted did not mind.

He liked the warm sun.

Teacher: This Student Page is intended as an *optional extension* of the lesson. After teaching the phonological awareness lesson orally, you can distribute or display this page to connect the phonological awareness skills (sounds) to phonics skills (sound-spelling).

Lesson 11   Identify Same and Different Initial Sounds

bat, fin   not, nap
fat, fog   net, cut
van, vet   fit, wet

met, mop   rat, bad   sit, so

Teacher: This Student Page is intended as an *optional extension* of the lesson. After teaching the phonological awareness lesson orally, you can distribute or display this page to connect the phonological awareness skills (sounds) to phonics skills (sound-spelling).

Lesson 11   Identify Same and Different Initial Sounds

take, tip
mop, man
cup, pup

win, vote
cat, dog
gas, go

led   lip   sip   lap

Teacher: This Student Page is intended as an *optional extension* of the lesson. After teaching the phonological awareness lesson orally, you can distribute or display this page to connect the phonological awareness skills (sounds) to phonics skills (sound-spelling).

Lesson 11 | Identify Same and Different Initial Sounds

cake	hat
van	pan
bed	tub

Teacher: This Student Page is intended as an *optional extension* of the lesson. After teaching the phonological awareness lesson orally, you can distribute or display this page to connect the phonological awareness skills (sounds) to phonics skills (sound-spelling).

| Lesson 12 | **Identify Same and Different Final Sounds** |

INTRODUCE Remind students that they can segment words into beginning sounds and ending sounds. Today we will listen for the last sound in a word. The last sound in a word is called the final sound. We will say two words. Then we will tell if the two words have the same final sound or different final sounds.

MODEL Display or share copies of the passage "Dan and Roy" from Student Page S93, and read it aloud.

RF.K.2.d Isolate and pronounce the initial, medial vowel, and final sounds (phonemes) in three-phoneme (consonant-vowel-consonant, or CVC) words. (This does not include CVCs ending with /l/, /r/, or /ks/.)

OBJECTIVES:
- Identify and pronounce the final sound in CVC words.
- Compare and distinguish among final sounds.
- Produce words with the same final sound.

Dan and Roy

Dan has a dog.
His dog is named Roy.
Roy is a big dog.
Dan takes Roy for a walk every day.
Dan and Roy have fun on their walks.
Dan loves his pet dog.

dog   big
same final sound (/g/)

fun   pet
different final sounds (/n/ and /t/)

TEACH After you read the passage aloud, demonstrate how to identify final sounds. Listen to these words: *dog, big.* As I say the words again, I will listen to their final sounds. Emphasize the final sounds as you blend the words. Now, I ask myself if both words end with the same sound or different sounds. **Repeat the words, drawing out the final sounds.** Say the words *dog* and *big* with me. Listen to make sure that students pronounce the words correctly. The words *dog* and *big* both have the final /g/ sound. **Repeat the process for the words** *fun* and *pet.* The words *fun* and *pet* have different final sounds. The word *fun* ends with the /n/ sound. The word *pet* ends with the /t/ sound.

Lesson 12 | Identify Same and Different Final Sounds

REMIND
STUDENTS
THAT...

• they can identify final sounds in words.

• they can pronounce final sounds in words.

• they can compare among final sounds.

PRACTICE 1 Make sure students can identify and pronounce final sounds in CVC words. Use the following routine.

Routine

1. Model.   Say the word: *tin.* /t//i//n/. Isolate and elongate the final sound as you pronounce it for students. I hear /n/ last. /n/ is the final sound in the word *tin.* /t//i//n/.

2. Practice together.   Let's say the word together: *tin.* /t//i//n/. What is the final sound in the word? Pause for responses. Yes! The final sound in the word *tin* is /n/.

3. Extend practice.   Repeat the routine with other CVC words with continuous final consonant sounds, such as *f, m, n,* and *s.*

For each of the following word pairs from Student Page S94, say the first word and have students repeat it: *gum* What is the final sound you hear in the word? (/m/) Then say the second word and have students repeat it: *fin.* What is the final sound you hear in the second word? (/n/) Do these words have the same final sounds or different final sounds? (different)

gum, fin (different)	beef, seem (different)
moon, ham (different)	van, pin (same)
pass, yes (same)	hiss, mess (same)

☑ **MONITOR PROGRESS** Say the following word pairs from Student Page S94:

hem, ram	his, pan	hen, win

What is the final sound you hear in the first word? Do you hear the same sound in the second word?

IF... students are unable to distinguish the final sound,
THEN... guide students in segmenting the words into initial, medial, and final sounds (for example, /h//e//m/). Ask them to repeat the final sound they hear. Have students perform these actions for both words and then compare the final sounds.

Lesson 12 | Identify Same and Different Final Sounds

PRACTICE 2 Before students compare sounds, make sure they can identify and pronounce final sounds in CVC words. Use the following routine.

Routine

1. Model. Say the word: *miss.* /m//i//s/. Isolate and elongate the final sound as you pronounce it for students. I hear /s/ last. /s/ is the final sound in the word *miss.* /m//i//s/.

2. Practice together. Say it with me: *miss.* /m//i//s/. What is the final sound in the word? Pause for responses. Yes! The final sound in the word *miss* is /s/.

3. Extend practice. Repeat the routine with other CVC words with stop final consonant sounds, such as *d, g, p,* and *t.*

Help students practice identifying same and different final sounds. I will say two words. If the words have the same final sound, we'll clap our hands. If the words have different final sounds, we won't clap our hands. Listen: *bag, pig.* **Clap** and make sure students do so. Then say *tip* and *dog.* Do not clap. The words *tip* and *dog* end with two different sounds, so we don't clap our hands.

Continue the activity with the following word pairs from Student Page S95.

nut, bet (clap)	log, cap (no clap)
hug, tag (clap)	top, rip (clap)
beg, lap (no clap)	met, ran (no clap)

☑ **MONITOR PROGRESS** Say the following words from Student Page S95:

get	bat	rug	hit

Have students repeat each word. Do you hear the /t/ sound at the end of *get, bat, rug,* or *hit*? What other final sounds do you hear?

IF... students misidentify the final sound,
THEN... have them segment the words into initial, medial, and final sounds and say each sound, focusing on the final sound they hear.

REMIND STUDENTS THAT ...

- they can identify the final sounds in words.
- they can pronounce the final sounds in words.
- they can compare and distinguish among final sounds.

| Lesson 12 | Identify Same and Different Final Sounds |

- they can identify and pronounce the final sounds in words.
- they can compare and distinguish among final sounds.
- they can produce words with the same final sound.

PRACTICE 3 Ensure that students can identify and pronounce final sounds in CVC words before comparing the final sounds of words. Use the following routine if needed.

Routine

1. Model. Say the word: *tub.* /t//u//b/. Isolate and pronounce the final sound for students. /b/ is the final sound in the word *tub.*

2. Practice together. Say it with me: *tub.* /t//u//b/. What is the final sound? Pause for responses. Right! The final sound in the word *tub* is /b/.

3. Extend practice. Repeat the routine with other CVC words with continuous and stop final consonant sounds.

Tell students that they will name words that end with the same sound. Listen to each word I say. Then say a new word that ends with the same final sound. Present the following words from Student Page S96. Say the word *jam* and have students repeat it. What other word has the same final sound as *jam?* (*ham, room,* and so on) Continue for the remaining words. If needed, help students produce appropriate words.

jam	bun	less	bib	red
bug	leg	hop	mat	pot

☑ **INDEPENDENT PRACTICE** Have students name one familiar word for each of the final /n/, /m/, /g/, and /t/ sounds. Then have students produce a new word with the same final sound.

IF... students have difficulty identifying words that have the final /n/, /m/, /g/, and /t/ sounds,
THEN... say a word as a model. Have students repeat the word and emphasize the final sound. Guide them in brainstorming new words with the same final sound.

Lesson 12 Identify Same and Different Final Sounds

Dan and Roy

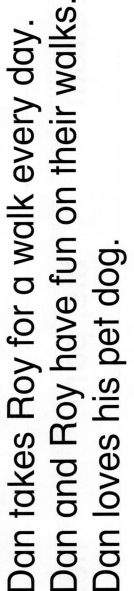

Dan has a dog.

His dog is named Roy.

Roy is a big dog.

Dan takes Roy for a walk every day.

Dan and Roy have fun on their walks.

Dan loves his pet dog.

Teacher: This Student Page is intended as an *optional extension* of the lesson. After teaching the phonological awareness lesson orally, you can distribute or display this page to connect the phonological awareness skills (sounds) to phonics skills (sound-spelling).

S • 93 Phonological Awareness

Lesson 12   Identify Same and Different Final Sounds

gum, fin
moon, ham
pass, yes

beef, seem
van, pin
hiss, mess

hem, ram   his, pan   hen, win

Teacher: This Student Page is intended as an *optional extension* of the lesson. After teaching the phonological awareness lesson orally, you can distribute or display this page to connect the phonological awareness skills (sounds) to phonics skills (sound-spelling).

Lesson 12   Identify Same and Different Final Sounds

nut, bet
hug, tag
beg, lap

log, cap
top, rip
met, ran

get   bat   rug   hit

Teacher: This Student Page is intended as an *optional extension* of the lesson. After teaching the phonological awareness lesson orally, you can distribute or display this page to connect the phonological awareness skills (sounds) to phonics skills (sound-spelling).

Lesson 12   Identify Same and Different Final Sounds

jam	bun	less	bib	red
bug	leg	hop	mat	pot

Teacher: This Student Page is intended as an *optional extension* of the lesson. After teaching the phonological awareness lesson orally, you can distribute or display this page to connect the phonological awareness skills (sounds) to phonics skills (sound-spelling).

Lesson 13 | Identify Same and Different Medial Sounds

INTRODUCE Remind students that they have listened to the beginning and ending sounds in words. Today we will listen for sounds in the middle of words. We will say two words. Then we will say if the two words have the same middle sound or different middle sounds.

MODEL Display or share copies of the passage "A Fun Day for Jan" from Student Page S97, and read it aloud.

RF.K.2.d Isolate and pronounce the initial, medial vowel, and final sounds (phonemes) in three-phoneme (consonant-vowel-consonant, or CVC) words. (This does not include CVCs ending with /l/, /r/, or /ks/.)

OBJECTIVES:
- Identify and pronounce the medial sound in CVC words.
- Compare and distinguish among medial sounds.
- Produce words with the same medial sound.

A Fun Day for Jan

Jan had a fun day.
She gave her mom a hug.
Then she got her bat.
She played baseball with her friends.
Then the fog came.
Jan went home.
She had a fig for a snack.

fun   hug
same medial sound
(/u/)

got   fig
different medial
sounds (/o/ and /i/)

TEACH After you read the passage aloud, show students how to identify medial sounds. Listen to these words: *fun, hug.* I will say the words again and listen to the middle sound in each one. Emphasize the medial sounds as you blend the words. Now I ask myself if both words have the same sound or different sounds in the middle. Repeat the words, drawing out the medial sounds. Let's say the words *fun* and *hug* together. Make sure that students pronounce the words correctly. The words *fun* and *hug* both have the /u/ sound in the middle.

Repeat the process for the words *got* and *fig.* The words *got* and *fig* have different middle sounds. The word *got* has the /o/ sound in the middle. The word *fig* has the /i/ sound in the middle.

Lesson 13 | Identify Same and Different Medial Sounds

REMIND STUDENTS THAT ...

- they can identify the medial sounds in words.
- they can pronounce medial sounds in words.
- they can compare among medial sounds.

PRACTICE 1 Before students compare sounds in CVC words, use the following routine to ensure students can identify and pronounce medial sounds.

Routine

1. Model.
Say the word: *fan.* /f//a//n/. Isolate and elongate the medial sound as you pronounce it for students.
I hear /a/ in the middle. /a/ is the middle sound in the word *fan.* /f//a//n/.

2. Practice together.
Let's say the word together: *fan.* /f//a//n/. What is the middle sound? Pause for responses. Yes! The middle sound in *fan* is /a/.

3. Extend practice.
Repeat the routine with other familiar CVC words.

Help students compare medial sounds in CVC words. Listen to these words: *cap, bat.* Say them with me: *cap, bat.* Do these words have the same middle sounds or different middle sounds? (same) Repeat the process with the words *bit* and *pot.*

For each of the following word pairs from Student Page S98, say the first word and have students repeat it. What is the middle sound in the word? Then say the second word and have students repeat it. Do you hear the same middle sound? Correct errors.

gum, bug (same)	wag, pan (same)
get, den (same)	rat, cup (different)
bed, had (different)	dog, leg (different)

☑ **MONITOR PROGRESS** Say the following word pairs from Student Page S98:

hog, big	pen, hem	mug, let	sit, pig

What is the middle sound you hear in the first word? Do you hear the same sound in the second word?

IF... students are unable to distinguish the medial sound,
THEN... guide students in segmenting the words into initial, medial, and final sounds (for example, /h//aw//g/). Ask them to repeat the medial sound they hear. Have students perform these actions for both words and then compare the medial sounds.

Lesson 13 | Identify Same and Different Medial Sounds

PRACTICE 2 Use the following routine to help students practice identifying and pronouncing medial sounds in CVC words.

Routine

1. Model. Say the word: *seed. /s//ē//d/.* Isolate and elongate the medial sound as you pronounce it for students. I hear /ē/ in the middle. /ē/ is the middle sound in the word *seed. /s//ē//d/.*

2. Practice together. Say it with me: *seed. /s//ē//d/.* What is the middle sound? Pause for responses. Yes! The middle sound in *seed* is /ē/.

3. Extend practice. Repeat the routine with other familiar and newly learned CVC words.

Practice comparing medial sounds in CVC words. I will say two words. If the words have the same middle sound, raise your hand. If the words have different middle sounds, don't raise your hand. Listen: *peel, meet.* Raise your hand. Repeat the process with the words *bun* and *dig.* Do not raise your hand.

Continue the activity with the following word pairs from Student Page S99. After students indicate whether the medial sounds are the same or different, have them identify the medial sound in each word.

> kit, fin (hands)   cat, map (hands)
> pit, fed (no hands)   bin, run (no hands)
> sad, hut (no hands)   tin, his (hands)

☑ **MONITOR PROGRESS** Say the following words from Student Page S99:

> bag   set   fit   web   hip   nap

Have students repeat each word after you. What sound do you hear in the middle of *bag?* Repeat the process for the remaining words. Then have students identify words with the same medial sound (bag, nap; set, web; fit, hip).

IF... students misidentify the medial sound,
THEN... have them segment the words into initial, medial, and final sounds and say each sound, focusing on the medial sound they hear.

- they can identify the medial sounds in words.
- they can pronounce the medial sounds in words.
- they can compare and distinguish among medial sounds.

Lesson 13 | Identify Same and Different Medial Sounds

REMIND STUDENTS THAT ...

- they can identify and pronounce the medial sounds in words.
- they can compare and distinguish among medial sounds.
- they can produce words with the same medial sound.

PRACTICE 3 Use the following routine if needed to ensure that students can identify and pronounce medial sounds in CVC words.

Routine

1. Model.   Say the word: *dot.* /dot/. Isolate and pronounce the medial sound for students. /o/ is the middle sound in the word *dot.*

2. Practice together.   Say it with me: *dot.* /dot/. What is the middle sound? Pause for responses. Right! The middle sound in *dot* is /o/.

3. Extend practice.   Repeat the routine with other familiar and newly learned CVC words.

Tell students that they will play a game. Pam, Ben, Kim, and Ron like words that have the same middle sound as the one in each of their names. Have students say the four names aloud and identify the medial sound in each name. I will say some words. Listen to each word. Then tell me who will like the word. You may wish to display the following words from Student Page S100 to help students connect medial sounds to spellings.

fit	hen	tag	hop
got	lap	dig	pet

Say the word *fit* and have students repeat it. Who likes the word *fit*—Pam, Ben, Kim, or Ron? Have students respond by saying *Kim likes the word* fit. Continue for the remaining words.

☑ **INDEPENDENT PRACTICE** Have students name one CVC word for each of these medial sounds: /a/, /e/, /i/, /o/, /u/. Then have students produce a new word with the same medial sound.

IF... students have difficulty identifying words,
THEN... say a correct word as a model. Have students repeat the word and emphasize the medial sound. Help them brainstorm a new word with the same medial sound.

Lesson 13   Identify Same and Different Medial Sounds

A Fun Day for Jan

Jan had a fun day.

She gave her mom a hug.

Then she got her bat.

She played baseball with her friends.

Then the fog came.

Jan went home.

She had a fig for a snack.

Teacher: This Student Page is intended as an *optional extension* of the lesson. After teaching the phonological awareness lesson orally, you can distribute or display this page to connect the phonological awareness skills (sounds) to phonics skills (sound-spelling).

Lesson 13   Identify Same and Different Medial Sounds

gum, bug
get, den
bed, had

wag, pan
rat, cup
dog, leg

hog, big   pen, hem   mug, let   sit, pig

Teacher: This Student Page is intended as an *optional extension* of the lesson. After teaching the phonological awareness lesson orally, you can distribute or display this page to connect the phonological awareness skills (sounds) to phonics skills (sound-spelling).

Lesson 13   Identify Same and Different Medial Sounds

kit, fin
pit, fed
sad, hut

cat, map
bin, run
tin, his

bag   set   fit   web   hip   nap

Teacher: This Student Page is intended as an *optional extension* of the lesson. After teaching the phonological awareness lesson orally, you can distribute or display this page to connect the phonological awareness skills (sounds) to phonics skills (sound-spelling).

Lesson 13   Identify Same and Different Medial Sounds

fit	hen	tag	hop
got	lap	dig	pet

Teacher: This Student Page is intended as an *optional extension* of the lesson. After teaching the phonological awareness lesson orally, you can distribute or display this page to connect the phonological awareness skills (sounds) to phonics skills (sound-spelling).

Lesson 14 | Isolate Initial, Final, and Medial Sounds

INTRODUCE Remind students that they have identified and pronounced the beginning, ending, and middle sounds in many words. Today we will listen closely to words and then say just their beginning sounds. Then we will listen closely and say just their final sounds. Next, we will listen closely and say just their middle sounds. Finally, we will say all the sounds together to make words.

MODEL Display or share copies of the passage "Tom Likes to Run" from Student Page S101. Read it aloud, emphasizing the word *run*.

Tom Likes to Run

Tom likes to run.
He runs everywhere he goes.
He runs to school.
He runs home from school, too!
His feet and legs help him to run.
Tom can run very fast!

run
initial sound (/r/)
final sound (/n/)
medial sound (/u/)

TEACH After you read the passage aloud, demonstrate isolating initial, final, and medial sounds in a word and then blending the sounds to say the word. Listen as I say a word: *run.* Say the word slowly. I ask myself what the beginning sound in *run* is. Let's say the word together: *run.* The word *run* begins with /r/. Repeat this process for the final sound /n/ and medial sound /u/. Then have the class say the word.

Repeat the process with other CVC words in the passage, such as *Tom, him,* and *can.* Help students identify the initial, final, and medial sounds in each word.

RF.K.2.d Isolate and pronounce the initial, medial vowel, and final sounds (phonemes) in three-phoneme (consonant-vowel-consonant, or CVC) words. (This does not include CVCs ending with /l/, /r/, or /ks/.)

OBJECTIVES:

- Recognize and isolate initial, final, and medial sounds in CVC words.
- Blend individual sounds in spoken words to make words.

Lesson 14 | Isolate Initial, Final, and Medial Sounds

REMIND STUDENTS THAT ...

- every word has a beginning sound and a final sound.
- they can identify and pronounce beginning and final sounds in words.

PRACTICE 1 Help students practice isolating initial and final sounds in CVC words with continuous initial or final consonant sounds, such as *f, m, n,* and *s.* Listen closely as I say a word: *man.* Say the word with me: *man.* Listen to the first sound: /m/. Say the first sound with me: /m/. Repeat this process for the final sound /n/.

Have students practice using the words below. Say the word *fed* and have students repeat it. What is the first sound you hear in the word *fed*? /f/. Repeat the procedure for *mop, nap,* and *sit.* Then use the same process to have students determine the final sounds in the words *miss, van, hum,* and *beef.*

After the oral exercise, you may wish to distribute or display Student Page S102 to help students connect initial and final sounds to specific letters.

Beginning Sound	Final Sound
fed (/f/)	miss (/s/)
mop (/m/)	van (/n/)
nap (/n/)	hum (/m/)
sit (/s/)	beef (/f/)

☑ **MONITOR PROGRESS** Say each of the following words from Student Page S102:

fan	mad	not	set
yes	pin	him	nod

What is the first sound you hear in the word [*fan, mad, not, set*]? What is the last sound you hear in the word [*yes, pin, him, nod*]?

IF... students make errors pronouncing initial and final sounds,
THEN... model the correct pronunciation and have students echo you. If necessary, provide other familiar CVC words to help students practice pronouncing initial and final sounds correctly.

| Lesson 14 | Isolate Initial, Final, and Medial Sounds |

PRACTICE 2 Help students practice isolating initial and final sounds in CVC words with stop initial or final consonant sounds, such as *b, d, g, k, p,* and *t.* Listen closely as I say a word: *pit.* Let's say the word together: *pit.* Listen to the first sound: /p/. Say the first sound with me: /p/. Repeat this process for the final sound /t/.

Tell students they will identify beginning and ending sounds in words. Say the word *bat* and have students repeat it. What is the first sound you hear in the word *bat?* Repeat the procedure for *dip, get, kit, pan,* and *tap.* Then use the same process for the final sounds in the words *rib, bed, pig, seek, hip,* and *sat.*

After the oral exercise, you may wish to distribute or display Student Page S103 to reinforce the connection between initial and final sounds and their corresponding letters.

REMIND STUDENTS THAT ...

- every word has a beginning sound and a final sound.
- they can identify and pronounce beginning and final sounds in words.

Beginning Sound

bat (/b/)	kit (/k/)
dip (/d/)	pan (/p/)
get (/g/)	tap (/t/)

Final Sound

rib (/b/)	bin (/n/)
bed (/d/)	hip (/p/)
pig (/g/)	sat (/t/)

☑ **MONITOR PROGRESS** Say each of the following words from Student Page S103:

tin	pot	cap	got	hid	map
bib	sad	hug	big	hop	set

What is the first sound you hear in the word [*tin, pot, jam, got, hid, map*]? What is the final sound you hear in the word [*bib, sad, hug, big, hop, set*]?

IF... students have difficulty identifying initial or final sounds,
THEN... have students say the word slowly; segment it into initial, medial, and final sounds; and then listen carefully as they repeat the initial and final sounds.

| **Lesson 14** | Isolate Initial, Final, and Medial Sounds |

REMIND STUDENTS THAT ...

- words have beginning sounds, final sounds, and middle sounds.
- they can identify and pronounce beginning, final, and middle sounds in words.
- they can blend beginning, middle, and final sounds to make words.

PRACTICE 3 First, review with students how to isolate initial and final sounds. Say the word *mat* and have students repeat it. Listen to the first sound: /m/. Say it with me: /m/. Now listen to the final sound: /t/. Say it with me: /t/. Remind students that words also have medial sounds. Repeat the word *mat*, emphasizing the medial sound /a/. Let's say the middle sound together: /a/. Now let's say the three sounds together to make the word: *mat*. Repeat this process with other CVC words, such as *hut* and *ram*.

Tell students that they will listen to words. Say the word *lap* and have students repeat it. What is the beginning sound in the word *lap*? What is the middle sound in the word *lap*? What is the final sound in the word *lap*? Now say the sounds together to make the word: *lap*. Repeat the process for the remaining words. You may wish to display the following words from Student Page S104 to help students connect initial, final, and medial sounds to spellings.

lap	peg	rip	sob	mud
can	not	lip	dot	rug

☑ **INDEPENDENT PRACTICE** Say these words aloud: *rat, led, tin, nod, sum, fib, bag,* and *fit.* Have students identify the initial, medial, and final sound in each word. Then have them blend the sounds to say the word.

IF... students have difficulty blending initial, medial, and final sounds into a word,
THEN... ask them to isolate the initial, medial, and final sound in the word and then practice saying the sounds several times, accelerating the pace until they have blended the sounds successfully.

Tom Likes to Run

Tom likes to run.

He runs everywhere he goes.

He runs to school.

He runs home from school, too!

His feet and legs help him to run.

Tom can run very fast!

Teacher: This Student Page is intended as an *optional extension* of the lesson. After teaching the phonological awareness lesson orally, you can distribute or display this page to connect the phonological awareness skills (sounds) to phonics skills (sound-spelling).

Lesson 14 | Isolate Initial, Final, and Medial Sounds

Beginning Sound

fed		
mop		
nap		
sit		

Final Sound

	miss	
	van	
	hum	
	beef	

fan	mad	not
yes	pin	him
		set
		nod

Teacher: This Student Page is intended as an *optional extension* of the lesson. After teaching the phonological awareness lesson orally, you can distribute or display this page to connect the phonological awareness skills (sounds) to phonics skills (sound-spelling).

Lesson 14   Isolate Initial, Final, and Medial Sounds

Beginning Sound

bat	kit	
dip	pan	
get	tap	

Final Sound

rib	bin	
bed	hip	
pig	sat	

tin	cap	got	hid	map
pot	hug	big	hop	set
sad	bib			

Teacher: This Student Page is intended as an *optional extension* of the lesson. After teaching the phonological awareness lesson orally, you can distribute or display this page to connect the phonological awareness skills (sounds) to phonics skills (sound-spelling).

Lesson 14 Isolate Initial, Final, and Medial Sounds

lap	peg	rip	sob	mud
can	not	lip	dot	rug

Teacher: This Student Page is intended as an *optional* extension of the lesson. After teaching the phonological awareness lesson orally, you can distribute or display this page to connect the phonological awareness skills (sounds) to phonics skills (sound-spelling).

ASSESSMENT
LESSONS 11–14

  Phonological Awareness

ASSESS MASTERY Use this Checkpoint to assess students' ability to identify initial, medial, and final sounds.

ADMINISTER THE TEST Administer the Checkpoint orally to each student. For each item, model the process as described, and then have the student use the process to respond to your prompts. Record responses on the scoring chart on the next page.

RF.K.2.d isolate and pronounce the initial, medial vowel, and final sounds (phonemes) in three-phoneme (consonant-vowel-consonant, or CVC) words. (This does not include CVCs ending with /l/, /r/, or /ks/.)

1. Identify Same and Different Initial Sounds (Lesson 11)
MODEL: I will say three words, and you will tell me which two words have the same beginning sound. For example, I could say the words *bell, den,* and *dip.* Which words have the same beginning sound? The words *den* and *dip* both start with the same sound, which is /d/.

ASSESS:	set, bug, sap	tip, tan, pat	hat, men, hen

2. Identify Same and Different Final Sounds (Lesson 12)
MODEL: I will say three words, and you will tell me which two words have the same final sound. For example, I could say the words *bat, bee,* and *let.* Which words have the same final sound? The words *bat* and *let* both end with the same final sound, which is /t/.

ASSESS:	ram, bus, him	met, men, sat	less, miss, mitt

3. Identify Same and Different Medial Sounds (Lesson 13)
MODEL: I will say three words, and you will tell me which two words have the same middle sound. For example, I could say the words *gum, mug,* and *get.* Which words have the same middle sound? The words *gum* and *mug* both have the same middle sound, /u/.

ASSESS:	fan, tin, rat	rod, rim, got	miss, lit, mud

4. Isolate Initial, Final, and Medial Sounds (Lesson 14)
MODEL: I will say a word and then ask you to say its beginning, final, or middle sound. For example, I could say the word *give.* What is the beginning sound of *give?* /g/ What is its final sound? /v/ What is its middle sound? /i/

ASSESS:			
Beginning and final sound:	lap	ten	book
Middle sound:	mat	fit	bake

ASSESSMENT
LESSONS 11–14

Phonological Awareness

SCORING

SKILL/LESSON	SCORE
1. Identify Same and Different Initial Sounds (Lesson 11) set/sap, /s/ tip/tan, /t/ hat/hen, /h/	_____ / 3
2. Identify Same and Different Final Sounds (Lesson 12) ram/him, /m/ met/sat, /t/ less/miss, /s/	_____ / 3
3. Identify Same and Different Medial Sounds (Lesson 13) fan/rat, /a/ rod/got, /o/ miss/lit, /i/	_____ / 3
4. Isolate Initial, Final, and Medial Sounds (Lesson 14) lap (/l/, /p/) ten (/t/, /n/) book (/b/, /k/) mat (/a/) fit (/i/) bake (/ā/)	_____ / 6

An overall score of 80% correct is typically considered mastery. Use your judgment and your individual students' needs as well to determine skill mastery.

IF... students score below the benchmark,
THEN... review those discrete skills, going back to the lessons to reteach and scaffold as needed.

Lesson 15 | Add Initial Phonemes

INTRODUCE Remind students that they have identified and pronounced the beginning, final, and middle sounds in words, and that they have blended these sounds to say words. Today we will say a word. We will listen to its sounds, especially at the beginning. Then we will add a sound at the beginning and say a new word.

MODEL Display or share copies of the passage "So Many Hats" from Student Page S107, and read it aloud.

RF.K.2.e Add or substitute individual sounds (phonemes) in simple, one-syllable words to make new words.

OBJECTIVES:
• Reinforce the concept of beginning sounds.
• Add single initial phonemes to make new words.

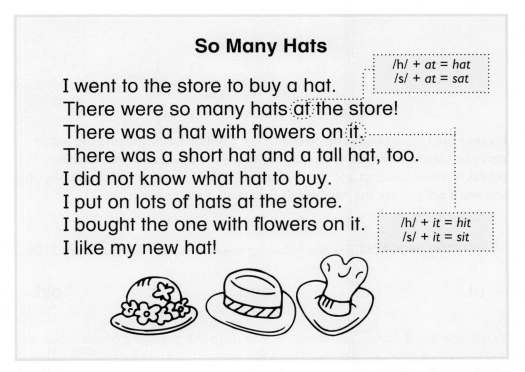

So Many Hats

I went to the store to buy a hat.
There were so many hats at the store!
There was a hat with flowers on it.
There was a short hat and a tall hat, too.
I did not know what hat to buy.
I put on lots of hats at the store.
I bought the one with flowers on it.
I like my new hat!

/h/ + at = hat
/s/ + at = sat

/h/ + it = hit
/s/ + it = sit

TEACH After you read the passage aloud, point out the word *at* in the second sentence. Listen as I say this word: *at*. Now I will add /h/ to the beginning of *at* to make a new word: *hat*. Say the new word with me: *hat*. Now I will add a /s/ to the beginning of *at* to make a different word: *sat*. Say it with me: *sat*. Repeat the process by adding first a /h/ and then a /s/ to the word *it* in the third sentence.

| Lesson 15 | Add Initial Phonemes |

REMIND STUDENTS THAT ...

- words are made of sounds in the beginning, middle, and end.

- adding a sound to the beginning of a word can make a new word.

PRACTICE 1 Show students how to construct new words by adding the continuous consonant sounds *f, m, n,* and *s* to the beginning of existing words. Listen closely as I say a word: *an.* Say the word with me: *an.* Listen to the first sound: /a/. Say it with me: /a/. Listen to the last sound: /n/. Let's say the last sound together: /n/. Now let's add the /f/ sound to the beginning of the word *an.* First, say the sound with me: /f/. Now let's say all the sounds together to make a new word: *fan.* **Repeat this process by adding the initial sound /m/ to the word** *an.*

Present the Elkonin boxes on Student Page S108 or have students use letter cards or tiles to make the word *eat.* Say the word aloud and have students repeat it. Have students add the /f/, /m/, /n/, and /s/ sound to the beginning of the word *eat* and say the new words *feat, meat, neat,* and *seat.*

☑ **MONITOR PROGRESS** Say the following five words from Student Page S108:

| at | eel | end | it | old |

What new word do you get when you add /f/ to the beginning of the words *at* and *eel?* What new word do you get when you add /s/ to the beginning of the words *end, it,* and *old?*

IF... students have trouble identifying the new word created by adding an initial phoneme,
THEN... model the correct response by saying the original word, saying the added initial phoneme, and then blending the sounds into the new word. Have students repeat these steps with one of the other four words.

Lesson 15 | Add Initial Phonemes

PRACTICE 2 Show students how to construct new words by adding stop consonant sounds, such as *b, d, g, k, p,* and *t,* to the beginning of existing words. Listen as I say a word: *and.* Say it with me: *and.* Let's add the /b/ sound to the beginning of the word *and.* First, say the sound with me: /b/. Now let's say all the sounds together to make a new word: /band/. Repeat this process by adding the initial sound /k/ to the word *it.*

Display the Elkonin boxes on Student Page S109 or have students use letter cards or tiles to make the word *art.* Say the word aloud and have students repeat it. Have students add the /d/, /p/, and /t/ sound to the beginning of the word *art* and say the new words *dart, part,* and *tart.*

☑ **MONITOR PROGRESS** Say the following seven words from Student Page S109:

am	ate	ill
an	end	
in	up	

What new words do you make when you add /d/ to the beginning of the words *am* and *ate*? What new words do you make when you add /b/ to the beginning of the words *an* and *end*? What new words do you make when you add /p/ to the beginning of the words *in*, *up*, and *ill*?

IF... students have difficulty saying the new word after adding the initial phoneme,
THEN... say the initial phoneme, the original word, and the new word and have students repeat after you. Have students follow these steps with one of the other six words.

REMIND STUDENTS THAT …

• words are made of sounds in the beginning, middle, and end.

• adding a sound to the beginning of a word can make a new word.

Lesson 15 | Add Initial Phonemes

REMIND STUDENTS THAT ...

- words are made of sounds in the beginning, middle, and end.

- adding a sound to the beginning of a word can make a new word.

- there may be more than one sound at the beginning of a word.

PRACTICE 3 Remind students that they have added sounds to the beginnings of words to make new words. Listen to this word: *an*. Say it with me: *an*. Let's add the /t/ sound to the beginning of the word *an*. First, say the sound with me: /t/. Now let's say all the sounds together to make a new word: /tan/. Repeat this process by adding the /t/ sound to the beginning of the word *wig*. There are now two sounds at the beginning of the word *twig*: /t/ and /w/.

Tell students that they will listen to words. Say the following words aloud, displaying Student Page S110 if desired.

pot	way	lip
rip	ray	rap

Say *pot* aloud and have students echo you. Let's add the /s/ sound to the beginning of the word. What new word do we make? (**spot**) What are the two sounds at the beginning of the new word? (/s/ and /p/) Have students add the /s/ sound to the beginning of *way* and *lip* to make the new words *sway* and *slip*. Repeat this process by having students add the /t/ sound to the beginning of *rip*, *ray*, and *rap*.

☑ **INDEPENDENT PRACTICE** Say the words *in, it, or, eat, lot,* and *nap* aloud. Have students add the /f/ sound to the first three words and the /s/ sound to the last three words. Have them say each new word aloud and identify the sound or sounds at the beginning of each word.

IF... students have difficulty distinguishing the two sounds at the beginning of *slot* and *snap*,
THEN... have them say the /s/ sound and the original word separately, focusing on the initial sound in the original word. Then have them blend the sounds to say the new word, emphasizing the two new sounds at the beginning of the word.

Add Initial Phonemes

So Many Hats

I went to the store to buy a hat.

There were so many hats at the store!

There was a hat with flowers on it.

There was a short hat and a tall hat, too.

I did not know what hat to buy.

I put on lots of hats at the store.

I bought the one with flowers on it.

I like my new hat!

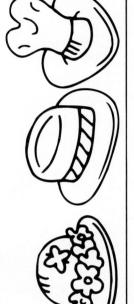

Teacher: This Student Page is intended as an *optional extension* of the lesson. After teaching the phonological awareness lesson orally, you can distribute or display this page to connect the phonological awareness skills (sounds) to phonics skills (sound-spelling).

Lesson 15 | **Add Initial Phonemes**

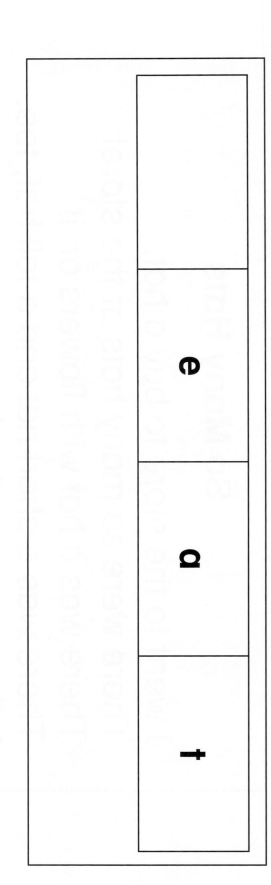

	e	a	t

at   eel   end   it   old

Teacher: This Student Page is intended as an *optional extension* of the lesson. After teaching the phonological awareness lesson orally, you can distribute or display this page to connect the phonological awareness skills (sounds) to phonics skills (sound-spelling).

Lesson 15   Add Initial Phonemes

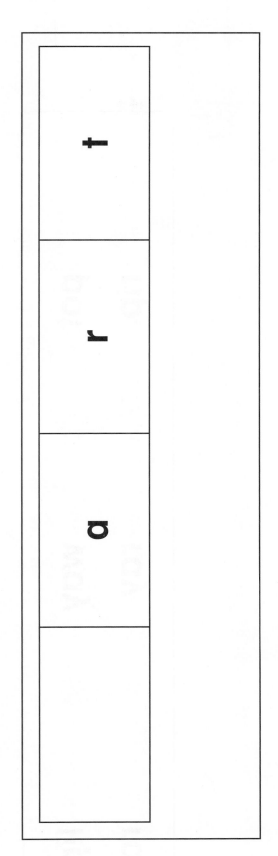

		r	t
	a		

am   ate   ill
an   end
in   up

Teacher: This Student Page is intended as an *optional extension* of the lesson. After teaching the phonological awareness lesson orally, you can distribute or display this page to connect the phonological awareness skills (sounds) to phonics skills (sound-spelling).

Lesson 15 | Add Initial Phonemes

pot	way	lip
rip	ray	rap

Teacher: This Student Page is intended as an *optional extension* of the lesson. After teaching the phonological awareness lesson orally, you can distribute or display this page to connect the phonological awareness skills (sounds) to phonics skills (sound-spelling).

Lesson 16 | Add Final Phonemes

INTRODUCE Remind students that they have been saying words and making new words. We know how to say a word and add a sound at the beginning of the word to make a new word. Think of the word *am*. When we add the /h/ sound to the beginning of the word *am*, we make the word *ham*. Today we will say a word. Then we will add a sound at the end of the word and say the new word.

MODEL Display or share copies of "A Trip to the Zoo" from Student Page S111, and read it aloud.

A Trip to the Zoo

My family and I went to the zoo. ...... *zoo + /m/ = zoom*
We saw so many animals there!
We saw a tall animal with a long neck.
We saw lions and monkeys, too.
The monkeys at the zoo did funny things.
They jumped on things and hung from bars.
I saw a big bee in the garden.
We had a fun time at the zoo!

bee + /f/ = beef

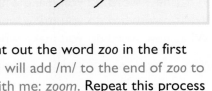

TEACH After you read the passage aloud, point out the word *zoo* in the first sentence. Listen as I say this word: *zoo*. Now I will add /m/ to the end of *zoo* to make a new word: *zoom*. Say the new word with me: *zoom*. Repeat this process by adding /f/ to the word *bee* in the seventh sentence.

RF.K.2.e Add or substitute individual sounds (phonemes) in simple, one-syllable words to make new words.

OBJECTIVES:
- Review naming final phonemes.
- Add final phonemes to make new words.
- Make blends by adding final phonemes.

Lesson 16 | Add Final Phonemes

REMIND STUDENTS THAT ...

- every word has a final sound.
- adding a sound to the end of a word can make a new word.

PRACTICE 1 Demonstrate how to make a new word by adding a sound to the end of an existing word. Listen as I say a word: *see*. Say the word with me: *see*. Listen to the first sound: /s/. Say it with me: /s/. Listen to the last sound: /ē/. Let's say the last sound together: /ē/. Now let's add the /m/ sound to the end of *see*. First, say the sound with me: /m/. Now let's say all the sounds together to make a new word: *seem*.

Display the Elkonin boxes on Student Page S112 or have students use letter cards or tiles to make the word *fee*. Say the word aloud and have students repeat it. Have students add the /d/, /l/, and /t/ sound to the end of the word *fee* and say the new words *feed, feel,* and *feet*.

☑ **MONITOR PROGRESS** Say each of the following words from Student Page S112:

| moo | see | tea | too |

What new word do you make when you add /n/ to the end of *moo*?
What new word do you make when you add /d/ to the end of *see*?
What new word do you make when you add /m/ to the end of *tea*?
What new word do you make when you add /l/ to the end of *too*?

IF... students have trouble identifying the new word created by adding a final phoneme,
THEN... model the correct response by saying the original word, saying the added final phoneme, and then blending the sounds into the new word. Have students repeat the process with one of the other words.

Lesson 16 | Add Final Phonemes

PRACTICE 2 Have students say the word *ten* and identify the final /n/ sound. Let's add /t/ to the end of *ten*. First, say the sound with me: /t/. Now let's say the sounds together to make a new word: *tent*. Point out that there are two sounds at the end of *tent*: /n/ and /t/. Repeat this process by adding the final sound /d/ to *ten*. Have students identify the final sounds /n/ and /d/ in the new word *tend*.

REMIND STUDENTS THAT ...
• adding a sound to the end of a word can make a new word.
• there may be more than one sound at the end of a word.

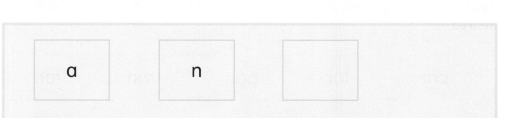

| a | n | |

Display the Elkonin boxes on Student Page S113 or have students use letter cards or tiles to make the word *an*. Have students say the word aloud. Then have them add /d/ and /t/ to the end of *an* and say the new words *and* and *ant*. What are the two sounds at the end of [*and, ant*]?

☑ **MONITOR PROGRESS** Say each of the following words from Student Page S113:

dam	hum	
far	fir	for
ban	pin	tan

What new words do you make when you add /p/ to the end of *dam* and *hum*? What new words do you make when you add /m/ to the end of *far, fir,* and *for*? What new words do you make when you add /k/ to the end of *ban, pin,* and *tan*? Have students identify the two sounds at the end of each new word.

IF... students have difficulty identifying the two sounds at the end of the new word,
THEN... say the new word slowly, emphasizing the two distinct final sounds, and have students repeat after you. Have students follow these steps with one of the other words you presented.

Lesson 16 | Add Final Phonemes

REMIND
STUDENTS
THAT ...

- adding a sound to the end of a word can make a new word.
- there may be more than one sound at the end of a word.

PRACTICE 3 Have students say *bar* and identify the final sound in the word. Let's add /k/ to the end of *bar* to make a new word. When we add /k/ to the end of *bar*, we make the word *bark*. Let's say the words together: *bar, bark.* Have students identify the two distinct sounds at the end of the word. Then repeat the process by adding /d/ to the end of *ten* and *men.*

Read the following words from Student Page S114 aloud, displaying them if desired.

car	for	pan	ran	tar

Repeat each word aloud with students. Now add the /t/ sound to the end of each word. What new words do we make? What are the two sounds at the end of each new word?

☑ **INDEPENDENT PRACTICE** Say these words aloud: *sun, bun, mass,* and *stun.* Have students add /k/ to the end of each word, say each new word aloud, and identify the two sounds at the end of each word.

IF... students have difficulty identifying the two sounds at the end of the new word,
THEN... have them say the original word, emphasizing the final sound, and then say the added final phoneme separately. Then have them combine the two parts into the new word, emphasizing the two distinct final sounds as they say the new word aloud.

A Trip to the Zoo

My family and I went to the zoo.

We saw so many animals there!

We saw a tall animal with a long neck.

We saw lions and monkeys, too.

The monkeys at the zoo did funny things.

They jumped on things and hung from bars.

I saw a big bee in the garden.

We had a fun time at the zoo!

Teacher: This Student Page is intended as an *optional extension* of the lesson. After teaching the phonological awareness lesson orally, you can distribute or display this page to connect the phonological awareness skills (sounds) to phonics skills (sound-spelling).

Lesson 16 | Add Final Phonemes

f	e	e	

moo   see   tea   too

Teacher: This Student Page is intended as an *optional* extension of the lesson. After teaching the phonological awareness lesson orally, you can distribute or display this page to connect the phonological awareness skills (sounds) to phonics skills (sound-spelling).

Lesson 16   Add Final Phonemes

a	n	

dam   hum   for

far   fir   tan

ban   pin

Teacher: This Student Page is intended as an *optional extension* of the lesson. After teaching the phonological awareness lesson orally, you can distribute or display this page to connect the phonological awareness skills (sounds) to phonics skills (sound-spelling).

Lesson 16   Add Final Phonemes

car   for   pan   ran   tar

Teacher: This Student Page is intended as an *optional extension* of the lesson. After teaching the phonological awareness lesson orally, you can distribute or display this page to connect the phonological awareness skills (sounds) to phonics skills (sound-spelling).

Lesson 17 | Delete or Change Initial Phonemes

INTRODUCE Remind students that words have beginning, middle, and ending sounds. We know how to add a beginning sound to a word and say the new word. We can add /s/ to the beginning of *end* and say the new word: *send*. We can also take away or change the beginning sound in a word to make a new word. Today we will say a word. Then we will take away or change the beginning sound and say the new word.

MODEL Display or share copies of the passage "A Day at the Beach" from Student Page S115, and read it aloud.

RF.K.2.e Add or substitute individual sounds (phonemes) in simple, one-syllable words to make new words.

OBJECTIVES:

- Reinforce the concepts of beginning sounds.

- Delete or change initial phonemes to make new words.

A Day at the Beach

Nan went to the beach today.
She sat in the sun and played in the sand.
She went for a swim in the sea.
Her mom and dad helped her fly a kite.
It was such a nice day at the beach!
Nan wants to go back very soon.

sat − /s/ = at
sat /s/ to /h/ = hat

sand − /s/ = and
sand /s/ to /b/ = band

TEACH After you read the passage aloud, point out the word *sat* in line 2. Listen as I say this word: *sat*. I will take away the /s/ to make another new word: *at*. Say it with me: *at*. Now I will change the /s/ to /h/ to make a new word: *hat*. Let's say the new word together: *hat*. **Repeat the process with the word** *sand* by first deleting the /s/ and then changing the /s/ to a /b/.

Lesson 17 | Delete or Change Initial Phonemes

REMIND STUDENTS THAT ...

- words have beginning sounds.
- deleting a word's beginning sound makes a new word.

PRACTICE 1 Help students focus on isolating and deleting initial sounds. Listen as I say a word. Then we'll say the word together. We will name the beginning sound. After that, we'll take away the beginning sound and say the new word.

Listen as I say the word: *fin*. Say the word with me: *fin*. Repeat the word, blending each sound slowly. The beginning sound in the word *fin* is /f/. Now let's take away the beginning /f/ sound and say the new word: *in*. Repeat this procedure for the word *man*.

Follow the above procedure with the words below, which appear on Student Page S116. Listen to each word I say. First, say the word. Then tell me the first sound in the word. Next, take away the first sound in the word and say the new word.

can (an)	win (in)	lend (end)	cart (art)

☑ **MONITOR PROGRESS** Say the following words from Student Page S116:

wall	meat	hill	sink
mask	self	hand	wax

Have students say the word *wall* and identify the beginning sound.

What new word do you make when you take away the beginning sound in *wall*? (all) Repeat this procedure for the remaining words.

IF... students have difficulty identifying the new word created after deleting the initial phoneme,
THEN... model the correct response with one of the words in the activity, and have students repeat after you. Return to the same word later in the practice and invite students to delete the initial phoneme and say the new word.

Lesson 17 | Delete or Change Initial Phonemes

PRACTICE 2 Review with students initial, medial, and final sounds. Let's practice making a new word by taking away the beginning sound of the old word. Listen as I say a word: *ham*. Say it with me: *ham*. **Repeat the word, blending each sound slowly.** Now let's take away the /h/ sound from the beginning of *ham*. Say the new word: *am*.

Help students recall that some words have more than one beginning sound. Listen to this word: *stop*. What are the two sounds at the beginning of *stop*? (/s/ and /t/) Now let's take away the /s/ sound from the beginning of *stop*. Say the new word: *top*.

Say the following words, displaying Student Page S117 if desired. Listen to each word I say. Repeat each word after me. Tell me the first sound or sounds you hear in the word. Then take away the very first sound in the word and say the new word. Guide and assist students as needed.

> bin (in)   kit (it)   spot (pot)   tray (ray)   year (ear)

☑ **MONITOR PROGRESS** Say the following words from Student Page S117:

> | | | | | |
> |---|---|---|---|---|
> | jam | stub | ran | grow | pup |
> | part | sway | flip | task | glow |

Have students say each word and identify its beginning sound(s). Then have them omit the very first sound they hear and say the new word.

IF... students have difficulty determining which sound they should omit in a word with two distinct initial sounds,
THEN... model how to omit the very first initial sound in one of the words they are having trouble with. Revisit the same word later in the practice and have students try deleting the initial phoneme and saying the new word on their own.

REMIND STUDENTS THAT ...
- words are made up of sounds.
- there may be more than one sound at the beginning of a word.
- deleting a word's beginning sound makes a new word.

Lesson 17 | Delete or Change Initial Phonemes

REMIND STUDENTS THAT ...

- words have one or more beginning sounds.
- changing a word's beginning sound makes a new word.

PRACTICE 3 Isolate an initial sound. The word *dip* has three sounds: /d//i//p/. The beginning sound is /d/. If I change the /d/ to a /t/, I make a new word: *tip*. Isolate the two initial sounds in *drip*. If I change the /d/ to a /t/, I make a new word: *trip*.

Listen as I say a word: *fan*. Say it with me: *fan*. The beginning sound in *fan* is /f/. Let's change the /f/ to /t/: /t//a//n/. The new word is *tan*. Let's say it together: *tan*. Present the word *slow*, identifying the two beginning sounds. Replace /s/ with /g/ to produce the word *glow*.

Say the following words from Student Page S118:

had /h/ to /p/ (pad)
sun /s/ to /r/ (run)
jump /j/ to /b/ (bump)
slip /s/ to /f/ (flip)

Say the word *had*. Have students repeat it and identify the initial /h/ sound. Change the /h/ sound to a /p/ sound. What new word do you get? Repeat the procedure for the remaining words. Make sure students identify the two distinct initial sounds in *slip*.

☑ **INDEPENDENT PRACTICE** Say *keep, grip, tar,* and *glow*. Have students identify the beginning sound(s) in each word. Ask them to replace the beginning sound in *keep* and *grip* with /d/ and the beginning sound in *tar* and *glow* with /f/. Have them say the new words.

IF... students have difficulty replacing initial phonemes to create new words, THEN... model the correct response by saying the original word, naming the sound to be replaced as well the new initial sound, and then saying the new word. Have them use this procedure with one or more of the other featured words.

Lesson 17 Delete or Change Initial Phonemes

A Day at the Beach

Nan went to the beach today.

She sat in the sun and played in the sand.

She went for a swim in the sea.

Her mom and dad helped her fly a kite.

It was such a nice day at the beach!

Nan wants to go back very soon.

Teacher: This Student Page is intended as an *optional extension* of the lesson. After teaching the phonological awareness lesson orally, you can distribute or display this page to connect the phonological awareness skills (sounds) to phonics skills (sound-spelling).

Lesson 17   Delete or Change Initial Phonemes

can	win	lend	cart

wall	meat	hill	sink
mask	self	hand	wax

Teacher: This Student Page is intended as an *optional extension* of the lesson. After teaching the phonological awareness lesson orally, you can distribute or display this page to connect the phonological awareness skills (sounds) to phonics skills (sound-spelling).

Lesson 17   Delete or Change Initial Phonemes

bin   kit   spot   tray   year

jam   stub   ran   grow   pup

part   sway   flip   task   glow

Teacher: This Student Page is intended as an *optional extension* of the lesson. After teaching the phonological awareness lesson orally, you can distribute or display this page to connect the phonological awareness skills (sounds) to phonics skills (sound-spelling).

Lesson 17 Delete or Change Initial Phonemes

had

sun

jump

slip

Teacher: This Student Page is intended as an *optional extension* of the lesson. After teaching the phonological awareness lesson orally, you can distribute or display this page to connect the phonological awareness skills (sounds) to phonics skills (sound-spelling).

Lesson 18 | Delete or Change Final Phonemes

INTRODUCE Remind students that they have practiced hearing the final sound in a word. When we say *bat*, the final sound is /t/. We say words slowly to hear the sounds.

MODEL Let's say the word *cup* together and listen for its sounds. Say it with me: *cup*. It has the sounds /k//u//p/.

Here is another word: *seed*. It has the sounds /s//ē//d/. If I take away the last sound, I make a new word: *see*. If I add the sound /n/ to the end, I have a new word, *seen*.

Read the first column of words from Student Page S119 aloud. Repeat the words *beef* and *bee* and ask: What sound did I take away? Pause for responses. Yes, I took the /f/ sound away and made the word *bee*. Repeat *beef* and *beet* and ask: What sound did I change? Pause. Yes, I changed /f/ to /t/ at the end and made the word *beet*.

RF.K.2.e Add or substitute individual sounds (phonemes) in simple, one-syllable words to make new words.

OBJECTIVES:

• Identify individual sounds in spoken words.

• Produce a spoken word when the final phoneme is removed.

• Recognize a spoken word when the final phoneme is replaced.

beef	seam	feel
bee	sea	fee
beet	seat	feed

TEACH Repeat the process with the other two columns of words. Then help students delete phonemes on their own, using the words below. I will say a word. You take away the last sound and say the new word. For example, I will say *feet*. You take away the last sound and say *fee*.

boot (boo)   seem (see)   weed (wee)   ink (in)

Lesson 18 | Delete or Change Final Phonemes

REMIND STUDENTS THAT ...

- they can hear the sounds that make up a word.
- they can take away sounds to make new words.

PRACTICE 1 Review isolating final sounds. We know how to hear the sounds in short words. Here is a word: *tap*. If I say it very slowly, you can hear all the sounds: /t//a//p/. Tell me the sounds that you heard. **Pause for responses.** That's right. *Tap* has three sounds: /t/ (pause) /a/ (pause) /p/. Now listen as I say another word: *sit*. What are the sounds in *sit*? **Pause for responses.** The sounds in sit are /s//i//t/.

Listen as I say another word: *mine*. Now let's say the sounds slowly together: /m//ī//n/. The last sound is /n/. If we take it away, what word do we have? *My.* Say it with me: *my.*

Present the following words from Student Page S120. I will say a word. We will say the word together, slowly, so we can hear the sounds. Then we will take away the last sound and say the new word. After practicing each deletion orally, you may wish to write the original words on the board and erase the final letter to emphasize deleting it.

seed	zoom	team
see	zoo	tea
moon	week	fort
moo	wee	for

☑ **MONITOR PROGRESS** Ask students to repeat the words *tool, heap,* and *light* with you, and to then remove the final sound of each. Have students say the new words on their own.

IF... students have difficulty saying a new word,
THEN... model orally segmenting the sounds in the original word, and then say the new word. Have students repeat the new word after you. Provide other suitable words for additional practice as needed.

Lesson 18	Delete or Change Final Phonemes

PRACTICE 2 Have students review adding final phonemes. I will say a word, and then you add a sound to the end and make a new word. For example, if I say *sea*, you can add /l/ to make the new word *seal*. Say the following words, and have students add final phonemes to make new words, such as the ones suggested in parentheses.

for
(form, fort, fork)
go
(goat, goal, ghost)

moo
(moon, mood, move, moose)
say
(sail, safe, same, sake, save)

Tell students that instead of adding a final sound, now they will change a final sound to make a new word. Earlier, we made the word *seal*. If we change the /l/ at the end of *seal* to /t/, what word will we have? **(seat)** What if we change the /t/ at the end of *seat* to /m/? **(seam)**

Use the routine below to have students change the final phonemes of the following words from Student Page S121.

Routine

1. **Say a word.**	Here is the beginning word: *mat.*
2. **Give the new sound.**	Change the /t/ at the end of *mat* to /d/.
3. **Elicit the new word.**	What will the new word be? **(mad)**

mat /d/ (mad)   hit /m/ (him)
web /t/ (wet)   jam /b/ (jab)
run /g/ (rug)   bag /d/ (bad)
hot /p/ (hop)   dim /p/ (dip)

☑ **MONITOR PROGRESS** Have students change the following final phonemes as indicated to make new words: *tan* /p/, *kit* /n/, *pat* /n/, and *ham* /d/.

IF… students have trouble saying the new word,
THEN… say the beginning part of the original word and have students repeat it. Then add the new final sound, say the new word, and have students repeat it. If necessary, provide other familiar CVC words for additional practice.

Lesson 18 | Delete or Change Final Phonemes

REMIND
STUDENTS
THAT …

• they can change final sounds to make new words.

PRACTICE 3 Demonstrate changing a final phoneme. Listen as I say a word: *hat*. The sounds in the word are /h//a//t/. The last sound is /t/: *hat*. If I change the final sound from /t/ to /z/, I can make a new word, /h//a//z/, *has*. I made the word *has*.

We can change the ending again, from /z/ to /m/. That makes another new word, /h//a//m/, *ham*.

Say each of the following words from Student Page S122. For each word, have students change the final phoneme to make at least two new words. Provide guidance and assistance as needed.

cat cab, can, cap	**bag** bad, ban, bat
hub hug, hum, hut	**cod** cob, cop, cot
dig did, dim, dip	**pan** pad, pal, pat

If students falter, suggest that they try different final sounds to see if one makes a real word. For example, students could say *cab, caf, caj, cak,* and so on.

☑ **INDEPENDENT PRACTICE** Have students change the final phonemes of the following words to make at least two new words: *bed, big, map, him,* and *sat*.

IF… students have trouble identifying appropriate final phonemes to use to create new words,
THEN… say the original word, repeating it without the final sound, and then encourage students to try various letters to see which ones can replace the existing final phoneme to create a new word.

Lesson 18   Delete or Change Final Phonemes

beef   seam   feel

bee   sea   fee

beet   seat   feed

Teacher: This Student Page is intended as an *optional extension* of the lesson. After teaching the phonological awareness lesson orally, you can distribute or display this page to connect the phonological awareness skills (sounds) to phonics skills (sound-spelling).

S • 119 Phonological Awareness

Lesson 18   Delete or Change Final Phonemes

seed	**zoom**	**team**
see	**zoo**	**tea**
moon	**week**	**fort**
moo	**wee**	**for**

Teacher: This Student Page is intended as an *optional extension* of the lesson. After teaching the phonological awareness lesson orally, you can distribute or display this page to connect the phonological awareness skills (sounds) to phonics skills (sound-spelling).

Lesson 18   Delete or Change Final Phonemes

mat   hit

web   jam

run   bag

hot   dim

Teacher: This Student Page is intended as an *optional extension* of the lesson. After teaching the phonological awareness lesson orally, you can distribute or display this page to connect the phonological awareness skills (sounds) to phonics skills (sound-spelling).

Lesson 18   Delete or Change Final Phonemes

cat	bag
hub	cod
dig	pan

Teacher: This Student Page is intended as an *optional extension* of the lesson. After teaching the phonological awareness lesson orally, you can distribute or display this page to connect the phonological awareness skills (sounds) to phonics skills (sound-spelling).

| Lesson 19 | Change Medial Phonemes |

INTRODUCE You know that words are made of sounds. Different sounds make different words. You can change the sounds in a word and make a new word. For example, think about the word *tug*. Say it with me: *tug*. If you change the beginning sound in *tug* to /m/, you make a new word, *mug*.

MODEL Display or share copies of Student Page S123, which features the chart below. These are pictures of words that have the same beginning sounds, /b/, and the same final sounds, /g/. Their middle sounds are different. Listen as I say the words: *bag, beg, big, bog, bug*.

We can say the word *bag* and listen to the sounds. The middle sound is /a/. We can change the middle sound to /e/. The new word is *beg*.

RF.K.2.e Add or substitute individual sounds (phonemes) in simple, one-syllable words to make new words.

OBJECTIVES:

- Recognize a spoken word when a phoneme is replaced with a different phoneme.

| bag | beg | big | bog | bug |

TEACH Use the chart to demonstrate changing medial phonemes. I will say each word slowly. After I say a word, we will say the word together *very* slowly. Listen for the sound in the middle.

The first word is *bag*. Draw out the vowel as you say the word. Say it slowly with me: *bag*. What is its middle sound? **Pause.** Yes, the middle sound is /a/. Repeat with the other four words. After each, say: The middle sound changed from [previous middle sound] to [present middle sound].

Lesson 19 | Change Medial Phonemes

REMIND
STUDENTS
THAT …

* words are made of different sounds they can hear.
* by saying a word slowly, they can hear the middle sound.

PRACTICE 1 Use the routine to have students isolate and then change medial short vowels. First, model listening for a middle phoneme. I am going to say a word very slowly so I can hear its middle sound. Listen with me: *red*. I will say the sounds in the word: /r/ (pause) /e/ (pause) /d/. The middle sound is /e/.

Routine

1. **Segment the word.**	Listen as I say the word very slowly: *tag*. The sounds are /t//a//g/.
2. **Isolate the middle sound.**	The middle sound I hear is /a/.
3. **Name a new sound.**	Let's change the middle sound to /u/. Say it with me: /u/.
4. **Say the new sounds together.**	Let's say the sounds of the new word: /t//u//g/.
5. **Blend the sounds.**	Now say the sounds together without stopping: *tug*.

Continue the activity using the following words and phonemes from Student Page S124.

pod, /a/, pad	pig, /e/, peg	fan, /i/, fin
hop, /i/, hip	lip, /a/, lap	pen, /a/, pan
rag, /u/, rug	at, /i/, sit	dug, /o/, dog

☑ **MONITOR PROGRESS** Guide students to isolate the middle sound in the following words. Then tell them to change the middle sound, as shown, and say the new word.

hit, /u/, (hut)   bud, /e/, (bed)   sad, /e/, (said)

IF… students have trouble distinguishing the middle sound,
THEN… slowly sound out the word together several times until students can identify it successfully.

Lesson 19 | Change Medial Phonemes

PRACTICE 2 Demonstrate changing one medial short vowel to another medial short vowel. Listen as I say a word: /h//o//t/, *hot*. Wave your hand as if fanning your face and repeat the word, drawing out the vowel. The sound in the middle of *hot* is /o/. If I change the middle sound from /o/ to /i/, I can make a new word, /h//i//t/, *hit*. Bump your fists together and repeat the word, drawing out the vowel.

Let's try another: *leg*. Say it with me slowly: /l//e//g/. What is the middle sound? Pause for responses. The sound in the middle of *leg* is /e/. Now let's change that middle sound to /a/: /l//a//g/, *lag*. The new word is *lag*. Say it with me: *lag*. Repeat the procedure with the following words from Student Page S125. When possible, use gestures to reinforce the differences between words.

REMIND STUDENTS THAT …

• by saying a word slowly, they can hear the middle sound.

• they can change the middle sound in a word to make a new word.

hum, /i/, him	pan, /i/, pin
pat, /e/, pet	wig, /a/, wag
cup, /a/, cap	bat, /i/, bit

☑ **MONITOR PROGRESS** Have students try changing some medial sounds on their own. I will say a word and we'll say it together. You say the middle sound. I will tell you a new middle sound to use. Then you say the new word. Ready? The word is *net*. Say it with me: *net*. What is the middle sound? (/e/) Now change the middle sound to /u/. What is the new word? (*nut*) Repeat with the following words:

cut, /a/, (cat)   mop, /a/, (map)   fix, /o/, (fox)

IF… students have trouble remembering the beginning and ending sounds of a word,
THEN… prompt them by voicing the beginning sound, asking for the new middle sound, and voicing the ending sound. Then have students echo you as you blend the sounds into the new word.

Lesson 19 | Change Medial Phonemes

REMIND
STUDENTS
THAT …

• changing the middle
sound in a word
makes a new word.

PRACTICE 3 Demonstrate how to say the middle sound in a word, change the middle sound, and say a new word. I am going to say a word, and I want to know its middle sound. The word is *rap*. I will say it slowly: /r//a//p/. The middle sound is /a/.

Now I want to change the middle sound to /i/. The beginning sound is /r/, the new middle sound is /i/, and the ending sound is /p/. That's /r//i//p/. The new word is *rip*.

Now you try. I will say a word. You tell me the middle sound. Then I will say a new middle sound, and you say the new word. Here is the word: *zip*. What is the middle sound? **Pause for responses.** Right, the middle sound is /i/. Change the middle sound to /a/. What is the new word? **Pause for responses.** Yes, the new word is *zap*.

Continue by substituting vowels in the middle of the word frames below, which also appear on Student Page S126.

p__t	h__m	h__t	c__t

☑ **INDEPENDENT PRACTICE** Have students try substituting short vowels as middle phonemes in the spoken words below. Encourage them to experiment in order to find new real words.

him (ham, hum)   tip (top, tap)   net (not, nut)
flip (flap, flop)   bet (bat, bit, but)   map (mat, man)
pop (pep, pup)   get (got, gut)   bed (bad, bid, bud)

IF… students make an error,
THEN… model the correct response by saying the original word, the new medial sound, and the new word. Revisit the word later in the practice.

Lesson 19   Change Medial Phonemes

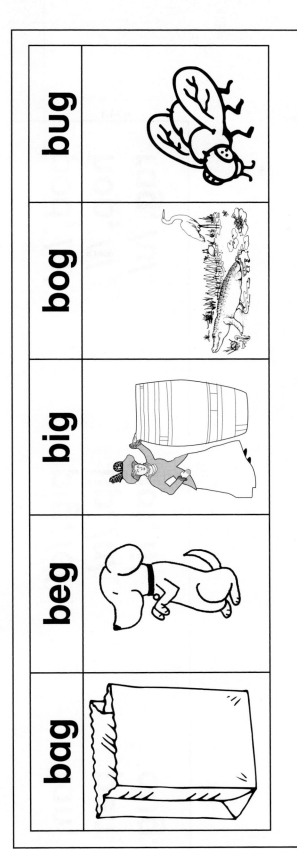

bag	beg	big	bog	bug

Teacher: This Student Page is intended as an *optional extension* of the lesson. After teaching the phonological awareness lesson orally, you can distribute or display this page to connect the phonological awareness skills (sounds) to phonics skills (sound-spelling).

Lesson 19 | Change Medial Phonemes

pod, /a/   pig, /e/   fan, /i/
hop, /i/   lip, /a/   pen, /a/
rag, /u/   sat, /i/   dug, /o/

Teacher: This Student Page is intended as an *optional extension* of the lesson. After teaching the phonological awareness lesson orally, you can distribute or display this page to connect the phonological awareness skills (sounds) to phonics skills (sound-spelling).

Lesson 19 Change Medial Phonemes

hum, /i/
pat, /e/
cup, /a/

pan, /i/
wig, /a/
bat, /i/

Teacher: This Student Page is intended as an *optional extension* of the lesson. After teaching the phonological awareness lesson orally, you can distribute or display this page to connect the phonological awareness skills (sounds) to phonics skills (sound-spelling).

Lesson 19   Change Medial Phonemes

p _ t   h _ m   h _ t   c _ t

Teacher: This Student Page is intended as an *optional extension* of the lesson. After teaching the phonological awareness lesson orally, you can distribute or display this page to connect the phonological awareness skills (sounds) to phonics skills (sound-spelling).

Lesson 20 | Blend Two to Three Phonemes Into Words

INTRODUCE Remind students that by listening closely, they can hear the separate sounds in words. We learned that words are made of sounds. Some very short words have just two sounds. Many words have more than two sounds. We will put sounds together to make words.

MODEL I am going to say the sounds that make up a word: /m/ (pause) /ē/. Now I will blend the sounds together to make the word. To do this, I will say the sounds quickly without stopping: *me.*

Repeat the process to model blending /y/ and /ōō/ into *you,* /w/ and /ē/ into *we,* and /m/ and /ā/ into *may.* Then display the passage from Student Page S127.

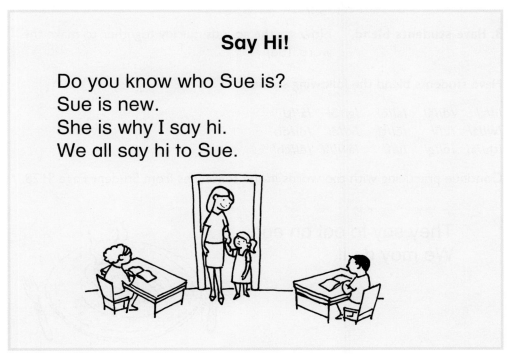

Say Hi!

Do you know who Sue is?
Sue is new.
She is why I say hi.
We all say hi to Sue.

RF.K.2.c Blend and segment onsets and rimes of single-syllable spoken words.

RF.K.2.d Isolate and pronounce the initial, medial vowel, and final sounds (phonemes) in three-phoneme (consonant-vowel-consonant, or CVC) words.

OBJECTIVES:

- Blend two phonemes into spoken words.
- Blend three phonemes into spoken words.

TEACH Have students blend two phonemes into words. I am going to say two sounds. You will make a word from the sounds. For example, I will say /i/ (pause) /t/. The sounds are /i//t/. You will make a word by saying the sound quickly without stopping: *it.* Have students make words from the following sounds:

/n//ō/   /s//ā/   /aw//l/   /wh//ī/   /sh//ē/

After students say the words, point to the word in the passage.

We can also blend three sounds into a word. For example, we can blend /m/ (pause) /a/ (pause) /p/ into the word *map.* Use the sounds below.

/h//a//t/   /w//i//n/   /b//ō//t/   /s//e//d/   /t//ā//k/

Lesson 20 | Blend Two to Three Phonemes Into Words

REMIND
STUDENTS
THAT ...

• words are made of sounds.

• some words have just two sounds.

• saying sounds together without stopping makes a word.

PRACTICE I Some short words, such as *me, my,* and *you,* have just two sounds. Can you hear them? The word *me* has the sounds /m/ and /ē/. What are the sounds in *my*? **Pause for responses.** Yes, the sounds are /m//ī/; *my*. The sounds in *you* are /y//ōō/; *you*. **Use the routine to have students blend two sounds into words.**

Routine

1. Model.   I can blend two sounds to make a word. For example, the sounds /b//ē/ can make a word. When I say them quickly without stopping, they make *be.*

2. Voice two sounds.   Listen to these two sounds: /t//ī/. The sounds are /t//ī/.

3. Have students blend.   Now say the sounds quickly together to make the word. (tie)

Have students blend the following sounds:

/i//z/   /d//ā/   /s//ē/   /g//ō/   /a//t/
/w//ā/   /l//ī/   /ē//t/   /k//ē/   /d//ōō/
/th//ā/   /e//g/   /i//f/   /aw//f/   /ē//ch/

Continue practicing with the words in the sentences from Student Page S128.

They say to eat an egg.
We may do it.

☑ **MONITOR PROGRESS** Give students the following sounds, and ask them to blend the sounds into a word.

/a//m/   /ā//k/   /b//ī/   /r//ō/   /o//n/

IF... students have trouble blending the sounds,
THEN... tell them the word and have them repeat it after you. Then have them try to blend the sounds again.

Lesson 20 | Blend Two to Three Phonemes Into Words

PRACTICE 2 Let's try blending some sounds into words. We will say the sounds, and then we will make the word by blending the sounds together. Here are the sounds: /ā/ (pause) /m/. Say the sounds with me: /ā/ (pause) /m/. Now let's say the sounds quickly without stopping: *aim*. The word is *aim*. **Repeat the process with the following words.**

/th//ā/   /m//ā/   /i//t/   /a//t/   /m//ē/

Now, let's make some words out of three sounds. We will do it the same way. I will say the sounds. Then we will say the sounds together. After that, we will blend the sounds together into a word. The first sounds we will say are /b//aw//l/. Say them with me: /b//aw//l/. Now we will say them quickly without stopping: *ball*. The word is *ball*. **Repeat the process with the following words.**

/k//i//k/   /g//ā//m/   /w//i//n/   /b//a//k/   /t//ē//m/

Display Student Page S129 and read it aloud.

REMIND STUDENTS THAT …
• some words have just two or three sounds.
• blending sounds together makes a word.

They may aim it at me.
I will kick it back.

☑ **MONITOR PROGRESS** Give students the following sounds, and have them blend the sounds into words.

/r//u//n/   /s//o//k/   /d//ā/   /s//u//n/   /l//e//g/

/b//ī/   /n//ē/   /b//ī//t/   /n//ē//l/   /g//ō//l/

IF… students have trouble blending three phonemes,
THEN… have them blend the first two and then add the third.

Lesson 20 | Blend Two to Three Phonemes Into Words

REMIND
STUDENTS
THAT ...

- blending sounds together makes a word.
- they can blend two sounds together to make a word.
- some short words have three sounds.

PRACTICE 3 Review the blending process. We will blend sounds into words. I will say some sounds. Then we will say the sounds together. After that, we will make the word by blending the sounds without stopping. Here are three sounds: /r/ (pause) /u/ (pause) /n/. Say the sounds with me: /r/ (pause) /u/ (pause) /n/. Now let's blend the sounds together without stopping: *run*. The word is *run*. Repeat the process with the following sounds.

/m//o//m/	/s//e//d/	/h//a//t/	/k//ō//t/
/b//a//t/	/b//aw//l/	/s//i//t/	/s//ē//t/
/r//ā//s/	/s//o//k/	/p//l//ā/	/n//ōō//n/
/s//u//n/	/r//ā//n/	/w//i//sh/	/t//o//p/

If desired, display Student Page S130 to reinforce the connection between sounds and letters.

mom	said	hat	coat
bat	ball	sit	seat
race	sock	play	noon
sun	rain	wish	top

☑ **INDEPENDENT PRACTICE** Mix practicing with two sounds and three sounds. Have students blend the following sounds into words.

/b//ē/	/s//ā//f/	/wh//e//n/	/y//ōō/
/t//ī/	/b//ō/	/b//ō//l/	/ē//t//s/
/m//e//t/	/l//ō/	/k//u//p/	/l//ā//s/
/sh//ōō/	/th//a//t/	/p//i//n/	/m//ī/

IF... students make an error,
THEN... model the correct response by repeating the sounds and then blending them into a word.

Say Hi!

Do you know who Sue is?
Sue is new.
She is why I say hi.
We all say hi to Sue.

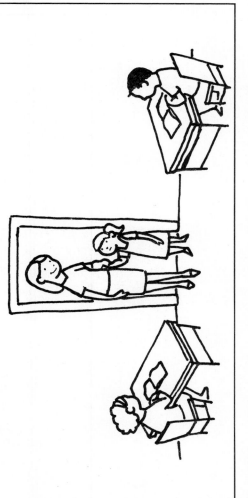

Teacher: This Student Page is intended as an *optional extension* of the lesson. After teaching the phonological awareness lesson orally, you can distribute or display this page to connect the phonological awareness skills (sounds) to phonics skills (sound-spelling).

Lesson 20   Blend Two to Three Phonemes Into Words

**They say to eat an egg.
We may do it.**

Teacher: This Student Page is intended as an *optional* extension of the lesson. After teaching the phonological awareness lesson orally, you can distribute or display this page to connect the phonological awareness skills (sounds) to phonics skills (sound-spelling).

Lesson 20   **Blend Two to Three Phonemes Into Words**

They may aim it at me.
I will kick it back.

Teacher: This Student Page is intended as an *optional extension* of the lesson. After teaching the phonological awareness lesson orally, you can distribute or display this page to connect the phonological awareness skills (sounds) to phonics skills (sound-spelling).

Lesson 20 | Blend Two to Three Phonemes Into Words

mom	said	hat	coat
bat	ball	sit	seat
race	sock	play	noon
sun	rain	wish	top

Teacher: This Student Page is intended as an *optional extension* of the lesson. After teaching the phonological awareness lesson orally, you can distribute or display this page to connect the phonological awareness skills (sounds) to phonics skills (sound-spelling).

ASSESSMENT
LESSONS 15–20

Phonological Awareness

ASSESS MASTERY Use this Checkpoint to assess students' mastery of phonemes.

ADMINISTER THE TEST Administer the Checkpoint orally to each student. For each item, model the process as described and then have the student use the process to respond to your prompts. Record responses using the scoring chart on the next page.

1. Add Initial Phonemes (Lesson 15)
MODEL: I will ask you to add a new sound at the beginning of some words. For example, I could add /s/ to the beginning of the word *at*: *sat*. I want you to add /p/ to the beginning of these words.

ASSESS:	it	an	at	in	eel

2. Add Final Phonemes (Lesson 16)
MODEL: I will ask you to add a new sound at the end of some words. For example, I could add /t/ to the end of the word *go*: *goat*. I want you to add /m/ to the end of these words.

ASSESS:	bee	say	tie	far	hoe

3. Delete or Change Initial Phonemes (Lesson 17)
MODEL: I am going to have you take away a beginning sound to make a new word. For example, take /f/ away from *fit* to make *it*. Then you will add a new beginning sound to make another word. Add /b/ to *it* to make *bit*.

ASSESS:	cat, /p/	bone, /f/	game, /s/	ball, /w/

4. Delete or Change Final Phonemes (Lesson 18)
MODEL: I want you to take away an ending sound to make a new word. For example, take /p/ away from *heap* to make *he*. Then I will have you add a new ending sound. Add /l/ to *he* to make the word *heel*.

ASSESS:	bike, /t/	rope, /d/	mail, /n/	tool, /b/

5. Change Medial Phonemes (Lesson 19)
MODEL: I will say a word, such as *tag*. Then I will say a new middle sound, such as /u/. You will use the new middle sound to make a new word. In the example, the new word is *tug*.

ASSESS:	pen, /a/	dog, /i/	not, /e/	fizz, /u/

6. Blend Two or Three Phonemes Into Words (Lesson 20)
MODEL: I will say some sounds. I want you to blend the sounds together into a word. For example, if I say /b//u//g/, you will say *bug*.

ASSESS:	/s//ō/	/w//aw//k/	/n//ē/	/m//ī//s/	/b//e//l/

RF.K.2.c Blend and segment onsets and rimes of single-syllable spoken words.

RF.K.2.d Isolate and pronounce the initial, medial vowel, and final sounds (phonemes) in three-phoneme (consonant-vowel-consonant, or CVC) words.

RF.K.2.e Add or substitute individual sounds (phonemes) in simple, one-syllable words to make new words.

ASSESSMENT	Phonological Awareness
LESSONS 15–20	

SCORING

SKILL/LESSON	SCORE

1. Add Initial Phonemes (Lesson 15)
  pit
  pan
  pat
  pin
  peel
	_____ / 5

2. Add Final Phonemes (Lesson 16)
  beam
  same
  time
  farm
  home
	_____ / 5

3. Delete or Change Initial Phonemes (Lesson 17)
  cat, at, pat
  bone, own, phone
  game, aim, same
  ball, all, wall
	_____ / 4

4. Delete or Change Final Phonemes (Lesson 18)
  bike, by, bite
  rope, row, rode
  mail, may, main
  tool, too, tube
	_____ / 4

5. Change Medial Phonemes (Lesson 19)
  pen, pan
  dog, dig
  not, net
  fizz, fuzz
	_____ / 4

6. Blend Two to Three Phonemes Into Words (Lesson 20) so; walk; knee; mice; bell	_____ / 5

An overall score of 80% correct is typically considered mastery. Use your judgment and your individual students' needs as well to determine skill mastery.

IF... students score below the benchmark,
THEN... review those discrete skills, going back to the lessons to reteach and scaffold as needed.

Lesson 21 | Connect Sounds and Letters: Consonants 1

INTRODUCE Write the letters *Mm*, say the name *(m)*, and have students repeat after you. Explain that *m* is a consonant and spells the sound /m/. Point to something that begins with *m*, such as a map. What sound do you hear at the beginning of *map*? Write the word *map*. In this lesson, we'll learn how letters and sounds connect.

MODEL Display or share copies of the following passage, "Mac and Sam," from Student Page S133, and read it aloud. The words in this story have the letters and sounds *l* /l/, *r* /r/, *s* /s/, *m* /m/, *t* /t/, and *p* /p/.

RF.K.3.a Demonstrate basic knowledge of one-to-one letter-sound correspondences by producing the primary sound or many of the most frequent sounds for each consonant.

OBJECTIVES:

- Recognize letters *l, r, s, m, t, p* and sounds *l* /l/, *r* /r/, *s* /s/, *m* /m/, *t* /t/, and *p* /p/.
- Connect letters and sounds *l* /l/, *r* /r/, *s* /s/, *m* /m/, *t* /t/, and *p* /p/.
- Identify *l* /l/, *r* /r/, *s* /s/, *m* /m/, *t* /t/, *and p* /p/ in words.

Mac and Sam

I have a tiny pup.
His name is Mac.
Mac likes to run for his ball.
I have a tiny cat.
Her name is Sam.
Sam likes to sit on my lap!

TEACH Use examples of words to help students recognize letter-sound correspondences. The first word in the title is *Mac*. It begins with the letter *M*. The other name in the title is *Sam*. It begins with the letter *S*. The letter *M* stands for the sound /m/ and the letter *S* stands for the sound /s/. Point out letter-sound correspondences in the story for *l* /l/, *r* /r/, *t* /t/, and *p* /p/.

Lesson 21 | Connect Sounds and Letters: Consonants 1

PRACTICE 1 Follow the routine below to teach one-to-one letter-sound correspondences for *l* /l/ and *r* /r/.

Routine

1. Teach the letters and sounds.	Write capital and lowercase *Ll*. This is the letter *l*. It stands for the sound /l/. Write capital and lowercase *Rr*. This is the letter *r*. It stands for the sound /r/.
2. Model letter-sound correspondence.	Write the word *log* and circle the *l*. The word *log* begins with the letter *l* and the sound /l/. Write the word *red* and circle the *r*. The word *red* begins with the letter *r* and the sound /r/.
3. Practice letter-sound correspondence.	Write *lot, lid,* and *lap*. Have students circle the letter *l* in each word. What sound does *l* make in each word? Write *rid, run,* and *rag*. Have students follow the same process for letter *r*.

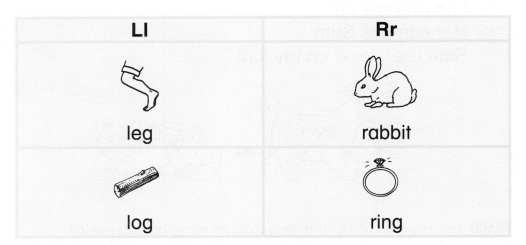

Ll	**Rr**
leg	rabbit
log	ring

Distribute Student Page S134. Have students cut out the picture cards. Pairs put letter cards *Ll* and *Rr* face up and mix the picture cards face down. They select picture cards, say the word for the picture, say the first sound of each word, and match the card to *Ll* or *Rr*.

☑ **MONITOR PROGRESS** Display the following sentence from Student Page S134. Have students identify each example of *l* /l/ and *r* /r/.

> Lions like to roar, and robins like to sing.

IF... students cannot connect the letters and sounds in the words,
THEN... review key steps in the routine, and provide additional words beginning with *l* /l/ and *r* /r/ for practice.

| **Lesson 21** | **Connect Sounds and Letters: Consonants 1** |

PRACTICE 2 Follow the routine below to teach one-to-one letter-sound correspondences for *s* /s/ and *m* /m/.

Routine

1. Teach the letters and sounds.	Write capital and lowercase *Ss*. This is the letter *s*. It stands for the sound /s/. Write capital and lowercase *Mm*. This is the letter *m*. It stands for the sound /m/.
2. Model letter-sound correspondence.	Write the word *sun* and circle the *s*. The word *sun* begins with the letter *s* and the sound /s/. Write the word *men* and circle the *m*. The word *men* begins with the letter *m* and the sound /m/.
3. Practice letter-sound correspondence.	Write the words *sip, sit,* and *sat*. Have students circle the letter *s* in each word. What sound is connected with the letter *s* in each word? Write the words *map, mop,* and *mat*. Have students follow the same process for letter *m*.

REMIND STUDENTS THAT ...

- they can recognize the letters *s* and *m* and the sounds /s/ and /m/.
- they can connect the letters and sounds *s* /s/ and *m* /m/.
- they can identify *s* /s/ and *m* /m/ in words.

Ss	**Mm**
six	man
sock	map

Distribute Student Page S135. Have students cut out the picture cards. Pairs put letter cards *Ss* and *Mm* face up and mix the picture cards face down. They select picture cards, say the word for the picture, say the first sound of each word, and match the card to *Ss* or *Mm*.

☑ **MONITOR PROGRESS** Display the following sentence from Student Page S135. Have students identify each example of *s* /s/ and *m* /m/.

Sis can mix the salad, and Mike can make jam.

IF... students cannot identify the letter-sound correspondences,
THEN... review key steps in the routine, and have students practice with other *s* /s/ and *m* /m/ words.

Lesson 21 | Connect Sounds and Letters: Consonants 1

REMIND STUDENTS THAT …

• they can recognize the letters *t* and *p* and the sounds /t/ and /p/.

• they can connect the letters and sounds *t* /t/ and *p* /p/.

• they can identify *t* /t/ and *p* /p/ in words.

PRACTICE 3 Tell students you will focus on the letters and sounds *t* /t/ and *p* /p/. Follow this routine.

Routine

1. Teach the letters and sounds.

Write capital and lowercase *Tt.* This is the letter *t.* It stands for the sound /t/. Write capital and lowercase *Pp.* This is the letter *p.* Its sound is /p/.

2. Model letter-sound correspondence.

Write the word *ten* and circle the *t.* The word *ten* begins with the letter *t* and the sound /t/. Write the word *pin* and circle the *p.* The word *pin* begins with the letter *p* and the sound /p/.

3. Practice letter-sound correspondence.

Write the words *tan, tip,* and *tub.* Have students circle the letter *t* in each word. What sound is connected with the letter *t* in each word? Write the words *pot, pat,* and *pet.* Have students circle the letter *p* in each word. What sound is connected with the letter *p* in each word?

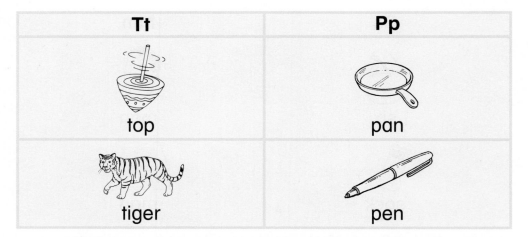

Tt	**Pp**
top	pan
tiger	pen

Distribute Student Page S136. Have students cut out the picture cards. Pairs put letter cards *Tt* and *Pp* face up and mix the picture cards face down. They select picture cards, say the word for the picture, say the first sound of each word, and match the card to *Tt* or *Pp.*

☑ **INDEPENDENT PRACTICE** Display the following sentence from Student Page S136. Have individuals identify each example of *t* /t/ and *p* /p/, one at a time.

> Ten pet pigs play tag.

IF… students cannot identify the one-to-one letter-sound correspondences, **THEN…** review key steps in the routine, and have students practice with additional words that contain *t* /t/ and *p* /p/.

Mac and Sam

I have a tiny pup.
His name is Mac.
Mac likes to run for his ball.
I have a tiny cat.
Her name is Sam.
Sam likes to sit on my lap!

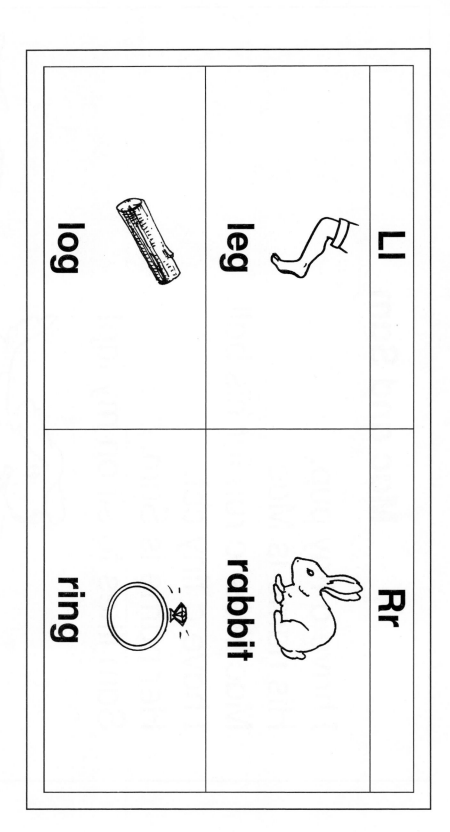

Ll	Rr
leg	rabbit
log	ring

Lions like to roar, and robins like to sing.

Mm

man

map

Ss

six

sock

Sis can mix the salad, and Mike can make jam.

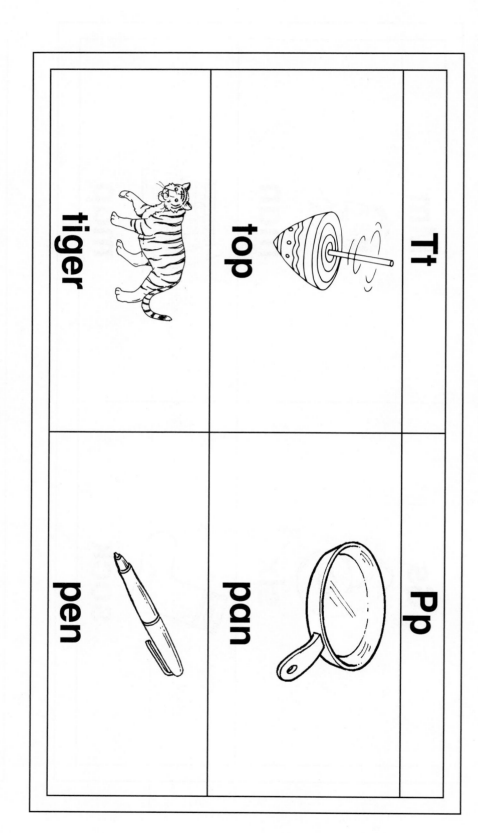

Tt	Pp
top	pan
tiger	pen

Ten pet pigs play tag.

Lesson 22 | Connect Sounds and Letters: Consonants 2

INTRODUCE Write the letters *Nn*, say the name *n*, and have students repeat after you. Explain that *n* is a consonant and spells the sound /n/. Point to a student whose name begins with *N*, such as *Nat*. What sound do you hear at the beginning of *Nat*? Write the name *Nat*. In this lesson, we'll connect sounds and consonant letters.

MODEL Display or share copies of the passage "Who Fits in the Car?" from Student Page S137, and read it aloud. Say: The words in this story have the letters and sounds *n* /n/, *b* /b/, *c* /k/, *f* /f/, *d* /d/, and *g* /g/.

Who Fits in the Car?

The dog got in the car.
The duck got in the car.
The goat got in the car.
The fox with the big bag
did not fit in the car!

TEACH Use examples to help students recognize letter-sound correspondences. Say: We read the word *dog*. The first letter in *dog* is *d*. The letter *d* stands for the sound /d/. Point to other words in the story that begin with *d* /d/. Help students identify the words *duck* and *did* as words beginning with *d* /d/. Circle each *d*. Continue the process for *n* /n/, *b* /b/, *c* /k/, *f* /f/, and *g* /g/, circling each letter as you identify it.

RF.K.3.a Demonstrate basic knowledge of one-to-one letter-sound correspondences by producing the primary sound or many of the most frequent sounds for each consonant.

OBJECTIVES:

• Recognize letters *n, b, c, f, d, g* and sounds /n/, /b/, /k/, /f/, /d/, /g/.

• Connect letters and sounds *n* /n/, *b* /b/, *c* /k/, *f* /f/, *d* /d/, and *g* /g/.

• Identify *n* /n/, *b* /b/, *c* /k/, *f* /f/, *d* /d/, and *g* /g/ in words.

Lesson 22 | Connect Sounds and Letters: Consonants 2

REMIND
STUDENTS
THAT …

- they can recognize the letters *n* and *b* and the sounds /n/ and /b/.
- they can connect the letters and sounds *n* /n/ and *b* /b/.
- they can identify *n* /n/ and *b* /b/ in words.

PRACTICE I Follow this routine to teach one-to-one letter-sound correspondences for *n* /n/ and *b* /b/.

Routine

I. Teach the letters and sounds.	Write capital and lowercase *Nn*. This is the letter *n*. It stands for the sound /n/. Write capital and lowercase *Bb*. This is the letter *b*. It stands for the sound /b/.
2. Model letter-sound correspondence.	Write the word *nap* and circle the *n*. The word *nap* begins with the letter *n* and the sound /n/. Repeat the word *nap* after me. Write the word *bat* and circle the *b*. The word *bat* begins with the letter *b* and the sound /b/. Say the word *bat*.
3. Practice letter-sound correspondence.	Write the words *not, nip,* and *net*. Have students circle the letter *n* in each word. What sound is connected with the letter *n* in each word? Write the words *bad, big,* and *bit*. Have students circle the letter *b* in each word. What sound is connected with the letter *b* in each word?
4. Extend practice.	Extend practice by having students find examples of the letters *Nn* and *Bb* in words in the titles of classroom books. Have them read the words and identify the sound.

Distribute Student Page S138. Have students cut apart the word cards. Have pairs place the cards face down and take turns picking a card. They identify the first letter of the word, say the sound of the first letter, read the word, and use the word in a sentence.

net	bat	ball
nut	bed	not
bud	nod	nip

☑ **MONITOR PROGRESS** Display the following sentence from Student Page S138. Have students identify all instances of *n* /n/ and *b* /b/. Then check that students can print each letter.

> ### Ben has the bat, but Ned does not have a ball.

IF… students confuse the letters,
THEN… read the sentence aloud, emphasizing each *b* /b/ and *n* /n/ word. Ask students to identify the first letter. Offer corrective feedback and repeat with other words as needed.

| Lesson 22 | Connect Sounds and Letters: Consonants 2 |

PRACTICE 2 Follow this routine to teach one-to-one letter-sound correspondences for *c* /k/ and *f* /f/.

REMIND STUDENTS THAT …

Routine

1. Teach the letters and sounds.

Write capital and lowercase *Cc*. This is the letter *c*. It stands for the sound /k/. Write capital and lowercase *Ff*. This is the letter *f*. It stands for the sound /f/.

2. Model letter-sound correspondence.

Write the word *cat* and circle the *c*. The word *cat* begins with the letter *c* and the sound /k/. Repeat the word *cat* after me. Write the word *fan* and circle the *f*. The word *fan* begins with the letter *f* and the sound /f/. Say the word *fan*.

3. Practice letter-sound correspondence.

Write the words *cap, car,* and *cab*. Have students circle the letter *c* in each word. What sound is connected with the letter *c* in each word? Write the words *fit, fun,* and *fin*. Have students circle the letter *f* in each word. What sound is connected with the letter *f* in each word?

4. Extend practice.

Extend practice by having students say the names of objects they see in the room that begin with *c* /k/ and *f* /f/.

- they can recognize the letters *c* and *f* and the sounds /k/ and /f/.
- they can connect the letters and sounds *c* /k/ and *f* /f/.
- they can identify *c* /k/ and *f* /f/ in words.

Distribute Student Page S139. Have students cut apart the word cards. Have pairs place the cards face down and take turns picking a card. They identify the first letter of the word, say the sound of the first letter, read the word, and use the word in a sentence.

can	fun	fib
cub	cut	fan
fin	fox	cat

☑ **MONITOR PROGRESS** Display the following sentence from Student Page S139. Have students identify all instances of each of the letters taught. Then check that students can print each letter.

> Can you find the cat and fix her food?

IF... students struggle to identify *c* /k/ and *f* /f/,
THEN... give students additional words for practice writing these letters. Review the steps of the routine as needed.

| **Lesson 22** | **Connect Sounds and Letters: Consonants 2** |

REMIND
STUDENTS
THAT …

- they can recognize the letters *d* and *g* and the sounds /d/ and /g/.
- they can connect the letters and sounds *d* /d/ and *g* /g/.
- they can identify *d* /d/ and *g* /g/ in words.

PRACTICE 3 Follow this routine to teach one-to-one letter-sound correspondences for *d* /d/ and *g* /g/.

Routine

I. Teach the letters and sounds.

Write capital and lowercase *Dd*. This is the letter *d*. It stands for the sound /d/. Write capital and lowercase *Gg*. This is the letter *g*. It stands for the sound /g/.

2. Model letter-sound correspondence.

Write the word *dip* and circle the *d*. The word *dip* begins with the letter *d* and the sound /d/. Write the word *gab* and circle the *g*. The word *gab* begins with the letter *g* and the sound /g/.

3. Practice letter-sound correspondence.

Write the words *did, dot,* and *dog*. Have students circle the letter *d* in each word. What sound is connected with the letter *d* in each word? Write the words *got, get,* and *gas*. Have students circle the letter *g* in each word. What sound is connected with the letter *g* in each word?

4. Extend practice.

Have students write the letters *Dd* and *Gg* on sticky notes. Ask them to find an object in the classroom that begins with *d* /d/ and put the *Dd* sticky note on it. Have them repeat the process with the *Gg* sticky note.

Distribute Student Page S140. Have students cut apart the word cards. Have pairs place the cards face down and take turns picking a card. They identify the first letter of the word, say the sound of the first letter, read the word, and use the word in a sentence.

dad	good	dot
dim	gag	gap
Don	gave	duck

☑ **INDEPENDENT PRACTICE** Display the following sentence from Student Page S140. Have individuals identify all instances of *d* /d/ and *g* /g/.

> Gram gave Dot a doll for a gift.

IF… students struggle to identify the words with *d* /d/ and *g* /g/,
THEN… give students additional words beginning with *d* /d/ and *g* /g/ to practice writing the letters. Review the steps of the routine as needed.

Who Fits in the Car?

The dog got in the car.
The duck got in the car.
The goat got in the car.
The fox with the big bag
did not fit in the car!

net	bat	ball
nut	bed	not
bud	nod	nip

Ben has the bat, but Ned does not have a ball.

Lesson 22 **Connect Sounds and Letters: Consonants 2**

can	fun	fib
cub	cut	fan
fin	fox	cat

Can you find the cat and fix her food?

Lesson 22   Connect Sounds and Letters: Consonants 2

dad	good	dot
dim	gag	gap
Don	gave	duck

Gram gave Dot a doll for a gift.

| Lesson 23 | Connect Sounds and Letters: Consonants 3 |

INTRODUCE Write the letters *Hh* and say the name *(h)*. Explain that *h* is a consonant and spells the sound /h/. Ask students to hold up a hand. The word *hand* begins with the letter *h* and the sound /h/. Write or display the word *hand*. In this lesson, we'll learn to connect more sounds and consonant letters.

MODEL Display or share copies of the passage "Can You Do It?" from Student Page S141, and read it aloud. The words in this passage have the letters and sounds *h* /h/, *v* /v/, *k* /k/, *j* /j/, *z* /z/, *w* /w/, *y* /y/, *q* /kw/ and *x* /ks/.

Can You Do It?

Can you hug a hippo?
Can you kiss a zebra?
Can you jog with an ox to the vet?
Yes, I can!
I am the queen!

TEACH Use examples to help students recognize letter-sound correspondences. We read the word *hug*. The first letter in *hug* is *h*. The letter *h* stands for the sound /h/. Do the words *hug* and *hippo* begin with the same sound or different sounds? Circle each *h*. Continue the process until you have identified the relevant letter and sound in each of the following words: *you, kiss, zebra, jog, with, ox, vet, Yes,* and *queen*. Explain to students that the letter *x* and sound /ks/ usually come at the end of the word.

RF.K.3.a Demonstrate basic knowledge of one-to-one letter-sound correspondences by producing the primary sound or many of the most frequent sounds for each consonant.

OBJECTIVES:

- Recognize letters *h, v, k, j, z, w, y, q, x* and sounds /h/, /v/, /k/, /j/, /z/, /w/, /y/, /kw/, /ks/.

- Connect letters and sounds *h* /h/, *v* /v/, *k* /k/, *j* /j/, *z* /z/, *w* /w/, *y* /y/, *q* /kw/, and *x* /ks/.

- Identify *h* /h/, *v* /v/, *k* /k/, *j* /j/, *z* /z/, *w* /w/, *y* /y/, *q* /kw/, and *x* /ks/ in words.

Lesson 23 | Connect Sounds and Letters: Consonants 3

REMIND STUDENTS THAT …

- they can recognize the letters *h, v,* and *k* and the sounds /h/, /v/, and /k/.
- they can connect the letters and sounds *h*/h/, *v*/v/, and *k*/k/.
- they can identify *h*/h/, *v*/v/, and *k*/k/ in words.

PRACTICE 1 Follow this routine to teach one-to-one letter-sound correspondences for *h* /h/, *v* /v/, and *k* /k/.

Routine

1. Teach the letters and sounds.
Write capital and lowercase *Hh*. This is the letter *h*. It stands for the sound /h/. Repeat for *Vv* and *Kk*.

2. Model letter-sound correspondence.
Write the word *hid* and circle the *h*. The word *hid* begins with the letter *h* and the sound /h/. Say the word *hid* after me. Repeat the process with the words *van* and *kit*.

3. Practice letter-sound correspondence.
Write the words *hip, hat,* and *him*. Have students circle the letter *h* in each word. What sound is connected with the letter *h* in each word? Write the words *vent, vest, kid,* and *Kim*. Have students circle the letters *v, k,* and *K* and identify the sounds /v/ and /k/.

4. Extend practice.
Have students write the letters *h, v,* and *k* and one example of a word that begins with each letter. They can use words from the lists in steps 2 and 3.

Distribute Student Page S142. Have students cut apart the word cards. Pairs place the cards face down and take turns selecting a card. They identify the first letter of the word, say the sound of the first letter, read the word, and then use it in a sentence.

hop	kid	vet
vent	kit	her
ham	hum	hid
hat	kind	van

☑ **MONITOR PROGRESS** Display the following sentence from Student Page S142. Have students identify all instances of *h* /h/, *v* /v/, and *k* /k/. Then check that students can print each letter.

> Kit has a helmet, and Kim has a vest.

IF… students struggle with the words,
THEN… help them find additional words with those letters in signs or posters in the room. Review steps from the routine as needed.

| **Lesson 23** | **Connect Sounds and Letters: Consonants 3** |

PRACTICE 2 Follow this routine to teach one-to-one letter-sound correspondences for *j* /j/, *z* /z/, and *w* /w/.

REMIND STUDENTS THAT …

Routine

1. Teach the letters and sounds.	Write capital and lowercase *Jj*. This is the letter *j*. It stands for the sound /j/. Repeat for *Zz* and *Ww*.
2. Model letter-sound correspondence.	Write the word *jam* and circle the *j*. The word *jam* begins with the letter *j* and the sound /j/. Say the word *jam* after me. Repeat the process with the words *zip* and *win*.
3. Practice letter-sound correspondence.	Write the words *jet, jog,* and *job*. Have students circle the letter *j* in each word. What sound is connected with the letter *j* in each word? Write the words *zap, zoo, was,* and *web*. Have students circle the letters *z* and *w* and identify the sounds /z/ and /w/.
4. Extend practice.	Have students write *j, z,* and *w* and say a word that begins with each letter. Ask them to use the word in a sentence.

- they can recognize the letters *j, z,* and *w* and the sounds /j/, /z/, and /w/.
- they can connect the letters and sounds *j* /j/, *z* /z/, and *w* /w/.
- they can identify *j* /j/, *z* /z/, and *w* /w/ in words.

Distribute Student Page S143. Have students cut apart the word cards. Pairs place the cards face down and take turns selecting a card. They identify the first letter of the word, say the sound of the first letter, read the word, and then use it in a sentence.

Zak	jot	jet
wed	will	zap
wig	jar	Jon
zest	were	went

☑ **MONITOR PROGRESS** Display the following sentence from Student Page S143. Have students identify all instances of *j* /j/, *z* /z/, and *w* /w/. Then check that students can print each letter.

| We just went to the zoo to see the baby zebra. |

IF… students struggle with the words,
THEN… help them hunt for additional words with these letters in classroom books. Review steps from the routine as needed.

Lesson 23 | Connect Sounds and Letters: Consonants 3

REMIND STUDENTS THAT …

- they can recognize the letters *y, q,* and *x* and the sounds /y/, /kw/, and /ks/.

- they can connect the letters and sounds *y* /y/, *q* /kw/, and *x* /ks/.

- they can identify *y* /y/, *q* /kw/, and *x* /ks/ in words.

PRACTICE 3 Follow this routine to teach one-to-one letter-sound correspondences for *y* /y/, *q* /kw/, and *x* /ks/.

Routine

1. Teach the letters and sounds. — Write capital and lowercase *Yy.* This is the letter *y.* It stands for the sound /y/. Repeat for *Qq* and *Xx.*

2. Model letter-sound correspondence. — Write the word *yet* and circle the *y.* The word *yet* begins with the letter *y* and the sound /y/. Say the word *yet* after me. Repeat the process with the words *quiz* and *fix.*

3. Practice letter-sound correspondence. — Write the words *yum, yap,* and *yes.* Have students circle the letter *y* in each word. What sound is connected with the letter *y* in each word? Write the words *quit, queen, ax,* and *ox.* Have students circle the letters *q* and *x* in each word. What sounds are connected with the letters *q* and *x?*

4. Extend practice. — Have students write *y, q,* and *x* and say a word that begins with each letter. Have them write a word for each letter using the lists in steps 2 and 3.

Distribute Student Page S144. Have students cut apart the word cards. Pairs place the cards face down and take turns selecting a card, reading the word, and using it in a sentence. Point out that *x* /ks/ is at the end of a word in this lesson.

quit	wax	fox
yes	Max	you
yank	fix	yellow
quick	mix	quiet

☑ **INDEPENDENT PRACTICE** Display the following sentence from Student Page S144. Have students identify all instances of *y* /y/, *q* /kw/, and *x* /ks/. Then check that students can print each letter.

> The fox gave the queen a yard of yellow yarn.

IF… students struggle with the words,
THEN… guide them as they look for additional words with these letters in classroom books. Review steps from the routine as needed.

Connect Sounds and Letters: Consonants 3

Can You Do It?

Can you hug a hippo?
Can you kiss a zebra?
Can you jog with an ox to the vet?
Yes, I can!
I am the queen!

| Lesson 23 | Connect Sounds and Letters: Consonants 3 |

hop	kid	vet
vent	kit	her
ham	hum	hid
hat	kind	van

Kit has a helmet, and Kim has a vest.

Connect Sounds and Letters: Consonants 3

Zak	jot	jet
wed	will	zap
wig	jar	Jon
zest	were	went

We just went to the zoo to see the baby zebra.

quit	wax	fox
yes	Max	you
yank	fix	yellow
quick	mix	quiet

The fox gave the queen a yard of yellow yarn.

Lesson 24 | Spelling: Soft Consonant Sounds

INTRODUCE Explain that some sounds can be spelled in more than one way. This lesson focuses on new spellings for the sounds /s/, /j/, and /z/.

MODEL Display or share copies of the following passage, "At the Circus," from Student Page S145, and read it aloud. The words in this passage have some sounds we know but with different spellings for the sounds.

At the Circus

He has a big, red nose.
He wears a hat with a rose.
You see him in the center of a big ring.
When he walks on tall poles, he is a giant.
Can you say who he is?

TEACH Connect to previously learned sound-spellings. Write *see* and *say*. What do you know about reading these words? Elicit from students that both begin with /s/ spelled *s*. Repeat /s/ with me: /s/. Today you will learn how to spell and read words with /s/ spelled *c*. Write the word *center*. This is the word *center*. What is the first letter? How do you say the sound? Help students recognize that the first letter is *c* but the sound is /s/. You will also learn how to read words with /j/ spelled *g* as in *giant* and /z/ spelled *s* as in *nose, rose, poles,* and *is*.

RF.K.3.a Demonstrate basic knowledge of one-to-one letter-sound correspondences by producing the primary sound or many of the most frequent sounds for each consonant.

OBJECTIVES:
• Recognize multiple sounds of consonants.
• Connect letters and sounds *c* /s/, *g* /j/, *s* /z/.
• Identify *c* /s/, *g* /j/, *s* /z/ in words.

Lesson 24 | Spelling: Soft Consonant Sounds

PRACTICE 1 Use this routine to help students connect /s/ with c.

Routine

1. Connect sound to spelling.	Remind students that some sounds can be spelled in more than one way. The letter c can stand for /s/.
2. Model.	Write and say *cell.* What is the first sound in this word? Students should respond with /s/. In this word, the sound /s/ is spelled with c. The c is followed by e. Point to c and have students say /s/. Now let's read this word together: /s//e//l/.
3. Guide practice.	Have students identify the first letter in *cent, celery,* and *circus.* What sound do you hear for the letter c in *cent* and *celery?* What sound do you hear for the first letter c in *circus?* Point to the second c in *circus.* What sound do you hear for this letter c in *circus?*
4. Extend practice.	Write and say *cider, candle, certain, circle, cubby,* and *cereal.* Have students say each word and identify the sound of each c as /s/ or /k/.

Have students cut apart the word cards from Student Page S146 and sort them into two piles: one with words with the sound /s/ spelled c, the other with words with the sound /k/ spelled c.

cent	cup	cell	circle
cat	cabin	cement	city

☑ **MONITOR PROGRESS** Display the following word pairs from Student Page S146 and read them aloud. Have students read the words and then ask individuals to identify the word in the pair with the sound /s/ spelled c.

cat, city	cupcake, cement	center, color

IF… students struggle to identify the word with the sound /s/ spelled c, THEN… provide additional word pairs for practice and review the routine.

Lesson 24 | Spelling: Soft Consonant Sounds

PRACTICE 2 Use this routine to help students connect /j/ with *g*.

Routine

1. Connect sound to spelling.	Remind students that some sounds can be spelled in more than one way. The letter *g* can stand for /j/.
2. Model.	Write and say *jet* and *June*. What are the first sound and letter in these words? (/j/ and *j*). Write and say *gem*. In this word, the sound /j/ is spelled with *g*. Point to *g* and have students say /j/. Blend the word with students.
3. Guide practice.	Write and say *germ* and *giant*. Have students say the words and identify the first letter in each one. What sound do you hear for the letter *g* in each word?
4. Extend practice.	Write and say *giraffe, garden, gas, ginger, gerbil,* and *gorilla*. Have students say each word and identify the sound of each *g* as /g/ or /j/.

Have students cut apart the word cards from Student Page S147 and sort them into two piles: one with words with the sound /j/ spelled *g*, the other with words with the sound /g/ spelled *g*.

gem	grass	gerbil	giraffe
gum	glad	gentle	germ

☑ **MONITOR PROGRESS** Display the following word pairs from Student Page S147 and read them aloud. Have students read the words and then ask individuals to identify the word in the pair with the sound /j/ spelled *g*.

gentle, gallon	gap, gym	Gene, girl

IF… students struggle to identify the word with the sound /j/ spelled *g*, THEN… provide additional word pairs for practice and review the routine.

REMIND STUDENTS THAT …

- they can recognize multiple sounds of consonants.
- they can connect letters and sounds *g* /g/ and *g* /j/.
- they can identify *g* /g/ and *g* /j/ in words.

| Lesson 24 | Spelling: Soft Consonant Sounds |

REMIND STUDENTS THAT ...

- they can recognize multiple sounds of consonants.
- they can connect letters and sounds s /s/ and s /z/.
- they can identify s /s/ and s /z/ in words.

PRACTICE 3 Use this routine to help students connect /z/ with s.

Routine

I. Connect sound to spelling.
Remind students that some sounds can be spelled in more than one way. The letter s can stand for /z/.

2. Model.
Write and say *his*. Let's read this word together: /h//i//z/. Where do you hear the sound /z/ in *his*? Students should say they hear /z/ at the end. The sound /z/ is sometimes spelled with s.
When s has the sound /z/, it is often at the end of the word.

3. Guide practice.
Write and say *has, is,* and *dogs*. Have students repeat the words and identify the sound at the end of each one.

4. Extend practice.
Write and say *these, dress,* and *bells*. Have students identify the sound of each s as /s/ or /z/.

Have students cut apart the word cards from Student Page S148 and sort them into two piles: words with the sound /s/ spelled s and words with the sound /z/ spelled s.

is	less	frogs
grows	this	us

☑ **INDEPENDENT PRACTICE** Display the following word pairs from Student Page S148 and read them aloud. Have students read the words and then ask individuals to identify the word in the pair with the sound /z/ spelled s.

plays, books	bus, as	miss, rose

IF... students cannot identify words with /s/ and /z/ spelled s,
THEN... provide additional examples for practice and review the routine.

At the Circus

He has a big, red nose.
He wears a hat with a rose.
You see him in the center of a big ring.
When he walks on tall poles, he is a giant.
Can you say who he is?

cent	cup	cell	circle
cat	cabin	cement	

cat, city   cupcake, cement   center, color

Lesson 24   Spelling: Soft Consonant Sounds

gem	grass	gerbil	giraffe
gum	glad	gentle	germ

gentle, gallon   gap, gym   Gene, girl

is	less	frogs
grows	this	us

plays, books   bus, as   miss, rose

ASSESSMENT
LESSONS 21–24

Phonics and Word Recognition

ASSESS MASTERY Use this Checkpoint to assess students' mastery of one-to-one letter-sound correspondences for consonants.

ADMINISTER THE TEST Administer the Checkpoint orally to each student. Give each student a copy of the next page. Have students listen as you read each sentence aloud, and then have them circle each letter you name. Then have students say the sound each letter represents. For example, if students circle _r_ and _l_ in _real_, they should then say /r/ and /l/.

Print the next page for students.

1. Connect Sounds and Letters: Consonants 1 (Lesson 21)
Circle each of these letters in the sentence: _l, r, s, m, t, p._

2. Connect Sounds and Letters: Consonants 2 (Lesson 22)
Circle each of these letters in the sentence: _n, b, c, f, d, g._

3. Connect Sounds and Letters: Consonants 3 (Lesson 23)
Circle each of these letters in the sentence: _h, v, k, j, z, w, y, q, x._

4. Spelling: Soft Consonant Sounds (Lesson 24)
Circle each of these letters in the sentence: _c_ that sounds like /s/, _g_ that sounds like /j/, _s_ that sounds like /z/.

SCORING

SKILL/LESSON	SCORE
1. Connect Sounds and Letters: Consonants 1 (Lesson 21) <u>T</u>i<u>m</u> <u>t</u>asted a <u>r</u>ipe <u>l</u>emon <u>s</u>lice.	_____ / 11
2. Connect Sounds and Letters: Consonants 2 (Lesson 22) A <u>b</u>ug <u>c</u>rawle<u>d</u> out <u>f</u>rom the <u>bin</u>.	_____ / 7
3. Connect Sounds and Letters: Consonants 3 (Lesson 23) Ma<u>x</u> li<u>k</u>es the <u>z</u>oo <u>w</u>ith <u>y</u>ello<u>w</u> <u>w</u>asps <u>j</u>ust <u>h</u>overing abo<u>v</u>e a <u>q</u>uilt.	_____ / 12
4. Spelling: Soft Consonant Sounds (Lesson 24) The <u>g</u>iraffe put i<u>c</u>e cube<u>s</u> in tho<u>s</u>e glasse<u>s</u>.	_____ / 5

An overall score of 80% correct is typically considered mastery. Use your judgment and your individual students' needs as well to determine skill mastery.

IF... students score below the benchmark,
THEN... review those discrete letters and sounds, going back to the lessons to reteach and scaffold as needed.

RF.K.3.a Demonstrate basic knowledge of one-to-one letter-sound correspondences by producing the primary sound or many of the most frequent sounds for each consonant.

Phonics and Word Recognition

1. Tim tasted a ripe lemon slice.

2. A bug crawled out from the bin.

3. Max likes the zoo with yellow wasps just hovering above a quilt.

4. The giraffe put ice cubes in those glasses.

| **Lesson 25** | Short *a* |

INTRODUCE Remind students that words are made up of consonant and vowel sounds. You learned that /ă/ is spelled with the letter *a*, and you learned how to blend letters to read words with this sound. Today we will learn another way to read words with the short *a* sound.

MODEL Display or share copies of the following passage, "Pat and Sam," from Student Page S151, and read it aloud.

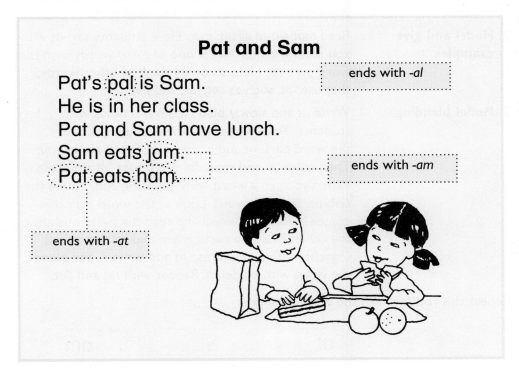

Pat and Sam

Pat's pal is Sam.
He is in her class.
Pat and Sam have lunch.
Sam eats jam.
Pat eats ham.

ends with -*al*

ends with -*am*

ends with -*at*

TEACH Point out the words with the short *a* sound. Explain that students can read more words when they learn how to recognize letter combinations that include a short *a*. *Jam* and *ham* both have a short *a* sound and end with -*am*. Now that I know -*am* has a short *a* sound, I can use this letter combination to make new words. Reinforce this idea by pointing out other words in the model that have the short *a* sound, such as *pal*, *Pat*, and *Sam*.

RF.K.3.b Associate the long and short sounds with the common spellings (graphemes) for the five major vowels.

OBJECTIVES:
• Read words with the short *a* sound.
• Form words using the short *a* sound.

Lesson 25 | Short *a*

REMIND STUDENTS THAT …

- they can recognize the short *a* sound.
- they can read words with the short *a* sound.
- they can make new words using -*at* and -*am*.

PRACTICE 1 Remind students that one way to read words is to break them into word parts and read the parts one after the other. Use the following routine to guide students as they identify words with the short *a* sound.

Routine

1. Connect.	Write and say *mat*. This is a word you know. Let's read it together. Knowing how to read -*at* can help you read many words with this word part.
2. Model and give examples.	Read *mat* aloud again: *mat*. Have students say -*at* with you several times. *Mat* is one of many words with the word part -*at*. Help students think of other words that use -*at*, such as *cat, rat,* and *flat*.
3. Model blending.	Write *at* and slowly blend it several times with students. Then write *m* at the beginning. Cover the word part -*at* and point to *m*. Say *m* aloud: /m/. Then cover *m* and read the word part -*at* aloud: *at*. When you see a word with -*at* at the end, notice the two parts in the word. Look at the word part that comes before the vowel and read the parts one after the other. The two parts are *m* and -*at*. Let's read together: *m, at, mat*. Erase *m* and write *c*, and blend the word with students. Repeat with *rat* and *flat*.

Repeat this routine with the word part -*am*.

	at		am

Display the Elkonin boxes from Student Page S152 and have students use them to create words. If needed, offer letters such as *b, h,* and *p*.

☑ **MONITOR PROGRESS** Display the following sentence from Student Page S152. Have students identify the words with the short *a* sound.

> ## Pam has a red hat.

IF… students misidentify words with the short *a* sound,
THEN… offer corrective feedback by pointing out the two words with the short *a* sound.

Lesson 25 | Short *a*

PRACTICE 2 Use the following routine to guide students as they identify words with the short *a* sound. Point out that students will focus on words that have the -*ad* and -*ag* word part.

REMIND STUDENTS THAT …

• they can recognize the short *a* sound.

• they can read words with the short *a* sound.

• they can make new words using -*ad* and -*ag*.

Routine

1. Connect.	Write and say *sad*. This is a word you know. Let's read it together. Knowing how to read -*ad* can help you read many words with this word part.
2. Model and give examples.	Read *sad* aloud again: *sad*. Have students say -*ad* with you several times. *Sad* is one of many words with the word part -*ad*. Help students think of other words that use -*ad*, such as *bad, mad,* and *glad*.
3. Model blending.	Write *ad* and slowly blend it several times with students. Then write *s* at the beginning. Cover the word part -*ad* and point to *s*. Say *s* aloud: /s/. Then cover *s* and read the word part -*ad* aloud: *ad*. When you see a word with -*ad* at the end, notice the two parts in the word. Look at the word part that comes before the vowel and read the parts one after the other. The two parts are *s* and -*ad*. Let's read together: *s, ad, sad*. Erase *s* and write *b*, and blend the word with students. Repeat with *mad* and *glad*.

Repeat this routine with the word part -*ag*.

ad	ag

Display the Elkonin boxes from Student Page S153 and have students use them to create words. If needed, offer letters such as *h, p,* and *t*. Then have students use one or two of the words in their own oral sentences.

☑ **MONITOR PROGRESS** Display the following sentence from Student Page S153. Have students identify the words with the short *a* sound.

> The bat had a tag.

IF… students misidentify words with the short *a* sound,
THEN… offer corrective feedback by pointing out the three words with the short *a* sound.

Lesson 25 | Short *a*

- they can recognize the short *a* sound.
- they can read words with the short *a* sound.
- they can make new words using -*ab*, -*an*, and -*ap*.

PRACTICE 3 Use the following routine to guide students as they identify words with the short *a* sound. Point out that students will focus on words that have the -*ab,* -*an,* or -*ap* word part.

Routine

1. Connect.	Write and say *cab.* This is a word you know. Let's read it together. Knowing how to read -*ab* can help you read many words with this word part.
2. Model and give examples.	Read *cab* aloud again: *cab.* Have students say -*ab* with you several times. *Cab* is one of many words with the word part -*ab.* Help students think of other words that use -*ab,* such as *lab, tab,* and *grab.*
3. Model blending.	Write *ab* and slowly blend it several times with students. Then write *c* at the beginning. Cover the word part -*ab* and point to *c.* Say *c* aloud: /k/. Then cover *c* and read the word part -*ab* aloud: *ab.* When you see a word with -*ab* at the end, notice the two parts in the word. Look at the word part that comes before the vowel and read the parts one after the other. The two parts are *c* and -*ab.* Let's read together: *c, ab, cab.* Erase *c* and write *l,* and blend the word with students. Repeat with *tab* and *grab.*

Repeat this routine with the word parts -*an* and -*ap.*

	ab
	an
	ap

Display the Elkonin boxes from Student Page S154 and have students use them to create words. If needed, offer letters like *c, m, n,* and *t.* Then have students use at least two of the words in their own oral sentences.

☑ **INDEPENDENT PRACTICE** Display the following sentence from Student Page S154. Have students identify the words with the short *a* sound.

> The cat sat on the man's cap.

IF… students misidentify words with the short *a* sound,
THEN… offer corrective feedback by pointing out the four words with the short *a* sound.

Pat and Sam

ends with -*al*

Pat's pal is Sam.

He is in her class.

Pat and Sam have lunch.

Sam eats jam.

Pat eats ham.

ends with -*am*

ends with -*at*

at		am

Pam has a red hat.

		ag
	ad	

The bat had a tag.

Lesson 25   Short *a*

	ab
	an
	ap

The cat sat on the man's cap.

| **Lesson 26** | Short *i* |

INTRODUCE Emphasize that words are made up of consonant and vowel sounds. You learned that /ĭ/ is spelled with the letter *i*, and you learned how to blend letters to read words with this sound. Today we will learn another way to read words with the short *i* sound.

MODEL Display or share copies of the following passage, "Sid Did," from Student Page S155, and read it aloud.

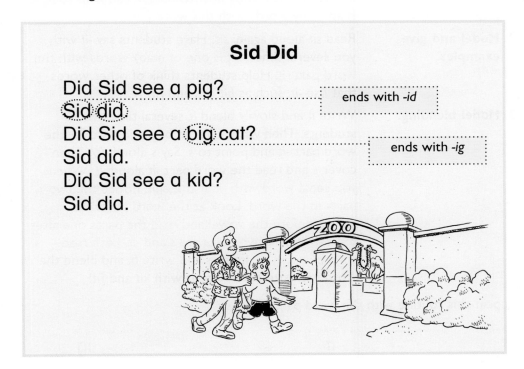

Sid Did

Did Sid see a pig?
Sid did.   ends with -*id*
Did Sid see a big cat?
Sid did.   ends with -*ig*
Did Sid see a kid?
Sid did.

TEACH Point out the words with the short *i* sound. Explain that students can read more words when they learn how to recognize letter combinations that include a short *i*. *Sid* and *did* both have a short *i* sound and end with -*id*. Now that I know that -*id* has a short *i* sound, I can use this letter combination to make new words. Reinforce this idea by pointing out other words in the model that have the short *i* sound, such as *big* and *kid*.

RF.K.3.b Associate the long and short sounds with the common spellings (graphemes) for the five major vowels.

OBJECTIVES:
• Read words with the short *i* sound.
• Form words using the short *i* sound.

Lesson 26 | Short *i*

REMIND STUDENTS THAT …

- they can recognize the short *i* sound.
- they can read words with the short *i* sound.
- they can make new words using *-ig* and *-it*.

PRACTICE 1 Remind students that one way to read words is to break them into word parts and read the parts one after the other. Use the following routine to guide students as they identify words with the short *i* sound.

Routine

1. Connect.	Write and say *sit*. This is a word you know. Let's read it together. Knowing how to read *-it* can help you read many words with this word part.
2. Model and give examples.	Read *sit* aloud again: *sit*. Have students say *-it* with you several times. *Sit* is one of many words with the word part *-it*. Help students think of other words that use *-it*, such as *bit*, *kit*, and *fit*.
3. Model blending.	Write *it* and slowly blend it several times with students. Then write *s* at the beginning. Cover the word part *-it* and point to *s*. Say *s* aloud: /s/. Then cover *s* and read the word part *-it* aloud: *it*. When you see a word with *-it* at the end, notice the two parts in the word. Look at the word part that comes before the vowel and read the parts one after the other. The two parts are *s* and *-it*. Let's read together: *s, it, sit*. Erase *s* and write *b*, and blend the word with students. Repeat with *kit* and *fit*.

Repeat this routine with the word part *-ig*.

	it		ig

Display the Elkonin boxes from Student Page S156 and have students use them to create words. If needed, offer letters such as *b* and *p*.

☑ **MONITOR PROGRESS** Have students read the following words from Student Page S156. Then have them make two new words: one with *-it* and one with *-ig*.

bit	lit	hit	___
rig	gig	dig	___

IF… students misread a word,
THEN… guide them to identify the letters and sounds in the word. Then have them blend the word with you and independently.

Lesson 26 | Short i

PRACTICE 2 Use the following routine to guide students as they identify words with the short *i* sound. Point out that students will focus on words that have the *-in* or *-ip* word part.

Routine

1. Connect.

Write and say *pin*. This is a word you know. Let's read it together. Knowing how to read *-in* can help you read many words with this word part.

2. Model and give examples.

Read *pin* aloud again: *pin*. Have students say *-in* with you several times. *Pin* is one of many words with the word part *-in*. Help students think of other words that use *-in*, such as *tin, fin,* and *win*.

3. Model blending.

Write *in* and slowly blend it several times with students. Then write *p* at the beginning. Cover the word part *-in* and point to *p*. Say *p* aloud: /p/. Then cover *p* and read the word part *-in* aloud: *in*. When you see *a* word with *-in* at the end, notice the two parts in the word. Look at the word part that comes before the vowel and read the parts one after the other. The two parts are *p* and *-in*. Let's read it together: *p,* in, pin. Erase *p* and write *t*, and blend the word with students. Repeat with *fin* and *win*.

Repeat this routine with the word part *-ip*.

	in		ip

Display the Elkonin boxes from Student Page S157 and have students use them to create words. If needed, offer letters such as *z, l,* and *t*. Then have students use one or two of the words in their own oral sentences.

☑ **MONITOR PROGRESS** Have students read the following words from Student Page S157. Then have them make two new words: one with *-in* and one with *-ip*.

bin	tin	win	___
lip	rip	dip	___

IF... students misread a word,
THEN...guide them as they sound out the word. Then have them blend the word with you and independently.

REMIND STUDENTS THAT ...
• they can recognize the short *i* sound.
• they can read words with the short *i* sound.
• they can make new words using *-in* and *-ip*.

Lesson 26 Short *i*

REMIND STUDENTS THAT ...

- they can recognize the short *i* sound.
- they can read words with the short *i* sound.
- they can make new words using -*ib*, -*im*, and -*is*.

PRACTICE 3 Use the following routine to guide students as they identify words with the short *i* sound. Point out that students will focus on words that have the -*ib*, -*im*, or -*is* word part.

Routine

1. Connect.

Write and say *him*. This is a word you know. Let's read it together. Knowing how to read -*im* can help you read many words with this word part.

2. Model and give examples.

Read *him* aloud again: *him*. Have students say -*im* with you several times. *Him* is one of many words with the word part -*im*. Help students think of other words that use -*im*, such as *dim, Jim,* and *rim*.

3. Model blending.

Write *im* and slowly blend it several times with students. Then write *h* at the beginning. Cover the word part -*im* and point to *h*. Say *h* aloud: /*h*/. Then cover *h* and read the word part -*im* aloud: *im*. When you see a word with -*im* at the end, notice the two parts in the word. Look at the word part that comes before the vowel and read the parts one after the other. The two parts are *h* and -*im*. Let's read together: *h, im, him*. Erase *h* and write *d*, and blend the word with students. Repeat with *Jim* and *rim*.

Repeat this routine with the word parts -*ib* and -*is*.

	ib
	im
	is

Display the Elkonin boxes from Student Page S158 and have students use them to create words. If needed, offer letters such as *b, h,* and *t*. Then have students use at least two of the words in their own oral sentences.

☑ **INDEPENDENT PRACTICE** Display the following sentences from Student Page S158. Have students identify the words with the short *i* sound.

> Jim and Kim have a bin.
> It is big.

IF... students misidentify words with the short *i* sound,
THEN... offer corrective feedback by identifying the six words with the short *i* sound.

Sid Did

Did Sid see a pig?

Sid did.   ⟵ ends with *-id*

Did Sid see a big cat?   ⟵ ends with *-ig*

Sid did.

Did Sid see a kid?

Sid did.

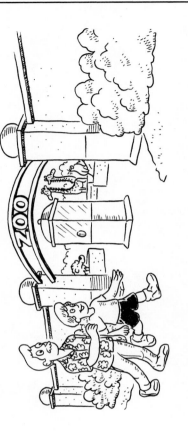

it		ig

bit	lit	hit	___
rig	gig	dig	___

Lesson 26 | **Short *i***

ip	in	

win	tin	bin
dip	rip	lip
___		
___		

		is
		im
ib		

Jim and Kim have a bin.

It is big.

ASSESSMENT	**Phonics and Word Recognition**

LESSONS 25–26

ASSESS MASTERY Use this Checkpoint to assess students' mastery of the short *a* sound and the short *i* sound.

ADMINISTER THE TEST Administer the Checkpoint orally to each student. For each item, model the process as described, and then have the student use the process to respond to your prompts. Record responses on the scoring chart on the next page.

RF.K.3.b Associate the long and short sounds with the common spellings (graphemes) for the five major vowels.

1. Short *a* (Lesson 25)
MODEL: I will display two words that have the short *a* sound. You will read them to me and tell me what short *a* word part is in both words. For example, I see the words *bad* and *mad*. When I read them, I can hear that the short *a* word part is *-ad*.

ASSESS:	jam, ham	cat, rat	bag, tag

2. Short *a* (Lesson 25)
MODEL: I will display two words that have the short *a* sound and you will make a word that has the same short *a* word part. For example, I read the words *pat* and *hat*. I can see that the short *a* word part is *-at*. I can use this word part to make the word *mat*.

ASSESS:	ban, pan, ____	tab, lab, ____	map, cap, ____

3. Short *i* (Lesson 26)
MODEL: I will display two words that have the short *i* sound. You will read them to me and tell me what short *i* word part is in both words. For example, I see the words *pig* and *big*. When I read them, I can hear that the short *i* word part is *-ig*.

ASSESS:	tin, pin	sit, kit	bib, rib

4. Short *i* (Lesson 26)
MODEL: I will display two words that have the short *i* sound and you will make a word that has the same short *i* word part. For example, I read the words *his* and *tis*. I can see that the short *i* word part is *-is*. I can use this word part to make the word *sis*.

ASSESS:	rip, nip, ____	Tim, rim, ____	did, hid, ____

ASSESSMENT
LESSONS 25–26

Phonics and Word Recognition

SCORING

SKILL/LESSON	SCORE
1. Short *a* (Lesson 25) jam, ham (-*am*) cat, rat (-*at*) bag, tag (-*ag*)	_____ / 3
2. Short *a* (Lesson 25) ban, pan, (Sample Answer: man) tab, lab, (Sample Answer: cab) map, cap, (Sample Answer: tap)	_____ / 3
3. Short *i* (Lesson 26) tin, pin (-*in*) sit, kit (-*it*) bib, rib (-*ib*)	_____ / 3
4. Short *i* (Lesson 26) rip, nip, (Sample Answer: lip) Tim, rim, (Sample Answer: him) did, hid, (Sample Answer: kid)	_____ / 3

An overall score of 80% correct is typically considered mastery. Use your judgment and your individual students' needs as well to determine skill mastery.

IF... students score below the benchmark,
THEN... review those discrete skills, going back to the lessons to reteach the scaffold as needed.

Lesson 27 | Short *o*

INTRODUCE Remind students that words are made up of consonant and vowel sounds. You learned that /ŏ/ is spelled with the letter *o*, and you learned how to blend letters to read words with this sound. Today we will learn another way to read words with the short *o* sound.

MODEL Display or share copies of the following passage, "Hot Pot," from Student Page S161, and read it aloud.

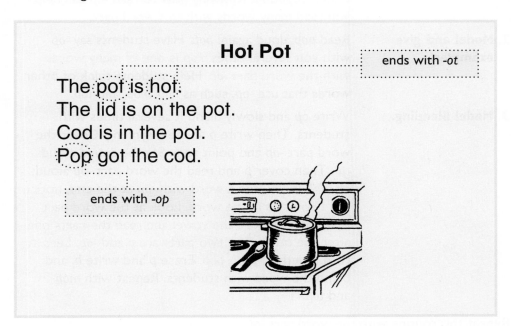

Hot Pot

ends with *-ot*

The pot is hot.
The lid is on the pot.
Cod is in the pot.
Pop got the cod.

ends with *-op*

TEACH Point out the words with the short *o* sound. Explain that students can read more words when they learn how to recognize letter combinations that include a short *o*. *Pot* and *hot* both have a short *o* sound and end with *-ot*. I can use the *-ot* letter combination to make new words that have the short *o* sound. Reinforce this idea by pointing out other words in the model that have the short *o* sound, such as *Pop*.

RF.K.3.b Associate the long and short sounds with the common spellings (graphemes) for the five major vowels.

OBJECTIVES:

• Read words with the short *o* sound.

• Form words using the short *o* sound.

Lesson 27　Short o

REMIND STUDENTS THAT ...

• they can recognize the short o sound.

• they can read words with the short o sound.

• they can make new words using -op and -ot.

PRACTICE I Remind students that they can read words by breaking them into word parts and reading the parts one after the other. Use the following routine to guide students as they identify words with the short o sound.

Routine

1. Connect.

Write and say *pop.* This is a word you know. Let's read it together. Knowing how to read *-op* can help you read many words with this word part.

2. Model and give examples.

Read *pop* aloud again: *pop.* Have students say *-op* with you several times. *Pop* is one of many words with the word part *-op.* Help students think of other words that use *-op,* such as *hop, mop,* and *top.*

3. Model blending.

Write *op* and slowly blend it several times with students. Then write *p* at the beginning. Cover the word part *-op* and point to *p.* Say the sound aloud: /p/. Then cover *p* and read the word part *-op* aloud: *op.* When you see a word with *-op* at the end, notice the two parts in the word. Look at the word part that comes before the vowel and read the parts one after the other. The two parts are *p* and *-op.* Let's read together: *p, op, pop.* Erase *p* and write *h,* and blend the word with students. Repeat with *mop* and *top.*

Repeat this routine with the word part *-ot.*

	op		ot

Display the Elkonin boxes from Student Page S162 and have students use them to create words. If needed, offer letters such as *c, g,* and *t.*

☑ **MONITOR PROGRESS** Display the following sentence from Student Page S162. Have students identify the words with the short o sound.

> Dot and Pop got a top.

IF... students misidentify words with the short o sound,
THEN... offer corrective feedback by pointing out the four words with the short o sound.

Lesson 27 | Short *o*

PRACTICE 2 Use the following routine to guide students as they identify words with the short *o* sound. Point out that students will focus on words that have the *-ob* and *-om* word part.

Routine

1. Connect.

Write and say *job*. This is a word you know. Let's read it together. Knowing how to read *-ob* can help you read many words with this word part.

2. Model and give examples.

Read *job* aloud again: *job*. Have students say *-ob* with you several times. *Job* is one of many words with the word part *-ob*. Help students think of other words that use *-ob*, such as *mob, sob,* and *rob*.

3. Model blending.

Write *ob* and slowly blend it several times with students. Then write *j* at the beginning. Cover the word part *-ob* and point to *j*. Say j aloud: /j/. Then cover *j* and read the word part *-ob* aloud: *ob*. When you see a word with *-ob* at the end, notice the two parts in the word. Look at the word part that comes before the vowel and read the parts one after the other. The two parts are *j* and *-ob*. Let's read together: *j, ob, job*. Erase *j* and write *m*, and blend the word with students. Repeat with *sob* and *rob*.

Repeat this routine with the word part *-om*.

	ob		om

Display the Elkonin boxes from Student Page S163 and have students use them to create words. If needed, offer letters such as *c* and *m*. Then have students use one or two of the words in their own oral sentences.

REMIND STUDENTS THAT ...

- they can recognize the short *o* sound.
- they can read words with the short *o* sound.
- they can make new words using *-ob* and *-om*.

☑ **MONITOR PROGRESS** Display the following sentence from Student Page S163. Have students identify the words with the short *o* sound.

> Mom and Tom got jobs.

IF... students misidentify words with the short *o* sound,
THEN... offer corrective feedback by pointing out the four words with the short *o* sound.

Lesson 27 | Short o

REMIND STUDENTS THAT ...

- they can recognize the short o sound.
- they can read words with the short o sound.
- they can make new words using -od, -og, and -on.

PRACTICE 3 Use the following routine to guide students as they identify words with the short o sound. Point out that students will focus on words that have the -od, -og, or -on word part.

Routine

1. Connect.

Write and say *fog*. This is a word you know. Let's read it together. Knowing how to read -og can help you read many words with this word part.

2. Model and give examples.

Read *fog* aloud again: *fog*. Have students say -og with you several times. Help students think of other words that use -og, such as *bog, dog,* and *log*.

3. Model blending.

Write *og* and slowly blend it several times with students. Then write *f* at the beginning. Cover the word part -og and point to *f*. Say *f* aloud: /f/. Then cover *f* and read the word part -og aloud: *og*. When you see a word with -og at the end, notice the two parts in the word. The two parts are *f* and -og. Let's read together: *f, og, fog*. Erase *f* and write *b*, and blend the word with students. Repeat with *dog* and *log*.

Repeat this routine with the word parts -od and -on.

	od
	og
	on

Display the Elkonin boxes from Student Page S164 and have students use them to create words. If needed, offer letters such as *c, h,* and *j*. Then have students use at least two of the words in their own oral sentences.

☑ **INDEPENDENT PRACTICE** Display the following sentences from Student Page S164. Have students identify the words with the short o sound.

> Fog is on the bog. The bog has a log.

IF... students misidentify words with the short o sound,
THEN... offer corrective feedback by pointing out the five words with the short o sound.

Hot Pot

ends with -ot

The pot is hot.
The lid is on the pot.
Cod is in the pot.
Pop got the cod.

ends with -op

	op		ot

Dot and Pop got a top.

	ob		om

Mom and Tom got jobs.

od	og	on

Fog is on the bog.

The bog has a log.

Lesson 28 | Short e

INTRODUCE Emphasize that words are made up of consonant and vowel sounds. You learned that /ĕ/ is spelled with the letter e, and you learned how to blend letters to read words with this sound. Today we will learn another way to read words with the short e sound.

MODEL Display or share copies of the following passage, "Ben's Pet," from Student Page S165, and read it aloud.

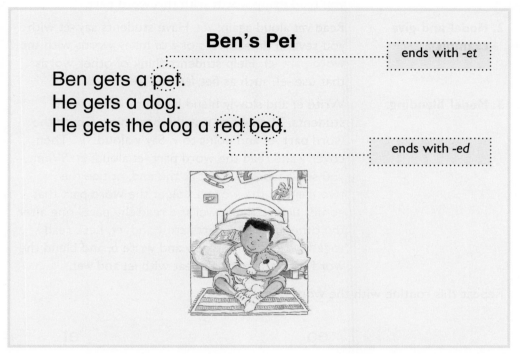

Ben's Pet

Ben gets a pet.   ends with -et
He gets a dog.
He gets the dog a red bed.   ends with -ed

TEACH Point out the words with the short e sound. Explain that students can read more words when they learn how to recognize letter combinations that include a short e. *Red* and *bed* both have a short e sound and end with *-ed*. Now that I know *-ed* has a short e sound, I can use this letter combination to make new words. Reinforce this idea by pointing out other words in the model that have the short e sound, such as *Ben* and *pet*.

RF.K.3.b Associate the long and short sounds with the common spellings (graphemes) for the five major vowels.

OBJECTIVES:

- Read words with the short e sound.
- Form words using the short e sound.

Lesson 28 | Short e

- they can recognize the short e sound.
- they can read words with the short e sound.
- they can make new words using -eg and -et.

PRACTICE I Remind students that one way to read words is to break them into word parts and read the parts one after the other. Use the following routine to guide students as they identify words with the short e sound.

Routine

I. Connect.

Write and say *vet.* This is a word you know. Let's read it together. Knowing how to read -et can help you read many words with this word part.

2. Model and give examples.

Read *vet* aloud again: *vet.* Have students say -et with you several times. *Vet* is one of many words with the word part -et. Help students think of other words that use -et, such as *bet, let,* and *wet.*

3. Model blending.

Write *et* and slowly blend it several times with students. Then write *v* at the beginning. Cover the word part -et and point to *v.* Say *v* aloud: /v/. Then cover *v* and read the word part -et aloud: *et.* When you see a word with -et at the end, notice the two parts in the word. Look at the word part that comes before the vowel and read the parts one after the other. The two parts are *v* and -et. Let's read together: *v, et, vet.* Erase *v* and write *b,* and blend the word with students. Repeat with *let* and *wet.*

Repeat this routine with the word part -eg.

	eg		et

Display the Elkonin boxes from Student Page S166 and have students use them to create words. If needed, offer letters such as *b* and *p.*

✔ **MONITOR PROGRESS** Have students read the following words from Student Page S166. Then have them make two new words: one with -eg and one with -et.

peg	beg	___
let	net	___

IF… students misread a word,
THEN… guide them to identify the letters and sounds in the word. Then have them blend the word with you and independently.

Lesson 28 | Short e

PRACTICE 2 Use the following routine to guide students as they identify words with the short e sound. Point out that students will focus on words that have the -*ed* or -*em* word part.

Routine

1. Connect.

Write and say *fed*. This is a word you know. Let's read it together. Knowing how to read -*ed* can help you read many words with this word part.

2. Model and give examples.

Read *fed* aloud again: *fed*. Have students say -*ed* with you several times. *Fed* is one of many words with the word part -*ed*. Help students think of other words that use -*ed*, such as *bed, red,* and *wed*.

3. Model blending.

Write *ed* and slowly blend it several times with students. Then write *f* at the beginning. Cover the word part -*ed* and point to *f*. Say *f* aloud: /f/. Then cover *f* and read the word part -*ed* aloud: *ed*. When you see a word with -*ed* at the end, notice the two parts in the word. Look at the word part that comes before the vowel and read the parts one after the other. The two parts are *f* and -*ed*. Let's read together: *f, ed, fed*. Erase *f* and write *b*, and blend the word with students. Repeat with *red* and *wed*.

Repeat this routine with the word part -*em*.

	ed		em

Display the Elkonin boxes from Student Page S167 and have students use them to create words. If needed, offer letters such as *g, h* and *l*. Then have students use one or two of the words in their own oral sentences.

☑ **MONITOR PROGRESS** Have students read the following words from Student Page S167. Then have them use one or two of the words in their own oral sentences.

fed	led	red
hem	gem	

IF... students misread a word,
THEN... guide them as they sound out the word. Then have them blend the word with you and independently.

Lesson 28 | Short e

REMIND STUDENTS THAT ...

- they can recognize the short e sound.
- they can read words with the short e sound.
- they can make new words using -eb, -el, and -en.

PRACTICE 3 Use the following routine to guide students as they identify words with the short e sound. Point out that students will focus on words that have the -eb, -el, or -en word part.

Routine

1. Connect.	Write and say *ten*. This is a word you know. Let's read it together. Knowing how to read -en can help you read many words with this word part.
2. Model and give examples.	Read *ten* aloud again: *ten*. Have students say -en with you several times. *Ten* is one of many words with the word part -en. Help students think of other words that use -en, such as *hen, Ken,* and *pen*.
3. Model blending.	Write *en* and slowly blend it several times with students. Then write *t* at the beginning. Cover the word part -en and point to *t*. Say *t* aloud: /t/. Then cover *t* and read the word part -en aloud: *en*. When you see a word with -en at the end, notice the two parts in the word. Look at the word part that comes before the vowel and read the parts one after the other. The two parts are *t* and -en. Let's read together: *t, en, ten*. Erase *t* and write *h*, and blend the word with students. Repeat with *Ken* and *pen*.

Repeat this routine with the word parts -eb and -el.

	eb
	el
	en

Display the Elkonin boxes from Student Page S168 and have students use them to create words. If needed, offer letters such as *d, g, m,* and *w*. Then have students use at least two of the words in their own oral sentences.

☑ **INDEPENDENT PRACTICE** Display the following sentence from Student Page S168. Have students identify the words with the short e sound.

> Mel the hen sits in a pen.

IF... students misidentify words with the short e sound,
THEN... offer corrective feedback by pointing out the three words with the short e sound.

Ben's Pet

ends with -et

Ben gets a pet.
He gets a dog.
He gets the dog a red bed.

ends with -ed

eg		et

peg	beg	___
let	net	___

	ed		em

fed	led	red
hem	gem	

eb	el	en

Mel the hen sits in a pen.

Lesson 29 | Short *u*

INTRODUCE Guide students to explain sounds in a word. You learned that words are made up of consonant and vowel sounds. You also learned that /ŭ/ is spelled with the letter *u*, and you learned how to blend letters to read words with this sound. Today we will learn another way to read words with the short *u* sound.

MODEL Display or share copies of the following passage, "Gus Hums," from Student Page S169, and read it aloud.

RF.K.3.b Associate the long and short sounds with the common spellings (graphemes) for the five major vowels.

OBJECTIVES:

- Read words with the short *u* sound.
- Form words using the short *u* sound.

Gus Hums

Gus hums for fun.
He hums on a rug.
He hums in a hut.
He hums in the sun.
Gus hums a lot!

ends with -*ut*

ends with -*un*

TEACH Point out the words with the short *u* sound. Explain that students can read more words when they learn how to recognize letter combinations that include a short *u*. *Fun* and *sun* both have a short *u* sound and end with -*un*. Now that I know -*un* has a short *u* sound, I can use this letter combination to make new words. Reinforce this idea by pointing out other words in the model that have the short *u* sound, such as *hut*.

Lesson 29   Short *u*

- they can recognize the short *u* sound.
- they can read words with the short *u* sound.
- they can make new words using -*ub* and -*ug*.

PRACTICE I Remind students that one way to read words is to break them into word parts and read the parts one after the other. Use the following routine to guide students as they identify words with the short *u* sound.

Routine

1. Connect.	Write and say *bug*. This is a word you know. Let's read it together. Knowing how to read -*ug* can help you read many words with this word part.
2. Model and give examples.	Read *bug* aloud again: *bug*. Have students say -*ug* with you several times. *Bug* is one of many words with the word part -*ug*. Help students think of other words that use -*ug*, such as *dug*, *rug*, and *tug*.
3. Model blending.	Write *ug* and slowly blend it several times with students. Then write *b* at the beginning. Cover the word part -*ug* and point to *b*. Say *b* aloud: /b/. Then cover *b* and read the word part -*ug* aloud: *ug*. When you see a word with -*ug* at the end, notice the two parts in the word. Look at the word part that comes before the vowel and read the parts one after the other. The two parts are *b* and -*ug*. Let's read together: *b, ug, bug*. Erase *b* and write *d*, and blend the word with students. Repeat with *rug* and *tug*.

Repeat this routine with the word part -*ub*.

	ub		ug

Display the Elkonin boxes from Student Page S170 and have students use them to create words. If needed, offer letters such as *c* and *t*.

☑ **MONITOR PROGRESS** Have students read the following words from Student Page S170. Then have them make two new words: one with -*ub* and one with -*ug*.

hub	sub	rub	___
mug	lug	jug	___

IF… students misread a word,
THEN… guide them to identify the letters and sounds in the word. Then have them blend the word with you and independently.

Lesson 29 | Short *u*

PRACTICE 2 Use the following routine to guide students as they identify words with the short *u* sound. Point out that students will focus on words that have the *-ud* or *-ut* word part.

REMIND STUDENTS THAT …
- they can recognize the short *u* sound.
- they can read words with the short *u* sound.
- they can make new words using *-ud* and *-ut*.

Routine

1. Connect.	Write and say *nut*. This is a word you know. Let's read it together. Knowing how to read *-ut* can help you read many words with this word part.
2. Model and give examples.	Read *nut* aloud again: *nut*. Have students say *-ut* with you several times. *Nut* is one of many words with the word part *-ut*. Help students think of other words that use *-ut*, such as *but* and *cut*.
3. Model blending.	Write *ut* and slowly blend it several times with students. Then write *n* at the beginning. Cover the word part *-ut* and point to *n*. Say *n* aloud: /n/. Then cover *n* and read the word part *-ut* aloud: *ut*. When you see a word with *-ut* at the end, notice the two parts in the word. Look at the word part that comes before the vowel and read the parts one after the other. The two parts are *n* and *-ut*. Let's read together: *n*, *ut*, *nut*. Erase *n* and write *b*, and blend the word with students. Repeat with *cut*.

Repeat this routine with the word part *-ud*.

	ud	ut

Display the Elkonin boxes from Student Pages S171 and have students use them to create words. Then have students use one or two of the words in their own oral sentences.

☑ **MONITOR PROGRESS** Have students read the following words from Student Page S171. Then have them make two new words: one with *-ud* and one with *-ut*.

mud	——	
cut	gut	——

IF… students misread a word,
THEN… guide them as they sound out the word. Then have them blend the word with you and independently.

Lesson 29 | Short *u*

REMIND STUDENTS THAT …

- they can recognize the short *u* sound.
- they can read words with the short *u* sound.
- they can make new words using -*um* and -*un*.

PRACTICE 3 Use the following routine to guide students as they identify words with the short *u* sound. Point out that students will focus on words that have the -*um* or -*un* word part.

Routine

1. Connect.
Write and say *run*. This is a word you know. Let's read it together. Knowing how to read -*un* can help you read many words with this word part.

2. Model and give examples.
Read *run* aloud again: *run.* Have students say -*un* with you several times. *Run* is one of many words with the word part -*un*. Help students think of other words that use -*un*, such as *pun* and *sun*.

3. Model blending.
Write *un* and slowly blend it several times with students. Then write *r* at the beginning. Cover the word part -*un* and point to *r*. Say *r* aloud: /r/. Then cover *r* and read the word part -*un* aloud: *un*. When you see a word with -*un* at the end, notice the two parts in the word. The two parts are *r* and -*un*. Let's read together: *r, un, run*. Erase *r* and write *p*, and blend the word with students. Repeat with *sun*.

Repeat this routine with the word part -*um*.

	um		un

Display the Elkonin boxes from Student Page S172 and have students use them to create words. Then have students use at least two of the words in their own oral sentences.

☑ **INDEPENDENT PRACTICE** Display the following sentence from Student Page S172. Have students identify the words with the short *u* sound.

> Dogs run in the mud for fun.

IF… students misidentify words with the short *u* sound,
THEN… offer corrective feedback by pointing out the three words with the short *u* sound.

Gus Hums

Gus hums for fun.
He hums on a rug.
He hums in a hut.
He hums in the sun.
Gus hums a lot!

ends with -*ut*

ends with -*un*

hub	sub	rub	___
mug	lug	jug	___

ub
ug

		ut
	ud	

mud		
cut	gut	___

	um		un

Dogs run in the mud for fun.

ASSESSMENT
LESSONS 27–29

Phonics and Word Recognition

ASSESS MASTERY Use this Checkpoint to assess students' mastery of the short *o* sound, the short *e* sound, and the short *u* sound.

ADMINISTER THE TEST Administer the Checkpoint orally to each student. For each item, model the process as described, and then have the student use the process to respond to your prompts. Record responses on the scoring chart on the next page.

RF.K.3.b Associate the long and short sounds with the common spellings (graphemes) for the five major vowels.

ACTIVITY A
MODEL: I will say two words and you will tell me what short vowel word part is in both words. For example, I might say *got* and *not*. I can hear that the short *o* word part is *-ot*.

1. Short o (Lesson 27)

ASSESS:	pop, top	job, Bob	pod, cod

2. Short e (Lesson 28)

ASSESS:	pet, wet	gel, Mel	hem, gem

3. Short u (Lesson 29)

ASSESS:	mud, bud	gum, hum	hub, sub

ACTIVITY B
MODEL: I will say two words and you will make a word that has the same short vowel word part. For example, I might say *bop* and *cop*. The short *o* word part is *-op*. I can use this word part to make the word *mop*.

4. Short o (Lesson 27)

ASSESS:	fog, hog, ___	rod, sod, ___	hot, lot, ___

5. Short e (Lesson 28)

ASSESS:	red, bed, ___	leg, peg, ___	Ken, pen, ___

6. Short u (Lesson 29)

ASSESS:	jug, mug, ___	cut, rut, ___	bun, sun, ___

ASSESSMENT
LESSONS 27–29

Phonics and Word Recognition

SCORING

SKILL/LESSON	SCORE
1. Short o (Lesson 27) pop, top (-op) job, Bob (-ob) pod, cod (-od)	_____ / 3
2. Short e (Lesson 28) pet, wet (-et) gel, Mel (-el) hem, gem (-em)	_____ / 3
3. Short u (Lesson 29) mud, bud (-ud) gum, hum (-um) hub, sub (-ub)	_____ / 3
4. Short o (Lesson 27) fog, hog, (Sample Answer: log) rod, sod, (Sample Answer: cod) hot, lot, (Sample Answer: pot)	_____ / 3
5. Short e (Lesson 28) red, bed, (Sample Answer: fed) leg, peg, (Sample Answer: beg) Ken, pen, (Sample Answer: hen)	_____ / 3
6. Short u (Lesson 29) jug, mug, (Sample Answer: bug) cut, rut, (Sample Answer: but) bun, sun, (Sample Answer: fun)	_____ / 3

An overall score of 80% correct is typically considered mastery. Use your judgment and your individual students' needs as well to determine skill mastery.

IF... students score below the benchmark,
THEN... review those discrete skills, going back to the lessons to reteach the scaffold as needed.

Lesson 30 | Long *a*, *i*, and *o*

INTRODUCE Connect today's lesson to short vowel sound-spellings by writing *cap* and *at* for students. You can read words like these. They both have short *a*, pronounced /a/, spelled *a*. Repeat the short *a* sound with me: /a/. Explain that students will learn how to spell and read words with long *a*, pronounced /ā/ as in *cape*. Use the same routine to review the short vowel sounds for *i* and *o*. Point out that students will also learn about long *i* and long *o* in this lesson.

MODEL Display or share copies of "Bike Ride" from Student Page S175, and read it aloud.

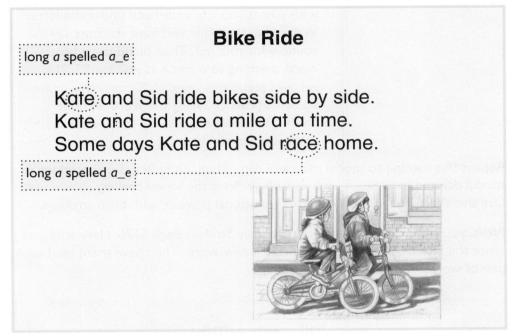

Bike Ride

long *a* spelled *a_e*

Kate and Sid ride bikes side by side.
Kate and Sid ride a mile at a time.
Some days Kate and Sid race home.

long *a* spelled *a_e*

TEACH Explain that students can read more words when they learn how long vowel sounds are spelled. Remind students that long vowels say their name. Long *a* sounds like the name of the letter: *a*.

Write *a_e* and say its sound: /ā/. Point out *Kate* and *race*. *Kate* and *race* both have a long *a* sound spelled *a_e*. The letter *e* is silent but gives the vowel *a* its long sound. The blank shows where a consonant will go. Write *K* and blend the sounds /k//ā/. Have students blend with you as you run your hand under the letters. Write *t* in the blank and have students say its sound with you. Then blend the whole word, pointing to *a* and *e* as you say /ā/. This is how I blend this word: /k//ā//t/, *Kate*. Have students practice saying the word without pausing between sounds. Repeat the process with *race*.

Follow this procedure to model words with the long *i* sound and long *o* sound, such as *side* and *home*.

RF.K.3.b Associate the long and short sounds with the common spellings (graphemes) for the five major vowels.

OBJECTIVES:

- Teach concept of long vowel sounds.
- Introduce long *a* spelled *a_e* and *ay*.
- Introduce long *i* spelled *i*, *i_e*, and *y*.
- Introduce long *o* spelled *o* and *o_e*.

Lesson 30 | Long *a*, *i*, and *o*

REMIND STUDENTS THAT …

- they can recognize words with long vowel sounds.
- they can recognize words with the long *a* sound spelled *a_e* and *ay*.
- they can read words with the long *a* sound.

WORD LIST

late	date
take	make
face	pace
made	name
lay	ray

PRACTICE I: Long *a* (Spelled *a_e* and *ay*) Use the routine below to help students connect /ā/ with *a_e* and to blend words with two long *a* spelling patterns.

Routine

1. Connect sound and spelling.

Write *a_e*. The long *a* sound, /ā/, can be spelled *a_e*. Point to *a_e*. Have students say /ā/ several times as you point to *a_e*.

2. Model blending.

Write *a_e* and say its sound: /ā/. Write *c* and blend the sounds: /k//ā/. Have students blend with you as you run your hand under the letters. Write *m* in the blank and have students say its sound with you: /m/. Then blend the whole word, pointing to *a* and *e* as you say /ā/. This is how I blend this word: /k//ā//m/, *came*. Have students practice saying the word without pausing between sounds. Say the sounds quickly to say the word. What's the word? Yes, it's *came*.

Repeat this routine to model *male* and *date*. Then, complete the procedure to model *day* and *may*. Begin each word by writing the vowel spelling *ay* as a unit. Use the Word List in the sidebar for additional practice with both spellings.

Next, you may wish to distribute or display Student Page S176. Have students write the letter *e* in the boxes to make a new word. Then have them read each pair of words.

tap	→	tap**e**
cap	→	cap**e**
at	→	at**e**
mad	→	mad**e**

☑ **MONITOR PROGRESS** Use the Word List from Student Page S176 to check that students can read more words with /ā/.

cake	game	safe	race
say	hay	pay	way

IF… students have difficulty reading a word,
THEN… model blending as you run your hand under the letters. Then have students blend the word with you.

Lesson 30 | Long *a*, *i*, and *o*

PRACTICE 2: Long *i* (Spelled *i*, *i_e*, and *y*) Write or display the word *hi*. Point out its spelling. I can blend this word: /h//ī/. Then continue to teach long *i* spelling patterns using the following routine.

Routine

1. Connect sound and spelling.

Write *i_e*. The long *i* sound, /ī/, can be spelled *i_e*. Point to *i_e*. Have students say /ī/ several times as you point to *i_e*.

2. Model blending.

Write *i* and say its sound: /ī/. Write *r* and blend the sounds: /r//ī/. Have students blend with you as you run your hand under the letters. Write *c* in the blank and have students say its sound with you: /s/. Then blend the whole word, pointing to *i* and *e* as you say /ī/. This is how I blend this word: /r//ī//s/, *rice*. Have students practice saying the word without pausing between sounds. Say the sounds quickly to say the word. What's the word? Yes, it's *rice*.

Repeat the routine to model how to read words with long *i* spelled *y*, such as *my*. Then, use the Word List in the sidebar for additional practice with the long *i* vowel spellings.

Next, distribute or display Student Page S177. Have students write the letter *e* in the boxes to make a new word. Then have them read each pair of words.

pin → pine
fin → fine
rid → ride
dim → dime

☑ **MONITOR PROGRESS** Use the Word List from Student Page S177 to check that students can read more words with /ī/.

bike	dive	side	life
my	by		

IF… students have difficulty reading a word,
THEN… model blending as you run your hand under the letters. Then have students blend the word with you.

REMIND STUDENTS THAT …

- they can recognize words with long vowel sounds.
- they can recognize words with the long *i* sound spelled *i*, *i_e*, and *y*.
- they can read words with the long *i* sound.

WORD LIST:

I	side
nice	like
bite	time
my	by

Lesson 30 | Long *a*, *i*, and *o*

REMIND STUDENTS THAT …

- they can recognize words with long vowel sounds.
- they can recognize words with the long *o* sound spelled *o* and *o_e*.
- they can read words with the long *o* sound.

WORD LIST

go	home
Rome	bone
hope	tote

PRACTICE 3: Long *o* (Spelled *o* and *o_e*) Use the routine to teach the long *o* sound and how to read words spelled *o* and *o_e*.

Routine

1. Connect sound and spelling

Write or display the word *go*. Point out its spelling. I can blend this word: /g//ō/.

2. Model blending

Next, write or display *o_e* and have students say its sound: /ō/. Write *h* and blend the sounds /h//ō/. Write *m* in the blank and say its sound. Then blend the whole word, pointing to *o* and *e* as you say /ō/. This is how I blend this word: /h//ō//m/, *home*. Let's say it together several times. Remind students that when they see the *o_e* spelling pattern, they should try the long *o* sound.

Use other words from the Word List for additional practice with long *o* vowel spellings. Follow the routine above to model for students how to read these words.

After the routine, distribute or display Student Page S178. Have students write the letter *e* in the boxes to make new words. Then have them read each pair of words.

not ➞ note
cod ➞ code
mop ➞ mope
rob ➞ robe

☑ **INDEPENDENT PRACTICE** Use the Word List from Student Page S178 to check that students can read more words with /ō/.

rope	vote	nose	joke
go	no		

IF… students have difficulty reading the words,
THEN… model breaking each word into sounds. Help students say each sound and write its spelling.

Bike Ride

Kate and Sid ride bikes side by side.
Kate and Sid ride a mile at a time.
Some days Kate and Sid race home.

Lesson 30   Long *a*, *i*, and *o*

tap	↓	tap
cap	↓	cap
at	↓	at
mad	↓	mad

cake	game	safe	race
say	hay	pay	way

Lesson 30   Long *a*, *i*, and *o*

pin	→	pin	
fin	→	fin	
rid	→	rid	
dim	→	dim	

| bike | dive | side | life |
| my | by | | |

Lesson 30   Long *a*, *i*, and *o*

not	→	not
cod	→	cod
mop	→	mop
rob	→	rob

| | | | |

rope	vote	nose	joke
go	no		

Lesson 31 | Long e and u

INTRODUCE Remind students that vowel sounds can be short or long. You have learned how to read words with long *a* spelled *a_e* and *ay*; long *i* spelled *i*, *i_e*, and *y*; and long *o* spelled *o* and *o_e*. Today we will learn to read words with the long *e* and *u* sounds.

MODEL Display or share copies of the following passage, "My Rat Zeke" from Student Page S179, and read it aloud.

My Rat Zeke   long e spelled e_e

Zeke is my rat.   long e spelled y
He is very nice.
I made him a maze in a tube.   long u spelled u_e
He likes his maze.

RF.K.3.b Associate the long and short sounds with the common spellings (graphemes) for the five major vowels.

OBJECTIVES:

- Teach the concept of long vowel sounds.
- Introduce long *e* spelled *e* and *y*.
- Introduce long *e* spelled *e_e*.
- Introduce long *u* spelled *u_e*.

TEACH Explain that students can read more words when they learn how long vowel sounds are spelled.

Write *e_e* and say its sound: /ē/. Point out *Zeke*. *Zeke* has a long *e* sound spelled *e_e*. The letter *e* at the end of the word gives the vowel *e* its long sound, and the blank shows where a consonant will go. Write *Z* and blend the sounds /z//ē/. Have students blend with you as you run your hand under the letters. Write *k* in the blank and have students say its sound with you: /k/. Then blend the whole word, pointing to *e* and *e* as you say /ē/. This is how I blend this word: /Z/ē/k/, *Zeke*. Have students practice saying the word without pausing between sounds. Repeat the process with *he* (/ē/ spelled *e*) and *very* (/ē/ spelled *y*). Then, follow this routine to model words with the long *u* sound, such as *tube*.

Phonics and Word Recognition T • 179

Lesson 31	Long e and *u*

- they can recognize words with long vowel sounds.
- they can recognize words with the long e sound spelled e and y.
- they can read words with the long e sound.

WORD LIST

be	we
ruby	baby

PRACTICE 1: Long e (Spelled e and y) Use the routine below to help students connect /ē/ with e and y and to blend words with these two long e spellings.

Write e. Have children say /ē/ several times with you. Write m. Then blend the whole word: /m//ē/, me. When a word or a syllable ends with one vowel, the vowel sound is usually long.

Explain to children that vowel sounds can be spelled in different ways. Today we're going to learn that the sound /ē/ can be spelled with a y at the end of a word.

Write y. Explain that the long e sound can be spelled y. Write copy. When the letter y comes at the end of a word with more than one syllable, it usually stands for /ē/. Have children say copy. Use this procedure to help children read the words from the Word List in the sidebar.

Then distribute or display Student Page S180 to reinforce the long e sound. Have students read each pair of words and identify the word that has the long e sound.

> met, me (me)   be, bet (be)
> lady, lad (lady)   wet, we (we)

☑ **MONITOR PROGRESS** Use the Word List from Student Page S180 to check that students can read more words with /ē/.

> he   very   body   we

IF… students cannot read a word,
THEN… have them use sound-by-sound blending. For example, if students cannot read *body*, write out *body* and move your hand in a continuous motion from letter to letter /b//o//d//ē/.

Lesson 31 | Long e and *u*

PRACTICE 2: Long e (Spelled e_e) Use the routine below to help students connect /ē/ with e_e and to blend words with this long e spelling pattern.

Routine

1. Connect sound to spelling.

Write e_e and have students say /ē/ as you point to the letters. The letter e at the end of the word gives the first e its long sound, and the blank shows where a consonant will go.

2. Model blending.

Say the word *gene*, then write e_e and say its sound: /ē/. Write g and blend the sounds: /j//ē/. Have students blend with you as you point to the letters. Write *n* in the blank and have students say its sound with you: /n/. Then blend the whole word, pointing to the first and second e as you say /ē/. This is how I blend this word: /j//ē//n/, *gene*. Have students practice saying the word without pausing between sounds.

Follow this procedure to model the long e, /ē/, spelled e_e as in *eve*. Then distribute or display Student Page S181 to reinforce the long e sound spelled e_e. Have students read each word aloud.

eve	Pete	Zeke

☑ **MONITOR PROGRESS** Use the Word List from Student Page S181 to check that students can read more words with /ē/, spelled e_e.

Steve	here	gene

IF... students have difficulty reading a word,
THEN... help them identify the consonant and vowel sounds in each word. Guide students to blend the sounds together to read the word.

REMIND STUDENTS THAT ...
- they can recognize words with long vowel sounds.
- they can recognize words with the long e sound spelled e_e.
- they can read words with the long e sound.

Lesson 31 | Long e and *u*

REMIND STUDENTS THAT ...

- they can recognize words with long vowel sounds.
- they can recognize words with the long *u* sound spelled *u_e*.
- they can read words with the long *u* sound.

WORD LIST

tube   use
fume

PRACTICE 3: Long *u* (Spelled *u_e*) Write the first two words from the Word List in the sidebar and say each aloud several times. What do you know about reading *tube* and *use*? When you see the spelling *u_e* in a word, try the long *u* sound, /ū/. Say /ū/ aloud with students as you point to *u_e*. Then point to the initial consonant, say its sound, and blend the first two sounds: /t//ū/. Point to the next consonant and say its sound: /b/. Now blend the word with me: /t//ū//b/. Repeat the procedure with *use*.

Use other words from the Word List for additional practice. Follow the procedure above to model for students how to read these words.

Then distribute or display Student Page S182 to reinforce the long *u* sound. Have students write the letter e in the boxes to make new words. Then have them read each pair of words.

cub → cube   hug → huge
tub → tube   cut → cute

☑ **INDEPENDENT PRACTICE** Distribute Student Page S182. Have students read the Word List independently to check that they can read words with /ū/ and /ē/. Then have them identify the spelling of the long vowel sound in each word.

duke (u_e)   be (e)   baby (y)
eve (e_e)   June (u_e)

IF... students cannot read a word,
THEN... have them use sound-by-sound blending. For example, if students cannot read *duke*, write out *duke* and move your hand in a continuous motion from letter to letter: /d//ū//k/.

My Rat Zeke

Zeke is my rat.
He is very nice.
I made him a maze in a tube.
He likes his maze.

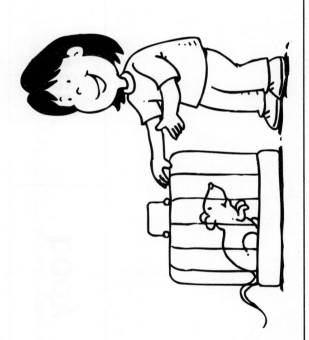

met, me   be, bet

lady, lad   wet, we

| he | very | body | we |

Long *e* and *u*

eve	Pete	Zeke

Steve	here	gene

Lesson 31 Long *e* and *u*

cub → cub	hug → hug
tub → tub	cut → cut

duke	be	baby
eve	June	

ASSESSMENT
LESSONS 30–31

Phonics and Word Recognition

ASSESS MASTERY Assess students' mastery of the long vowel sounds.

ADMINISTER THE TEST Administer the Checkpoint orally to each student. Give each student a copy of the next page. Instruct students as follows.

MODEL: I will display words that have a long vowel sound. You will tell me what long vowel spelling is in each word. For example, *day*: long *a* spelled *ay*.

RF.K.3.b Associate the long and short sounds with the common spellings (graphemes) for the five major vowels.

1. Long *a* (Lesson 30)

ASSESS:	make	say	face	way

2. Long *i* (Lesson 30)

ASSESS:	mile	hi	dive	by

3. Long *o* (Lesson 30)

ASSESS:	go	Rome	hope	no

4. Long *e* (Lesson 31)

ASSESS:	we	eve	baby	Pete

5. Long *u* (Lesson 31)

ASSESS:	cute	huge	cube	tube

SCORING

SKILL/LESSON	SCORE
1. Long *a* (Lesson 30) make (*a_e*), say (*ay*), face (*a_e*), way (*ay*)	_____ / 4
2. Long *i* (Lesson 30) mile (*i_e*), hi (*i*), dive (*i_e*), by (*y*)	_____ / 4
3. Long *o* (Lesson 30) go (*o*), Rome (*o_e*), hope (*o_e*), no (*o*)	_____ / 4
4. Long *e* (Lesson 31) we (*e*), eve (*e_e*), baby (*y*), Pete (*e_e*)	_____ / 4
5. Long *u* (Lesson 31) cute (*u_e*), huge (*u_e*), cube (*u_e*), tube (*u_e*)	_____ / 4

An overall score of 80% correct is typically considered mastery. Use your judgment and your individual students' needs as well to determine skill mastery.

IF... students score below the benchmark,
THEN... review those discrete skills, reteaching as needed.

ASSESSMENT
LESSONS 30–31

Phonics and Word Recognition

make	say	face	way

mile	hi	dive	by

go	Rome	hope	no

we	eve	baby	Pete

cute	huge	cube	tube

Lesson 32 | High-Frequency Words 1

INTRODUCE Remind students that we form words by putting letters together. We learn to read some words by saying the sounds that the letters make. Other words we have to learn just by remembering the letters. These are words that we see a lot. Let's look at some of these words.

MODEL Display or share copies of the following passage, "Jon and Max," from Student Page S185 and read it aloud.

RF.K.3.c Read common high-frequency words by sight (e.g., *the, of, to, you, she, my, is, are, do, does*).

OBJECTIVES:

- Recognize common high-frequency words by sight.
- Correctly pronounce and fluently read common high-frequency words in text.

Jon and Max

I am Jon.

I have a little cat.

His name is Max.

Max likes to sleep in the tub!

Words to learn and remember

TEACH Point out the first set of high-frequency words from the first word list on Student Page S186. Remind students that the words they are learning by sight are common words found in many texts. The words we are learning now are words we'll see a lot when reading new texts. Reinforce this idea by showing that almost half of the words in the model are high-frequency words.

Next, follow the routine on T186 to introduce high-frequency words. Teach the meaning, pronunciation, and spelling of these words. Help students apply this knowledge to independently recognize and read the words in new contexts.

Lesson 32 | High-Frequency Words 1

REMIND STUDENTS THAT …

- they can recognize the words *a, am, have, I, is, little, the,* and *to* by sight.
- they can identify and read these high-frequency words in texts.

PRACTICE 1 Display the words *a, am, have, I, is, little, the,* and *to* from Student Page S186. Follow the routine to teach each word. You may wish to create separate word cards for student practice.

a	am	have	I
is	little	the	to

Routine

1. Introduce the word.
Display the word card for *am*. This word is *am*.

2. Say and spell it.
Am has two letters. Touch each letter as you spell the word. It is spelled *a-m, am*. Have students say the word with you and without you. Ask: How do you spell *am*? Right, *a-m*. If students are still having trouble, then spell the word again.

3. Use the word.
I use the word in sentences to help me understand it: *I* am *a student. I* am *happy. I* am *ready for school.*

4. Read the word.
Display a sentence that includes the word, such as *I* am *happy*. Ask: Where is the word *am*? Circle it. Say the word and then read the complete sentence, emphasizing the word *am*.

Follow the routine for each word on the list.

☑ **MONITOR PROGRESS** Display high-frequency word cards in random order and have students read each of them. Then have students use one or two of the words in their own oral sentences. Display the following sentences from Student Page S186 and ask each student to identify the high-frequency words you say aloud.

> I am Kim.
> I have to go.
> I am a little late.

IF… students have trouble using the word in a sentence,
THEN… identify the word and model how to use it. For example, say: *The word is* to. *I go* to *the store.* Have students repeat the sentence and then say their own sentence.

Lesson 32 | High-Frequency Words 1

PRACTICE 2 Display the words *for, he, like, me, my, she, we,* and *with* from Student Page S187. Follow the routine to teach each word. You may wish to create separate word cards for student practice.

for	he	like	me
my	she	we	with

REMIND STUDENTS THAT …

- they can recognize the high-frequency words *for, he, like, me, my, she, we,* and *with* by sight.
- they can identify and read these high-frequency words in texts.

Routine

1. Introduce the word.

Display the *for* word card. This word is *for.*

2. Say and spell it.

For has three letters. Touch each letter as you spell the word. It is spelled *f-o-r, for.* Have students say the word with you and then without you. Ask: How do you spell *for*? Right, *f-o-r.*

3. Use the word.

I use the word in sentences to help me understand it: *I look* for *my coat. I have a toy* for *you. Are you ready* for *lunch?*

4. Read the word.

Display a sentence that includes the word, such as *I will go* for *a walk.* Ask: Where is the word *for*? Circle it. Say the word and then read the complete sentence, emphasizing the word *for.*

Follow the routine for each word on the list.

☑ **MONITOR PROGRESS** Choose a word from the list and have students use it in a sentence. Display a sentence that includes the word and have students identify the word in context. For each word on the list, display the word card and have students say the word. Then display the following sentences from Student Page S187 for students to read aloud with you.

> We like my dog, Bud.
> He likes to run with me.
> He can run a lot!

IF… students cannot read a particular word,
THEN… model how to say and spell any problematic high-frequency words, such as *like* or *with,* and use sound-by-sound blending for decodable words. Then have students read the sentence aloud independently.

Lesson 32 | High-Frequency Words 1

REMIND STUDENTS THAT ...

- they can recognize the high-frequency words *are, do, look, of, see, that, they,* and *you* by sight.

- they can identify and read these high-frequency words in texts.

PRACTICE 3 Display the words *are, do, look, of, see, that, they,* and *you* from Student Page S188. Follow the routine to teach each word. You may wish to create separate word cards for student practice.

are	do	look	of
see	that	they	you

Routine

1. Introduce the word.
Display the *are* word card. This word is *are.*

2. Say and spell it.
Are has three letters. Touch each letter as you spell the word. It is spelled *a-r-e, are.* Have students say the word with you and then without you. Ask: How do you spell *are?* Right, *a-r-e.*

3. Use the word.
I use the word in sentences to help me understand it: *We are home. Are you coming? They are my shoes.*

4. Read the word.
Display a sentence that includes the word, such as *You are so kind.* Ask: Where is the word *are?* Circle it. Say the word and then read the complete sentence, emphasizing the word *are.*

Follow the routine for any words on the list.

☑ **MONITOR PROGRESS** Display sentences including the high-frequency words and have students identify the words in context. For each word on the list, hold up a word card and have students say the word and then use it in a sentence. Then display the following sentences from Student Page S188 for students to read aloud with you.

> Do you see the little bugs?
> I like to look for bugs.
> They are fun!

IF... students have trouble using the words in sentences,
THEN... identify the word and model how to use it. For example, say: *The word is that. I want to play with that red ball.* Have students repeat the sentence and then say their own sentence.

Lesson 32 | High-Frequency Words 1

PRACTICE 4 Display the words *one, two, three, four, five, from, go,* and *here* from Student Page S189. Follow the routine to teach each word. You may wish to create separate word cards for student practice.

one	two	three	four
five	from	go	here

Routine

1. Introduce the word.
Display the word card for *one.* This word is *one.*

2. Say and spell it.
One has three letters. Touch each letter as you spell the word. It is spelled *o-n-e, one.* Have students say the word with you and then without you. Ask: How do you spell *one?* Right, *o-n-e.*

3. Use the word.
I use the word in sentences to help me understand it: *I have* one *book.* One *day I want to go to Africa.*

4. Read the word.
Display a sentence that includes the word, such as *I have* one *little fish.* Ask: Where is the word *one?* Circle it. Say the word and then read the complete sentence, emphasizing the word *one.*

Follow the routine for each word on the list. Point out the difference between the homophones *for/four* and *to/two.*

☑ **MONITOR PROGRESS** Choose the word cards *four* and *two* from the list and have students use them in oral sentences. Display sentences including the words *for, four, to,* and *two,* and ask students to identify the words in context. Then display the following sentences from Student Page S189 and ask students to read them aloud.

> Here we go!
> Here are three balls for you and two for me.
> I have to look for that one.

IF... students mix up *for/four* or *to/two,*
THEN... model how to say and spell the words, pointing out differences in spelling and meaning. Then have students create sentences using the words correctly.

REMIND STUDENTS THAT ...
• they can recognize the high-frequency words *one, two, three, four, five, from, go,* and *here* by sight.
• they can identify and read these high-frequency words in texts.

| Lesson 32 | High-Frequency Words 1 |

- they can recognize the high-frequency words *yellow, blue, green, come, said, was, what,* and *when* by sight.

- they can identify and read these high-frequency words in texts.

PRACTICE 5 Display the words *yellow, blue, green, come, said, was, what,* and *when* from Student Page S190. Follow the routine to teach each word. You may wish to create separate word cards for student practice.

yellow	blue	green	come
said	was	what	when

Routine

1. Introduce the word.	Display the word card for *blue.* This word is *blue.*
2. Say and spell it.	*Blue* has four letters. Touch each letter as you spell the word. It is spelled *b-l-u-e, blue.* Have students say the word with you and then without you.
3. Use the word.	I use the word in sentences to help me understand it: *I have a* blue *hat. The sky is* blue.
4. Read the word.	Display a sentence that includes the word, such as *She has a* blue *dress.* Ask: Where is the word *blue?* Circle it. Say the word and then read the complete sentence, emphasizing the word *blue.*

Follow the routine for other words on the list.

☑ **INDEPENDENT PRACTICE** Choose two words from the list and have students use them in oral sentences. Display a sentence including the words and have students identify both words in context. For each word on the list, hold up a word card and have students say the word and use it in a sentence. Then display the following sentences from Student Page S190 and have individual students read them aloud.

Do you see what I see?
Dad said that we have five hats.
Two are blue. Three are green.
What hat was yellow?

IF... students have trouble identifying the words,
THEN... review any problematic high-frequency words, reteaching as necessary.

Lesson 32   High-Frequency Words 1

Jon and Max

I am Jon.
I have a little cat.
His name is Max.
Max likes to sleep in the tub!

a	am	have	I
is	little	the	to

I am Kim.
I have to go.
I am a little late.

Lesson 32   High-Frequency Words I

for	he	like	me
my	she	we	with

We like my dog, Bud.
He likes to run with me.
He can run a lot!

are	do	look	of
see	that	they	you

Do you see the little bugs?
I like to look for bugs.
They are fun!

Lesson 32   **High-Frequency Words 1**

one	two	three	four
five	from	go	here

Here we go!
Here are three balls for you and two for me.
I have to look for that one.

yellow	blue	green	come
said	was	what	when

Do you see what I see?
Dad said that we have five hats.
Two are blue.
Three are green.
What hat was yellow?

Lesson 33 | High-Frequency Words 2

INTRODUCE Remind students that we form words by putting letters together. We learn to read some words by saying the sounds that the letters make. Other words we have to learn just by remembering the letters. These are words that we see a lot. We've learned some of these words. Let's look at more of them today.

MODEL Display or share copies of the following passage, "Kitten at Play," from Student Page S191, and read it aloud.

Kitten at Play

I need to get my pen.

Did it fall on the rug?

Is it in the den?

It must be here, but where?

Look at Mugs play with it!

RF.K.3.c Read common high-frequency words by sight (e.g., *the, of, to, you, she, my, is, are, do, does*).

OBJECTIVES:
- Recognize common high-frequency words by sight.
- Correctly pronounce and fluently read common high-frequency words in text.

TEACH Point out the first set of high-frequency words from the word list on Student Page S192. Remind students that the words they are learning by sight are common words found in many texts. The words we are learning now are words we'll see a lot when reading new texts. Reinforce this idea by pointing out how many of the words in the model are high-frequency words.

Next, follow the routine on T192 to introduce high-frequency words. Teach the meaning, pronunciation, and spelling of these words, and help students apply this knowledge to independently recognize and read the words in new contexts.

Lesson 33 | High-Frequency Words 2

REMIND
STUDENTS
THAT …

- they can recognize the words *and, but, get, did, be, in, on,* and *at* by sight.
- they can identify and read these high-frequency words in texts.

PRACTICE 1 Display the words *and, at, be, but, did, get, in,* and *on* for students using Student Page S192. You may wish to create separate word cards for student practice.

and	at	be	but
did	get	in	on

Follow the routine below to teach each word.

Routine

1. Introduce the word.
Display the word card for *and*.

2. Say and spell it.
And has three letters. Touch each letter as you spell the word. Have students say the word with you and without you. Ask: How do you spell *and*? Right, *a-n-d*. If students are still having trouble, then spell the word again.

3. Use the word.
I use the word in sentences to help me understand it: *Pal* and *Spot are my pets. Meg* and *I run together.*

4. Read the word.
Display a sentence that includes the word, such as *Pal and Spot are my pets.* Ask: Where is the word *and*? Circle it. Say the word and then read the complete sentence, emphasizing the word *and*.

Repeat the routine using the other words in the list.

☑ **MONITOR PROGRESS** Display the following sentences from Student Page S192 and ask individuals to identify the high-frequency words you say aloud.

He did get the ham and eggs.
The buns are in the pan.
Can you be here at six?

IF… students have trouble identifying a high-frequency word,
THEN… identify the word and model how to use it. For example, say:
The word is did. *I* did *clean my desk.*

Lesson 33 | High-Frequency Words 2

PRACTICE 2 Display the words *help, her, him, make, people, play, them,* and *water* for students using Student Page S193. You may wish to create separate word cards for student practice.

help	her	him	make
people	play	them	water

Follow the routine below to teach each word.

Routine

1. Introduce the word. Display the word card for *help.*

2. Say and spell it. *Help* has four letters. Touch each letter as you spell the word. Have students say the word with you and without you. Ask: How do you spell *help*? Yes, *h-e-l-p.*

3. Use the word. I use the word in sentences to help me understand it: *You* help *at home. I* help *students learn.*

4. Read the word. Display a sentence that includes the word, such as *You* help *at home.* Ask: Where is the word *help*? Circle it. Say the word and then read the complete sentence, emphasizing the word *help.*

Repeat the routine using the other words in the list.

☑ **MONITOR PROGRESS** For each word on the list, display the word card and have students say the word. Choose several of the words and have students use them in sentences. Then display the following sentences from Student Page S193 for students to read aloud with you.

> The people can play in the water.
> I will make up games for them.
> He can help me.

IF... students cannot read one of the words,
THEN... model how to say and spell it. Have the student read the sentence aloud independently.

REMIND STUDENTS THAT ...

• they can recognize the words *help, her, him, make, people, play, them,* and *water* by sight.

• they can identify and read these high-frequency words in texts.

| Lesson 33 | High-Frequency Words 2 |

REMIND STUDENTS THAT ...

- they can recognize the words *been, can, jump, many, ride, run, some,* and *take* by sight.

- they can identify and read these high-frequency words in texts.

PRACTICE 3 Display the words *been, can, jump, many, ride, run, some,* and *take* for students using Student Page S194. You may wish to create separate word cards for student practice.

been	can	jump	many
ride	run	some	take

Follow the routine below to teach each word.

Routine

1. Introduce the word. Display the word card for *been*.

2. Say and spell it. *Been* has four letters. Touch each letter as you spell the word. Have students say the word with you and without you. Ask: How do you spell *been?* Yes, *b-e-e-n.*

3. Use the word. I use the word in sentences to help me understand it: *I have* been *to a zoo. Have you* been *sick?*

4. Read the word. Display a sentence that includes the word, such as *Dad has* been *to see Gram.* Ask: Where is the word *been?* Circle it. Say the word and then read the complete sentence, emphasizing the word *been.*

Repeat the routine using the other words in the list.

☑ **MONITOR PROGRESS** Display the following sentences from Student Page S194 and have students read them aloud with you. Ask them to identify the high-frequency words.

Jan can run and jump into the water.
She can take a ride on a boat.
She has many ways to have fun.

IF... students have trouble identifying the high-frequency words,
THEN... identify the word and model using it. For example, say and write: *The word is* some. *I want* some *pens!*

Lesson 33 | High-Frequency Words 2

PRACTICE 4 Display the words *came, down, out, sit, this, these, up,* and *use* for students using Student Page S195. You may wish to create separate word cards for student practice.

came	down	out	sit
this	these	up	use

Follow the routine below to teach each word.

Routine

1. Introduce the word.
Display the word card for *came.*

2. Say and spell it.
Came has four letters. Touch each letter as you spell the word. Have students say the word with you and without you. Ask: How do you spell *came?* Yes, *c-a-m-e.* If students are still having trouble, then spell the word again.

3. Use the word.
I use the word in sentences to help me understand it: *Nan* came *to see us. She* came *at five.*

4. Read the word.
Display a sentence that includes the word, such as *She* came *to play a game with us.* Ask: Where is the word *came?* Circle it. Say the word and then read the complete sentence, emphasizing the word *came.*

Repeat the routine using the other words in the list.

REMIND STUDENTS THAT ...

• they can recognize the words *came, down, out, sit, this, these, up,* and *use* by sight.

• they can identify and read these high-frequency words in texts.

☑ **MONITOR PROGRESS** Display the following sentences from Student Page S195 and ask students to identify high-frequency words in context. Then ask students to read the sentences aloud.

> This old car did not make it up the hill.
> It slid back down.
> These people need a ride.

IF... students have trouble identifying the high-frequency words in sentences, THEN... identify the words and model using them.

Lesson 33 | High-Frequency Words 2

REMIND STUDENTS THAT ...

- they can recognize the words *black, brown, does, picture, red, show, were,* and *white* by sight.

- they can identify and read these high-frequency words in texts.

PRACTICE 5 Display the words *black, brown, does, picture, red, show, were,* and *white* for students using Student Page S196. You may wish to create separate word cards for student practice.

black	brown	does	picture
red	show	were	white

Follow the routine below to teach each word.

Routine

1. Introduce the word.	Display the word card for *black.*
2. Say and spell it.	*Black* has five letters. Touch each letter as you spell the word. Have students say the word with you and without you. Ask: How do you spell *black?* Right, *b-l-a-c-k.* If students are still having trouble, then spell the word again.
3. Use the word.	I use the word in sentences to help me understand it: *Jack has* black *hair. I need a* black *marker.*
4. Read the word.	Display a sentence that includes the word, such as *Ned has a* black *cat.* Ask: Where is the word *black?* Circle it. Say the word and then read the complete sentence, emphasizing the word *black.*

Repeat the routine using the other words in the list.

☑ **INDEPENDENT PRACTICE** Display the following sentences from Student Page S196. Then have students identify the high-frequency words and use them in an oral sentence.

> T.S. has a black cap.
> My cap is brown.
> Were their caps red or yellow?

IF... students have trouble using the high-frequency words in oral sentences, THEN... identify the words and model using them. For example, say: *The word is* white. *I need a piece of* white *paper.*

Kitten at Play

I need to get my pen.

Did it fall on the rug?

Is it in the den?

It must be here, but where?

Look at Mugs play with it!

and	at	be	but
did	get	in	on

He did get the ham and eggs.
The buns are in the pan.
Can you be here at six?

help	her	him	make
people	play	them	water

The people can play in the water.
I will make up games for them.
He can help me.

been	can	jump	many
ride	run	some	take

Jan can run and jump into the water.
She can take a ride on a boat.
She has many ways to have fun.

Lesson 33   High-Frequency Words 2

came	down	out	sit
this	these	up	use

This old car did not make it up the hill.

It slid back down.

These people need a ride.

black	brown	does	picture
red	show	were	white

T.S. has a black cap.
My cap is brown.
Were their caps red or yellow?

Lesson 34 | High-Frequency Words 3

INTRODUCE Remind students that we form words by putting letters together. We learn to read some words by saying the sounds that the letters make. We have been learning about other words by remembering the letters. We call these sight words. Let's learn more of these words.

MODEL Display or share copies of the passage "What Is It?" from Student Page S197, and read it aloud.

RF.K.3.c Read common high-frequency words by sight (e.g., *the, of, to, you, she, my, is, are, do, does*).

OBJECTIVES:

- Recognize common high-frequency words by sight.
- Correctly pronounce and fluently read common high-frequency words in text.

What Is It?

Soon it will be time to eat.
First you mix, and then you bake.
After it bakes, let it cool.
Before you cut it, find the butter.
Now give me a slice.

TEACH Point out the first set of high-frequency words from the word list on Student Page S198. Remind students that the words they are learning by sight are common words found in many texts. The words we are learning now are words we'll see a lot when we read. Reinforce this idea by pointing out how many of the words in the model are high-frequency words.

Next, follow the routine on T198 to introduce high-frequency words. Teach the meaning, pronunciation, and spelling of these words, and help students apply this knowledge to independently recognize and read the words in new contexts.

Lesson 34 | High-Frequency Words 3

REMIND
STUDENTS
THAT …

- they can recognize
  the words *after,
  before, first, now, soon,
  then, time,* and *when*
  by sight.

PRACTICE 1 Display the words *after, before, first, now, soon, then, time,* and *when* for students using Student Page S198. You may wish to create separate word cards for student practice.

after	before	first	now
soon	then	time	when

Follow the routine below to teach each word.

Routine

1. Introduce the word.	Display the word card for *after.*
2. Say and spell it.	*After* has five letters. Touch each letter as you spell the word. Have students say the word with you and without you. Ask: How do you spell *after?* Right, *a-f-t-e-r.* If students are still having trouble, then spell the word again.
3. Use the word.	I use the word in sentences to help me understand it: After *dinner, we will read a book. Tuesday comes* after *Monday.*
4. Read the word.	Display a sentence that includes the word, such as *We will swim* after *school.* Ask: Where is the word *after?* Circle it. Say the word and then read the complete sentence, emphasizing the word *after.*

Repeat the routine for each word on the list.

☑ **MONITOR PROGRESS** Display the following sentences from Student Page S198 and read them aloud. Ask each student to identify the high-frequency words.

Soon it will be time to race.
First, get in a line.
Then, listen to me.
You can go when I say, "Now!"

IF… students have difficulty identifying high-frequency words,
THEN… say the word and model how to use it. For example, say: The word is *first.* First, *you pick a color.*

Lesson 34 | High-Frequency Words 3

PRACTICE 2 Display the words *away, different, home, live, move, new, place,* and *same* using Student Page S199. You may wish to create separate word cards for student practice.

away	different	home	live
move	new	place	same

Follow the routine below to teach each word.

Routine

1. Introduce the word.

Display the word card for *away.*

2. Say and spell it.

Away has four letters. Touch each letter as you spell the word. Have students say the word with you and without you. Ask: How do you spell *away?* Right, *a-w-a-y.* If students are still having trouble, then spell the word again.

3. Use the word.

I use the word in sentences to help me understand it: *Please go* away *now. Gran is* away *on a trip.*

4. Read the word.

Display a sentence that includes the word, such as *Stay* away *from the stove.* Ask: Where is the word *away?* Circle it. Say the word and then read the complete sentence, emphasizing the word *away.*

Repeat the routine for each word on the list.

☑ **MONITOR PROGRESS** Display the following sentences from Student Page S199 and read them aloud. Ask each student to identify the high-frequency words.

> I will move to a different home.
> It is away from here.
> Do you live in the same place?

IF... students respond incorrectly,
THEN... offer corrective feedback for the high-frequency words they cannot identify.

REMIND STUDENTS THAT ...

• they can recognize the words *away, different, home, live, move, new, place,* and *same* by sight.

• they can identify and read these high-frequency words in texts.

| Lesson 34 | High-Frequency Words 3 |

• they can recognize the words *answer, ask, know, learn, read, study, work,* and *write* by sight.

• they can identify and read these high-frequency words in texts.

PRACTICE 3 Display the words *answer, ask, know, learn, read, study, work,* and *write* for students using Student Page S200. You may wish to create separate word cards for student practice.

answer	ask	know	learn
read	study	work	write

Follow the routine below to teach each word.

Routine

1. Introduce the word. Display the word card for *answer.*

2. Say and spell it. *Answer* has six letters. Touch each letter as you spell the word. Have students say the word with you and without you. Ask: How do you spell *answer?* Right, *a-n-s-w-e-r.* If students are still having trouble, then spell the word again.

3. Use the word. I use the word in sentences to help me understand it: *Who can* answer *the question? Your* answer *is correct.*

4. Read the word. Display a sentence that includes the word, such as *She will* answer *the bell.* Ask: Where is the word *answer?* Circle it. Say the word and then read the complete sentence, emphasizing the word *answer.*

Repeat the routine for each word on the list.

☑ **MONITOR PROGRESS** Display the following sentences from Student Page S200 for students to read aloud with you. Then have students identify the high-frequency words used.

> You can study and learn.
> Ask me what you do not know.
> Read the book, and write your answer.

IF... students cannot identify the high-frequency words or read the sentences, THEN... point out the high-frequency words and help student pronounce the words they cannot identify.

Lesson 34 | High-Frequency Words 3

PRACTICE 4 Display the words *eat, family, father, give, good, mother, our,* and *which* for students using Student Page S201. You may wish to create separate word cards for student practice.

eat	family	father	give
good	mother	our	which

Follow the routine below to teach each word.

Routine

1. Introduce the word.

Display the word card for *eat.*

2. Say and spell it.

Eat has three letters. Touch each letter as you spell the word. Have students say the word with you and without you. Ask: How do you spell *eat?* Right, *e-a-t.* If students are still having trouble, then spell the word again.

3. Use the word.

I use the word in sentences to help me understand it: *It is time to* eat. *What will your family* eat *for dinner?*

4. Read the word.

Display a sentence that includes the word, such as Eat *your corn now!* Ask: Where is the word *eat?* Circle it. Say the word and then read the complete sentence, emphasizing the word *eat.*

Repeat the routine for each word on the list.

☑ **MONITOR PROGRESS** Display the following sentences from Student Page S201 and ask students to identify the words in context.

> Our family is on a trip.
> We get to eat out.
> Father wants to show us a good time.

IF... students cannot identify the high-frequency words in the sentences, THEN... say the word and model how to use it. For example, say: The word is *eat. I* eat *lunch.*

REMIND STUDENTS THAT ...

- they can recognize the words *eat, family, father, give, good, mother, our,* and *which* by sight.
- they can identify and read these high-frequency words in texts.

Lesson 34 | High-Frequency Words 3

REMIND STUDENTS THAT …

- they can recognize the words *animal, because, change, land, need, over, try,* and *under* by sight.

- they can identify and read these high-frequency words in texts.

PRACTICE 5 Display the words *animal, because, change, land, need, over, try,* and *under* for students using Student Page S202. You may wish to create separate word cards for student practice.

animal	because	change	land
need	over	try	under

Follow the routine below to teach each word.

Routine

1. Introduce the word. Display the word card for *animal.*

2. Say and spell it. *Animal* has six letters. Touch each letter as you spell the word. Have students say the word with you and without you. Ask: How do you spell *animal?* Right, *a-n-i-m-a-l.* If students are still having trouble, then spell the word again.

3. Use the word. I use the word in sentences to help me understand it: *An elephant is an* animal. *It's fun to have a pet* animal.

4. Read the word. Display a sentence that includes the word, such as *A pig is an* animal. Ask: Where is the word *animal?* Circle it. Say the word and then read the complete sentence, emphasizing the word *animal.*

Repeat the routine for each word on the list.

☑ **INDEPENDENT PRACTICE** For each word on the list, hold up a word card and have students say the word and use it in a sentence. Then display the following sentences from Student Page S202 and have individual students read them aloud.

This animal lives on land.
That animal lives under water.
Animals eat because they need food.
It helps them grow and change.

IF… students have trouble identifying the words,
THEN… review any problematic high-frequency words and model how to use them.

What Is It?

Soon it will be time to eat.

First you mix, and then you bake.

After it bakes, let it cool.

Before you cut it, find the butter.

Now give me a slice.

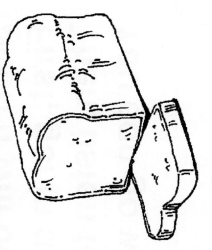

after	before	first	now
soon	then	time	when

Soon it will be time to race.
First, get in a line.
Then, listen to me.
You can go when I say, "Now!"

away	different	home	live
move	new	place	same

I will move to a different home.

It is away from here.

Do you live in the same place?

answer	ask	know	learn
read	study	work	write

You can study and learn.
Ask me what you do not know.
Read the book, and write your answer.

Lesson 34 High-Frequency Words 3

eat	family	father	give
good	mother	our	which

Our family is on a trip.
We get to eat out.
Father wants to show us a good time.

animal	because	change	land
need	over	try	under

This animal lives on land.

That animal lives under water.

Animals eat because they need food.

It helps them grow and change.

Lesson 35 | Similarly Spelled Words

INTRODUCE Explain that some word pairs are spelled almost alike. Ask students to repeat the words *cat* and *cut* after you: *cat, cut.* Say: *Cat* is spelled *c-a-t* and *cut* is spelled *c-u-t.* The difference is the letter and sound in the middle. *Cat* has the letter *a* and sound /a/, and *cut* has the letter *u* and sound /u/.

MODEL Display or share copies of the following passage, "Pat's Hat," from Student Page S203, and read it aloud. Look and listen for words that are spelled almost alike.

Pat's Hat

Pat is sad.   spelled *P-a-t*

She had a hat.

Sid put it on and set it down.   spelled *p-u-t*

Then he sat on it, and now Pat needs a new hat.

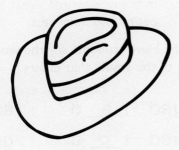

TEACH Explain that we can read similarly spelled words by identifying the sounds of the letters that are different. Point to *Pat* and *put.* Say: *Pat* is spelled *P-a-t.* What changes in the word *put*? Continue with the words *is/it, sad/Sid, she/he, and set/sat.*

Next, teach the one-to-one correspondence between letters and sounds and the spelling of these words. Help students apply this knowledge to independently recognize and read words with similar spelling patterns in new contexts.

RF.K.3.d Distinguish between similarly spelled words by identifying the sounds of the letters that differ.

OBJECTIVES:

- Identify the sounds that changed in similarly spelled words (e.g., After pronouncing *cat* and *cut,* identify that /a/ changed to /u/).
- Identify the sound that changed in similarly spelled high-frequency words (e.g., *love/live, she/he/me*).

| Lesson 35 | Similarly Spelled Words |

- they can identify sounds that changed in similarly spelled words by saying the sounds of the letters in each word, such as *cat* and *cut*.

- they can identify the sound that changed in similarly spelled words by remembering the letters in each word, such as *she* and *he*.

PRACTICE I Follow the routine to help students distinguish between similarly spelled words by identifying the sounds of the letters that differ.

Routine

1. **Display examples.** Write *bat* and *bit*. Say the words with me. Point to each word as you blend the sounds.

2. **Connect sound to spelling.** Explain that *bat* and *bit* begin with the letter *b* and the sound /b/. What letter and sound do you see and hear at the end of both words? How is each word spelled?

3. **Identify the sounds that differ.** Point out that the letter *a* stands for the sound /a/. What sound does the letter *i* stand for? Changing the letter *a* in *bat* to the letter *i* makes the word *bit*. *Bit* has the sound /i/.

4. **Extend the practice.** Write *rug*. Have students read it aloud and identify the sounds and letters. Erase *u* and replace it with *a*. What is the letter and sound in the new word? What is the word? Repeat for *pet/pit* and *miss/mess*.

Distribute Student Page S204. Have students say the words in each column and identify and write the letter of the sound that differs.

pot	p _o_ t	red	r _e_ d	same	_s_ ame
pit	p _i_ t	rod	r _o_ d	game	_g_ ame
pet	p _e_ t	rid	r _i_ d	tame	_t_ ame

☑ **MONITOR PROGRESS** Display this sentence from Student Page S204. Have pairs find two similarly spelled words and identify the letters that differ.

The fan had fun at the game.

IF… students do not find *fan* and *fun* and determine how they differ,
THEN… provide new examples for practice and review the routine.

Lesson 35 | Similarly Spelled Words

PRACTICE 2 Follow the routine to teach how to distinguish between similarly spelled words by identifying the sounds of the letters that differ.

Routine

1. Display examples.

Write *hot, hit* and *she, me.* Point to and say *hot* and *hit.* Read the words with me: *hot, hit.* Remind students that they learned the words *hot* and *hit* by saying the sounds of the letters. Repeat the process for *she* and *me,* words students learned by sight.

2. Connect sound to spelling.

Sweep your hand under the letters as you say *hot* and *hit.* Have students listen to the sounds. How is *hot* spelled? How is *hit* spelled? Repeat for *she* and *me.*

3. Identify the sounds that differ.

Point out that *hot* and *hit* have the same beginning and final sounds and letters. What sounds and letters differ in the two words? Repeat for *she* and *me,* pointing out that changing *sh*/sh/ to *m*/m/ forms the word *me.*

Distribute Student Page S205. Have students say the words in each column and identify and write the letter of the sound that differs.

land __l__ and	like __l__ ike	no __n__ o
band __b__ and	bike __b__ ike	so __s__ o
sand __s__ and	bake b__a__ ke	go __g__ o

☑ **MONITOR PROGRESS** Display the sentence below from Student Page S205. Have students find similarly spelled words and identify the letters that differ.

> ## We came yesterday and will come today.

IF... students do not find *came* and *come* and determine how they differ, THEN... provide new examples for practice and review the routine.

Lesson 35	Similarly Spelled Words

PRACTICE 3 Follow the routine to teach how to distinguish between similarly spelled words by identifying the sounds of the letters that differ.

Routine

1. Display examples.	Write *fix, fox* and *give, live.* Point to *fix* and *fox.* Read the words aloud: *fix, fox.* Remind students that they can read *fix* and *fox* by saying the sounds of the letters. Repeat the process for the sight words *give* and *live.*
2. Connect sound to spelling.	Sweep your hand under the letters as you repeat *fix* and *fox.* How is *fix* spelled? How is *fox* spelled? Repeat for *give* and *live.*
3. Identify the sounds that differ.	Point out that *fix* and *fox* have the same beginning and final letters and sounds. What letters and sounds differ in the two words? Repeat for *give* and *live.* Note that here *live* is pronounced /l/ /ĭ/ /v/, not /l/ /ī/ /v/.

Distribute Student Page S206. Have students say the words in each column and identify and write the letter or letters of the sound that differs.

then	th en	brown	br own	here	h e re
pen	p en	down	d own	hire	h i re
pan	p an	town	t own	hare	h a re

☑ **INDEPENDENT PRACTICE** Display the following letters from Student Page S206. Have students start with the word *him.* Using the letters displayed, they change one letter in *him* to form a new word. Then they choose another letter to form another word, building a new word each time. Possible answers: *him, hem, hum, ham, had, pad,* and *pat, him, ham, hat, cat, cap, cup, cut,* and so on.

e	u	a	d	p	t

| him | h__m | __im | hi__ | __ __ __ | __ __ __ |

IF... students have difficulty changing one letter at a time,
THEN... guide students to make words using prompts. *If I change the i in* him *to an a, I have the word* ham. *What word do I get if I change the a to a u?*

Pat's Hat

Pat is sad.

She had a hat.

Sid put it on and set it down.

Then he sat on it, and now

Pat needs a new hat.

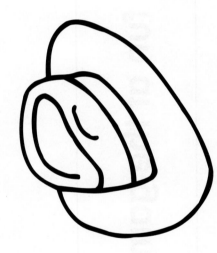

Lesson 35 | Similarly Spelled Words

pot	p _ t	red	r _ d	same	_ ame
pit	p _ t	rod	r _ d	game	_ ame
pet	p _ t	rid	r _ d	tame	_ ame

The fan had fun at the game.

land ___and	like	___ike	no	___o
band ___and	bike	___ike	so	___o
sand ___and	bake	b___ke	go	___o

We came yesterday and will come today.

then ___en   brown ___own   here h___re

pen ___en   down ___own   hire h___re

pan p___n   town ___own   hare h___re

---

him   h___m   ___im   hi___   ___ ___ ___

e   u   a   d   p   t

ASSESSMENT
LESSONS 32–35

Phonics and Word Recognition

ASSESS MASTERY Use this Checkpoint to assess students' mastery of high-frequency words and similarly spelled words.

ADMINISTER THE TEST Administer the Checkpoint to each student. Give each student a copy of the next page. Have students listen as you read each sentence aloud, and then have them identify each high-frequency or similarly spelled word. Then have students use one or more of the words in a new oral sentence.

RF.K.3.c Read common high-frequency words by sight (e.g., *the, of, to, you, she, my, is, are, do, does*).

RF.K.3.d Distinguish between similarly spelled words by identifying the sounds of the letters that differ.

1. High-Frequency Words 1 (Lesson 32)

ASSESS: There are two blue hats.

2. High-Frequency Words 2 (Lesson 33)

ASSESS: I saw this picture.

3. High-Frequency Words 3 (Lesson 34)

ASSESS: After today, we will live in a different place.

4. Similarly Spelled Words (Lesson 35)

ASSESS: Mike likes his new bike.

SCORING

SKILL/LESSON	SCORE
1. High-Frequency 1 (Lesson 32) There <u>are</u> <u>two</u> <u>blue</u> hats. (Answers will vary.)	_____ / 4
2. High-Frequency 2 (Lesson 33) <u>I</u> saw <u>this</u> <u>picture</u>. (Answers will vary.)	_____ / 4
3. High-Frequency 3 (Lesson 34) <u>After</u> today, <u>we</u> will <u>live</u> <u>in</u> <u>a</u> <u>different</u> <u>place</u>. (Answers will vary.)	_____ / 8
4. Similarly Spelled Words (Lesson 35) <u>Mike</u> <u>likes</u> his new <u>bike</u>. (Answers will vary.)	_____ / 4

An overall score of 80% correct is typically considered mastery. Use your judgment and your individual students' needs as well to determine skill mastery.

IF... students score below the benchmark,
THEN... review those discrete skills, going back to reteach as needed.

ASSESSMENT
LESSONS 32–35

Phonics and Word Recognition

1. There are two blue hats.

2. I saw this picture.

3. After today, we will live in a different place.

4. Mike likes his new bike.

Lesson 36 | Activate Prior Knowledge

INTRODUCE Tell students that when they read, they can use what they already know to help them understand what the author is saying. Let's say you read a story about a ladybug. What do you know about a ladybug? Pause for students to respond. Yes, it's small. It has wings. It's red. You can use what you know to help you understand the story.

MODEL Tell students that they will be reading a passage about a bear in the wintertime. Explain that you know some things about winter. In some places, winter can be very cold. The days are short. It might snow. Knowing that helps me get a picture in my mind.

Display or share copies of the following passage, "The Bear in Winter," from Student Page S209, and read it aloud.

The Bear in Winter

The bear woke up.
It was dark.
She was cold.
There was snow on her fur!
She curled up tight.
She went back to sleep.

Tell students that what you know about winter helped you understand the passage. You know about the cold, the dark, and the snow, so you can picture what winter looks like.

TEACH Remind students that the passage is about a bear. What do you know about bears? Ask guiding questions to help students explain what bears are like. For example, ask: Are bears big or small? Are they furry? What do bears like to do?

Reread the passage with students. Ask how they were able to use what they already know about bears to help them understand the passage better.

RF.K.4 Read emergent-reader texts with purpose and understanding.

RL.K.10 Actively engage in group reading activities with purpose and understanding.

RI.K.10 Actively engage in group reading activities with purpose and understanding.

OBJECTIVES:

• Activate prior knowledge before reading a text.

• Draw pictures to show prior knowledge.

• Discuss prior knowledge with classmates.

Lesson 36 | Activate Prior Knowledge

REMIND STUDENTS THAT …

- they can picture what they read about in their minds.
- they can use what they know to help them understand a text.

PRACTICE 1 Tell students that they are going to use what they know about a topic to help them understand a text. We are going to read a text about a lion. What do you know about lions? Are they big or small? What color can lions be? What do lions do? What do they look like? Tell students that they can draw a picture of a lion to help explain what they know about lions.

Have children draw pictures of lions. Then ask them to tell a partner what the picture shows. See if you and your partner agree about lions. Maybe you can learn something about lions from your partner.

Display the passage from Student Page S210 and read it with students.

> ### Lions
>
> Lions are big.
> They look a lot like big cats.
> They have tails and claws.
> Lions sleep a lot!

Reread the text one line at a time. Ask students to raise their hands if their pictures tell about that line. For instance, students whose pictures show an animal with a tail and claws should raise their hands when you read the third line.

☑ **MONITOR PROGRESS** Have students look at the following sentence from Student Page S210:

> I like to look at birds.

Ask students to name some things they know about birds.

IF… students have trouble thinking of facts about birds,
THEN… ask guiding questions, such as "How do birds get from one place to another?" or "How many legs do birds have?"

Lesson 36 | Activate Prior Knowledge

PRACTICE 2 Review with students that they can draw a picture to help them show what they know about a topic. Next we will read a passage about two animals. One animal is a rabbit. The other is a mouse. Think about what you know about these animals. Then draw a picture that shows both of them.

When students have completed their drawings, ask them to share their work with a partner. Then invite a volunteer to say one thing they know about rabbits. Have other students add ideas of their own as appropriate. Repeat the activity for the mice drawings.

Explain that students can use what they know about rabbits and mice to help them understand the passage from Student Page S211. Let's read the passage together. Picture in your mind what is happening.

REMIND STUDENTS THAT ...

• they can use what they know about a topic to help them understand what they read.

• they can draw pictures to show what they know.

The Rabbit and the Mouse

A rabbit met a mouse.
The rabbit had long ears.
The mouse had short ears.
The rabbit was big.
The mouse was small.
But they both could run fast!

Ask students how the pictures they drew helped them understand the passage better.

☑ **MONITOR PROGRESS** Have students draw a picture to show what they know about cows and horses. Ask them to tell about their pictures.

IF... students cannot tell what they know based on the picture,
THEN... model by saying something you see, such as: I can tell that cows have four legs.

Lesson 36 | Activate Prior Knowledge

REMIND STUDENTS THAT ...

- they can use what they know about a topic to help them understand what they read.

- they can draw pictures to show what they know about a topic.

- they can talk with a partner to share what they know and learn more about a topic.

PRACTICE 3 Tell students that they will be working in small groups to share what they know about a topic. Review that when students already know something about a topic, it is easier for them to understand a text about it.

Ask if anyone has ever seen a turtle. Think about what a turtle looks like. How many legs does it have? Think about what a turtle does. How does it move from one place to another? Think about what else you know about turtles.

Divide the class into groups of four. Ask them to take turns telling their group members some things they know about turtles. We will read a passage about turtles. It's good to know as much about turtles as we can before reading the passage.

When groups have finished discussion, have them share with the class one or two facts about turtles. Then read the following passage from Student Page S212 with students.

The Turtle

The turtle swam and swam.
Soon it was tired.
It found a rock in the sun.
It pulled its legs into its shell.
Now it was warm and dry!

Ask students how their discussions helped them learn more about turtles. Have students discuss how knowing about turtles can help them read and understand a text about turtles.

☑ **INDEPENDENT PRACTICE** Ask students to choose an animal they like. Have them use words and drawings to tell what they know about that animal.

IF... students have difficulty describing the drawing they made,
THEN... model by pointing to different features in the drawing and asking about those features.

The Bear in Winter

The bear woke up.

It was dark.

She was cold.

There was snow on her fur!

She curled up tight.

She went back to sleep.

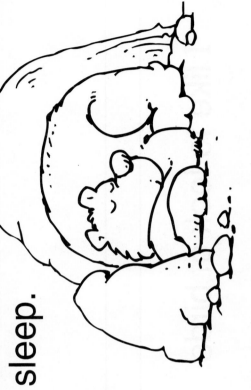

Lions

Lions are big.

They look a lot like big cats.

They have tails and claws.

Lions sleep a lot!

I like to look at birds.

The Rabbit and the Mouse

A rabbit met a mouse.

The rabbit had long ears.

The mouse had short ears.

The rabbit was big.

The mouse was small.

But they both could run fast!

The Turtle

The turtle swam and swam.

Soon it was tired.

It found a rock in the sun.

It pulled its legs into its shell.

Now it was warm and dry!

Lesson 37 | Make Predictions About Text

INTRODUCE Tell students that today they will learn how to make predictions. Explain that when you make a prediction, you use what you know to tell something you think is going to happen. You can make a prediction about the weather. Do you think it will be hot or cold today? Encourage students to make simple predictions about weather conditions based on what they know about current weather conditions.

You can also make predictions about books. You can use text clues to tell what you think a story will be about, or what might happen next.

MODEL Display the passage below, along with the art. Read the title aloud. Because the title is "My Pet," I can predict that the passage will be about a pet. I wonder what kind of a pet it is. Point out the picture. I'll use the picture to help me think about that part. I can see that the animal in the picture is hiding under a chair, so I can predict that the pet is small enough to hide under a chair.

My Pet

My pet is bigger than a mouse.
It's smaller than a dog.
I call my pet Kitty!
What kind of pet do you think I have?

My pet is…a cat!
(Meow!)

TEACH Read the first line of the passage with students. What pet might be bigger than a mouse? Remember to use what you already know. What could it be? Raise your hand if you would like to make a prediction about the pet.

Help students work their way through the passage line by line. Point out that each sentence gives more information about the pet. Then read the last lines of the passage with students. What kind of pet is it? Were you surprised? Did your prediction match the passage?

RF.K.4 Read emergent-reader texts with purpose and understanding.

RL.K.10 Actively engage in group reading activities with purpose and understanding.

RI.K.10 Actively engage in group reading activities with purpose and understanding.

OBJECTIVES:

- Use titles to make and confirm predictions about text.
- Use context to make and confirm predictions about text.
- Use pictures to make and confirm predictions about text.

| Lesson 37 | Make Predictions About Text |

REMIND STUDENTS THAT …

- they can make predictions to tell what happens in a story or text.
- they can use what they already know to make predictions.

PRACTICE I Display Student Page S214. Tell students that these are the titles and pictures from some books. What predictions can you make about these books? Can you guess what they will be about?

Read the title of the first book with students and point to the picture. Is this book going to be about kings and queens? How do you know? Point out that this topic would not make sense, because the title doesn't mention kings and queens and the pictures does not show a king or a queen. Guide students to realize that the book will probably be about making sandwiches. The title is "How to Make a Sandwich," and the picture is of a sandwich. You can predict that the book will be about making sandwiches!

How to Make a Sandwich

My Favorite Sport

The Ride

Repeat with the other two book titles. Guide students to recognize that they can use what they know about a topic as well as what the title says to make their predictions.

☑ **MONITOR PROGRESS** Distribute Student Page S214. Have students read the title of the book with you and then have them look at the image. Ask students to use these clues to predict what the story will be about.

The Girl and the Red Bird

IF... students are uncertain of what a prediction is,
THEN... review with them that a prediction is using text clues and what you know to make a good guess about what will happen.

Lesson 37 | Make Predictions About Text

PRACTICE 2 Tell students that they can make predictions about what will happen in a text. If possible, remind students of a time when someone made a prediction about what would happen in a book, or ask students to tell about a prediction they made. These guesses are called predictions. It can be fun to make predictions about what will happen next in a story! You can use clues in the story and what has already happened to make a good prediction.

Read the text on Student Page S215 with students.

- a prediction is a good guess about what will happen or what a book might be about.
- they can use what they know about a story or text so far to make predictions.

The Big Noise

Jeff was playing at home.
Then he heard a big noise.
The noise was very loud!
Jeff ran to the window.
He looked out.

Point out that the passage is not yet over. Ask students to predict what Jeff will see. Emphasize that what Jeff sees must be able to make a loud noise. Have students make predictions, and record them on the board or on chart paper.

☑ **MONITOR PROGRESS** Display Student Page S215. Ask students which of the endings to the passage would make the most sense.

Jeff saw a tiny little bug!
Jeff saw a dog asleep on the deck!
Jeff saw a big loud truck!

IF… students do not answer the question correctly,
THEN… point out the description in the text and ask them to tell which of those objects makes a big noise.

Lesson 37 | Make Predictions About Text

REMIND STUDENTS THAT ...

- they can make predictions about what a text will be about.
- they can make predictions about what will happen next in a passage.
- they can make predictions using the title and pictures.

PRACTICE 3 Explain that students can use clues in the text when they make predictions about a story. You can use the title. You can use any pictures that are in the text. You can use what happens at the beginning of the text.

Tell students that they will be reading another passage. Display Student Page S216 and cover everything but the title. Then read the title with students. Ask them to use the title to predict what the passage will be about. Record predictions if possible.

Then reveal the first line of the text. Ask students to predict what will happen next. Again, record predictions if you can.

Continue as above until one line remains. Reveal the last line of the passage. Ask students if they were surprised by the ending and why.

My Snack

First, I ate an apple.
Then, I ate some crackers.
Next, I ate some cheese.
After that, I ate two carrots.
And after that...

I wasn't hungry any more!

☑ **INDEPENDENT PRACTICE** Ask students what predictions they made that turned out to match the passage. Ask them how they knew to make that prediction.

IF... students have difficulty recalling the predictions they made,
THEN... review the passage with them.

My Pet

My pet is bigger than a mouse.

It's smaller than a dog.

I call my pet Kitty!

What kind of pet do you think I have?

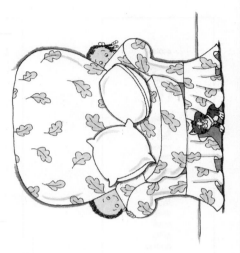

My pet is...a cat!

(Meow!)

How to Make a Sandwich

My Favorite Sport

The Ride

The Girl and the Red Bird

The Big Noise

Jeff was playing at home.
Then he heard a big noise.
The noise was very loud!
Jeff ran to the window.
He looked out.

My Snack

First, I ate an apple.

Then, I ate some crackers.

Next, I ate some cheese.

After that, I ate two carrots.

And after that...

I wasn't hungry any more!

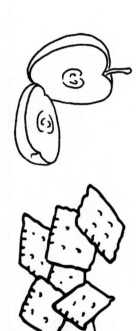

Lesson 38 | **Understand Read-Aloud, Echo-Read, and Choral-Read Text**

INTRODUCE Tell students that they can read and listen to texts in several different ways. You can listen to someone read a text out loud. You can read a text with other people, too.

MODEL Display or distribute Student Page S217. I'll read the first part of this text out loud. Listen carefully! This is called "reading aloud." Read the title and the first three sentences of the text aloud to students.

RF.K.4 Read emergent-reader texts with purpose and understanding.

OBJECTIVES:

- Understand texts that are read aloud.
- Echo-read texts with purpose and understanding.
- Choral-read texts with purpose and understanding.

Playing Soccer

Playing soccer can be a lot of fun!
You kick the ball, and you try to score a goal.
The other team tries to stop you.

Did you score a goal?
Then your team gets a point.
Good for you!

Ask students what the text was about. Explain that students can find out about new things when they listen to stories or other texts that are read aloud.

TEACH You can read text with other people, too. We're going to do something called echo reading. I'll read the text first. Then you be my echo and read it after me.

Read the sentence "Did you score a goal?" from Student Page S217, touching the words as you say them. Then have students repeat the sentence as you track the words again. Repeat with "Then your team gets a point."

Now we'll do something called choral reading. We'll all read the last sentence together. Ready? Help students read the sentence "Good for you!" Have them repeat it without you.

Explain that students will be learning about read-alouds, echo reading, and choral reading in these lessons.

Lesson 38 | Understand Read-Aloud, Echo-Read, and Choral-Read Text

REMIND STUDENTS THAT ...

- they can learn from and enjoy texts that are read aloud.
- they can answer questions about texts read aloud.

PRACTICE I Tell students that they will be listening to a passage. Listen closely. See what you can learn about the person in the passage.

Display Student Page S218. Read the sentences in turn. You may move your hand under the words if you wish.

The Man Who Played Baseball

Once there was a man who loved to play baseball.
He could throw hard, and he could run fast.
He also could hit the ball a very long way.
One day he hit the ball with his bat.
He hit the ball so hard, it went all the way around the world!
When it came back to him again, he reached up and caught it!

Ask students to tell a partner one thing they learned about the man who loved to play baseball. Invite students to share the results of their discussions. Remind students that they can learn a lot by listening carefully as someone else reads a passage.

☑ **MONITOR PROGRESS** Ask students if the man who loved baseball was fast or slow. Then ask if he could throw the ball hard.

IF... students do not recall the answer to the questions,
THEN... reread the story aloud, asking students to listen for the correct information.

Lesson 38 | Understand Read-Aloud, Echo-Read, and Choral-Read Text

PRACTICE 2 Review with students that they learned earlier about echo reading. When there is an echo, you hear a sound again after it has stopped. When you echo-read, you read the same words right after someone else says them.

Display or distribute Student Page S219. Point out that this selection is a poem. Ask students to listen for rhymes. Read aloud the title and have students repeat as you point to each word in turn. Then continue with the other sentences, saying each one as you point to the words and having students repeat. Remind students to look at the words as they say them and to read clearly and with expression.

REMIND STUDENTS THAT ...

• they can learn from and enjoy texts that are read aloud.

• they can echo-read after a teacher.

• they can answer questions about texts.

Running

How fast can you run?
Can you run over here?
Can you run like the wind?
Can you run like a deer?

One thing that I know:
It feels good when I run.
If I'm slow or I'm fast,
Running is fun.

☑ **MONITOR PROGRESS** Ask students how the speaker of the poem feels about running and how they know.

IF... students cannot answer the question,
THEN... read the poem aloud and have students focus on the speaker's feelings about running.

Lesson 38 | Understand Read-Aloud, Echo-Read, and Choral-Read Text

REMIND
STUDENTS
THAT …

• they can learn from
and enjoy texts that
are read aloud.

• they can choral-read
with other students.

• they can answer
questions about
texts.

PRACTICE 3 Explain that students can read a text aloud together. Remind them that this is often called choral reading.

Display Student Page S220. Read the first line aloud. Then invite students to join you. Next, have students read the line themselves without your assistance. *It can help to count to three together before you start. Listen: one, two, three! Pam likes…* You may wish to appoint a student to lead the group so they begin and end together.

Continue with the rest of the text, having students read one line at a time in choral fashion. Make sure they stay together. Remind them to listen to each other as they read to make sure they are saying the same thing at the same time.

Pam Swims

Pam likes to swim.
She likes to get wet.
She can swim fast!
She can swim far!

Pam gets out of the water.
She shakes her body.
Now she is dry.

Is Pam a girl?
No!
Pam is a dog!

☑ **INDEPENDENT PRACTICE** Ask students to tell something they learned about Pam from the passage.

IF… students cannot successfully answer the question,
THEN… have them echo-read the passage with you.

Understand Read-Aloud, Echo-Read, and Choral-Read Text

Playing Soccer

Playing soccer can be a lot of fun!
You kick the ball, and you try to score a goal.
The other team tries to stop you.

Did you score a goal?
Then your team gets a point.
Good for you!

The Man Who Played Baseball

Once there was a man who loved to play baseball.

He could throw hard, and he could run fast.

He also could hit the ball a very long way.

One day he hit the ball with his bat.

He hit the ball so hard, it went all the way around the world!

When it came back to him again, he reached up and caught it!

Running

How fast can you run?
Can you run over here?
Can you run like the wind?
Can you run like a deer?

One thing that I know:
It feels good when I run.
If I'm slow or I'm fast,
Running is fun.

Pam Swims

Pam likes to swim.
She likes to get wet.
She can swim fast!
She can swim far!

Pam gets out of the water.
She shakes her body.
Now she is dry.

Is Pam a girl?
No!
Pam is a dog!

ASSESSMENT	Fluency
LESSONS 36–38	

ASSESS MASTERY Use this checkpoint to assess students' mastery of skills related to grade-level reading comprehension, including reading (with support) emergent texts, activating prior knowledge, and making and confirming predictions about texts.

ADMINISTER THE TEST Administer the Checkpoint to each student.

1. Give each student a copy of the following page. Read the passage aloud and have students follow along.
2. Then read questions 1–4 and have students respond. Check their answers using the Scoring chart.
3. Finally, have the student echo-read the story with you, 2–3 times.

RF.K.4 Read emergent-reader texts with purpose and understanding.

RL.K.10 Actively engage in group reading activities with purpose and understanding.

RI.K.10 Actively engage in group reading activities with purpose and understanding.

SCORING

SKILL/LESSON	STANDARD	ANSWER	SCORING
1. Activate Prior Knowledge (Lesson 36)	**RF.K.4, RL.K.10**	A cat; possible answers: cats meow, they hide, and they can jump high.	_____ / 1
2. Make Predictions About Text (Lesson 37)	**RF.K.4 RL.K.10**	A cat is lost; someone will try to find it.	_____ / 1
3. Make Predictions About Text (Lesson 37)	**RF.K.4, RL.K.10**	Sam is up high, maybe on a shelf.	_____ / 1
4. Understand Read-Aloud Text (Lesson 38)	**RF.K.4**	Sam is a cat who likes to hide up high.	_____ / 1
5. Echo-Read Text (Lesson 38)	**RF.K.4**	Check the student's ability to echo-read.	_____ excellent _____ satisfactory _____ struggling

An overall score of 80% correct is typically considered mastery. Use your judgment and your individual students' needs as well to determine skill mastery.

IF... students struggle to answer the questions or to echo-read the text, THEN... review needed skills, going back to the lessons to reteach and scaffold as needed.

Lost Cat

Where was Sam?
Mia looked under the bed.
She looked in the box.
She looked on the mat.
"Meow?"
Then Mia looked up.
It was Sam!

1. What animal is this story about? What do you already know about this animal?

2. What can you predict the story will be about from the title and first sentence?

3. At the end of the story, where do you predict Sam is?

4. What do you learn about Sam in the story?

READING, WRITING, AND LANGUAGE

PART 2

Lesson 39 | **Ask and Answer Questions**

DIRECTIONS Follow along as your teacher reads aloud the title and the story, "A Chore for Angela." Look at the picture.

A Chore for Angela

"Come here, Angela!" Papa calls.

"Yes, come!" Mama says. They are in the kitchen.

Angela is busy with her stuffed animals. "What is it, Papa and Mama?" she calls. Her parents are quiet. Angela is curious. She goes to the kitchen.

"We are sending a letter to your sister. Would you like to sign it?" asks Papa.

"No," says Angela. Angela is mad at her sister for going away.

"Well then," says Mama, "would you please take the letter to the mailbox? Maybe you could ride your donkey to the mailbox."

A Chore for Angela, *continued*

"OK," Angela replies. She hates chores, but she loves her donkey. She likes to climb the stool and put the blanket and saddle on the donkey. Then Angela puts the bridle around the donkey's neck.

"Bye, Papa! Bye, Mama!" calls Angela.

"Wait! Here is the letter," says Papa. He waves for Angela to stop.

Papa and Mama then watch Angela ride her donkey to the end of the driveway. They smile when Angela puts the letter in the mailbox.

Lesson 39 | Ask and Answer Questions

INTRODUCE Say: When you hear or read a story, asking and answering questions will make the story easier to understand and remember.

MODEL Display and read aloud Student Page S225. After you read, model asking and answering questions about each set of highlighted words.

A Chore for Angela

details about events

details about Angela

Angela is busy with her stuffed animals.
"What is it, Papa and Mama?" she calls.
Her parents are quiet. Angela is curious.
She goes to the kitchen.
      "We are sending a letter to your sister. Would you like to sign it?" asks Papa.
      "No," says Angela. Angela is mad at her sister for going away.

multiple-meaning word

TEACH Ask: What is Angela like? Pause for responses. The story says she is *busy* with her stuffed animals. The story says she is *curious,* too, so she goes to find out what her parents want. The story also says Angela is *mad.* Why is Angela mad? **Read aloud the conversation about the letter.** What is the answer to my question? Pause for responses. I read what comes after "Angela is mad." I learn that Angela is mad at her sister for going away.

Point to the word *sign.* Say: Papa asks Angela if she would like to sign the letter. When I hear the word *sign,* I think of writing that gives information, such as on a street sign. I wonder what *sign* means here. Does anyone know? **Pause for responses.** In this story, the word *sign* means to write your name at the end of a letter so that people know who sent it.

Say: I just asked and answered questions about key details and a word in the story. You can do this too!

RL.K.1 With prompting and support, ask and answer questions about key details in a text. ***See also* RL.K.4, L.K.4.a**

OBJECTIVES:

- Ask questions about key details.
- Ask questions about unfamiliar words.
- Answer questions about a text.

BUILD VOCABULARY

Familiar Word Meanings

Point out the word *ride* in paragraph 6.

Say: When I read the word *ride,* I think of something you go on at an amusement park, such as a merry-go-round. But *ride* has another meaning.

Read aloud the sentence that contains *ride.* Mama says that Angela can ride her donkey to the mailbox. In this sentence, *ride* is something you do. It means "to sit and travel on something."

Have students use the same strategy to distinguish the meaning of the verb *calls* in paragraph 1 from that of the plural noun *calls.*

Lesson 39 | Ask and Answer Questions

REMIND STUDENTS THAT…

- they can ask and answer questions about a story.

- asking and answering questions about a story makes the story easier to understand and remember.

PRACTICE 1: Ask Questions About Key Details Say: To understand a story, you need to know what happens at the beginning, in the middle, and at the end. Things that happen are called *events*. In this story, Angela's parents ask her to do a chore. Angela doesn't want to do the chore. At the end, she does the chore. To understand and remember the events, ask questions about key details.

Display or distribute Student Page S226. Read it aloud.

> "Come here, Angela!" Papa calls.
> "Yes, come!" Mama says. They are in the kitchen.
> Angela is busy with her stuffed animals. "What is it, Papa and Mama?" she calls. Her parents are quiet. Angela is curious. She goes to the kitchen.

Ask: What part of the story is this? (the beginning) What details did you hear? Through discussion, guide students to see that the details tell about the characters and the setting. To understand the first event in the story, what other questions could you ask about these details? Help students formulate questions such as *Where are the characters? What makes Angela go to the kitchen?*

☑ **MONITOR PROGRESS** Read aloud paragraphs 4 through 6 on Teacher Page T223. Have students use *who, what, where, when, why,* and *how* to ask questions about key details in this section of the story.

IF… students cannot formulate questions about details,
THEN… model asking a question about the first sentence in paragraph 4, such as *What are Mama and Papa doing?* Then prompt students to use *who, what, where, when, why,* or *how* in a question about each remaining sentence.

Lesson 39 | **Ask and Answer Questions**

PRACTICE 2: Ask Questions About Unfamiliar Words Say: When you hear or read a word you don't know, ask questions about how the word is used in the story. Often the details in the story or a picture on the page will help you answer the questions. This will help you better understand the meaning of the word.

Display or distribute Student Page S227. Read it aloud.

"OK," Angela replies. She hates chores, but she loves her donkey. She likes to climb the stool and put the blanket and saddle on the donkey.

Say: I wonder what a *saddle* is. What questions could you ask to help me find out? Prompt students to use the story and illustration to generate *who, what, where, when, why,* and *how* questions about the word *saddle*.

☑ **MONITOR PROGRESS** Read aloud these sentences from the story: *She likes to climb the stool and put the blanket and saddle on the donkey. Then Angela puts the bridle around the donkey's neck.*

Ask students what questions could help them determine what *bridle* means. Remind them that they can use the story and the illustration for help. Model a question based on the illustration, such as *Where is the bridle?* or *Who wears it?*

IF... students struggle to ask questions about a word,
THEN... reread the sentence in which the word occurs, and help students explore context by asking why the author includes the word.

Lesson 39 | Ask and Answer Questions

REMIND
STUDENTS
THAT...

• they can ask
questions about key
details and unfamiliar
words in a story.

• asking about key
details will help them
understand story
events.

• knowing what words
mean will help them
understand a text.

PRACTICE 3: Answer Questions About a Text Say: The first time you hear a story, ask questions about it. Try to find the answers. When you hear the story again, use the answers to understand it.

Display or distribute Student Page S228. Read it aloud.

> "Well then," says Mama, "would you please take the letter to the mailbox? Maybe you could ride your donkey to the mailbox."
>
> "OK," Angela replies. She hates chores, but she loves her donkey. She likes to climb the stool and put the blanket and saddle on the donkey. Then Angela puts the bridle around the donkey's neck.

Pose some questions and pause for students to answer. Ask: What does Mama ask Angela to do? Even though Angela hates chores, what does she do? Remind students that their answers to the questions help make the story events clear. Help them use text and picture details to find the answers.

☑ **INDEPENDENT PRACTICE** Read aloud the last three paragraphs of the story on Teacher Page T224. Ask individual students these questions: Why does Papa say, "Wait"? (Angela has forgotten the letter.) What does *wait* mean here? (to stay in a place until something happens) What details in the text help you find out? (Papa waves for Angela to stop, or stay in a place.) What makes Papa and Mama smile? (seeing Angela put the letter in the mailbox) How will answering questions about the story help you remember it?

IF... students cannot answer the questions,
THEN... reread the story and help them ask their own questions about key details and unfamiliar words. Generate answers through discussion, and then return to the Independent Practice questions.

A Chore for Angela

Angela is busy with her stuffed animals. "What is it, Papa and Mama?" she calls. Her parents are quiet. Angela is curious. She goes to the kitchen.

"We are sending a letter to your sister. Would you like to sign it?" asks Papa.

"No," says Angela. Angela is mad at her sister for going away.

"Come here, Angela!" Papa calls.

"Yes, come!" Mama says. They are in the kitchen.

Angela is busy with her stuffed animals. "What is it, Papa and Mama?" she calls. Her parents are quiet. Angela is curious. She goes to the kitchen.

"OK," Angela replies. She hates chores, but she loves her donkey. She likes to climb the stool and put the blanket and saddle on the donkey.

"Well then," says Mama, "would you please take the letter to the mailbox? Maybe you could ride your donkey to the mailbox."

"OK," Angela replies. She hates chores, but she loves her donkey. She likes to climb the stool and put the blanket and saddle on the donkey. Then Angela puts the bridle around the donkey's neck.

Lesson 40 | **Retell Stories**

DIRECTIONS Follow along as your teacher reads aloud the title and the story, "A Steady Pace." Look at the picture.

A Steady Pace

Turtle and Rabbit were best friends, even though they were unalike. Rabbit loved trying new things—new foods, new dances, new vacation spots.

Turtle loved keeping everything the same—same foods, same dances, same vacation spots. Turtle felt happiest with things he knew all about. Turtle knew all about Rabbit.

A Steady Pace, *continued*

So when Rabbit shouted, "Let's race to the road!" Turtle just said, "Fine, fine." Turtle gasped when Rabbit jumped right over him to get ahead.

But Turtle was unsurprised when Rabbit ran back and said, "Come on! Come on!" Rabbit ran to the road again, and again, and again.

Turtle began to walk toward the road at a steady pace. When Turtle got to the road, Rabbit was way back at home.

Rabbit came hopping up, out of breath. "I won," Turtle said. "As I tell you every time, 'slow and steady wins the race.'"

"I know," smiled Rabbit. "I can count on you to say that."

Lesson 40 | Retell Stories

INTRODUCE Remind students that characters are the people and animals in a story. Say: When you read, look for details about each character. Also look for information about where and when the story takes place. Try to remember the main things that happen.

MODEL Display and read aloud Student Page S231.

---

details about Rabbit and Turtle

A Steady Pace

details about Rabbit

Turtle and Rabbit were best friends, even though they were unalike. Rabbit loved trying new things—new foods, new dances, new vacation spots.

Turtle loved keeping everything the same—same foods, same dances, same vacation spots. Turtle felt happiest with things he knew all about. Turtle knew all about Rabbit.

So when Rabbit shouted, "Let's race to the road!" Turtle just said, "Fine, fine."

details about Turtle

TEACH Ask students to name the characters. Then elicit details about them: What does Rabbit love? What does Turtle love? Affirm correct answers. How are Rabbit and Turtle unalike? Help students incorporate their previous answers into their responses.

Point out that the story is just beginning. Ask: What has happened so far? Affirm the correct response: Yes, Rabbit has challenged Turtle to a race, and Turtle has agreed. Remind students that the place and time of a story make up the setting. Read the passage aloud again, and then ask: Where does Rabbit want to race? What does that tell you about the setting? Guide students to state that the story takes place near a road.

RL.K.2 With prompting and support, retell familiar stories, including key details.

RL.K.3 With prompting and support, identify characters, settings, and major events in a story.

See also L.K.4.b

OBJECTIVES:
- Identify characters and settings.
- Identify major events and other key details.
- Retell a story.

BUILD VOCABULARY

Use Prefixes

Point out the word *unlike* in the first paragraph.

Say: To find out what *unlike* means, I can look for a familiar word part. The word *alike* is part of the word *unlike*. I know that *alike* means "almost the same."

The word part *un-* means "not." So *unlike* means "not almost the same." Rabbit and Turtle are not almost the same. They are very different.

Have students use a similar strategy to determine the meaning of *unsurprised* in the third paragraph.

Lesson 40 | Retell Stories

REMIND STUDENTS THAT...

- characters are the people and animals in a story.
- the setting is the place and time in which the story takes place.

PRACTICE 1: Identify Characters and Settings Point out that most stories are about characters. Have students identify a character from a familiar story to show they understand what a character is.

Read aloud the first two paragraphs of "A Steady Pace" on Teacher Page T229. **Ask:** Who are the characters in this story? Tell what you know about each character. Encourage students to include as many details about the characters as they can.

Display or distribute Student Page S232. Read it aloud.

So when Rabbit shouted, "Let's race to the road!" Turtle just said, "Fine, fine." Turtle gasped when Rabbit jumped right over him to get ahead.

But Turtle was unsurprised when Rabbit ran back and said, "Come on! Come on!" Rabbit ran to the road again, and again, and again.

Ask: Where do you think Turtle and Rabbit are when the race begins? Where does Rabbit go? How far away is that? Invite students to use details from the text to picture and describe the scene.

☑ **MONITOR PROGRESS** Read aloud the first sentence of the story on Teacher Page T229: *Turtle and Rabbit were best friends, even though they were unalike.* Have students tell you how they know that Turtle and Rabbit are unalike. Encourage them to use any information they remember from the whole story.

IF... students cannot explain why the characters are unalike,
THEN... reread the sentences about what each character loved, and help students describe how "new" and "the same" are unalike, or different.

Lesson 40 | Retell Stories

PRACTICE 2: Identify Major Events and Other Key Details Say: An event is something that happens. In "A Steady Pace," two friends have a race. What are the main things that happened in the story?

Display or distribute Student Page S233 and read it aloud.

So when Rabbit shouted, "Let's race to the road!" Turtle just said, "Fine, fine." Turtle gasped when Rabbit jumped right over him to get ahead.

But Turtle was unsurprised when Rabbit ran back and said, "Come on! Come on!" Rabbit ran to the road again, and again, and again.

Explain that *gasped* means Turtle nearly choked or lost his breath. Demonstrate a gasp for students. Point out that people (or animals) gasp when they are scared or surprised. Ask: What did Rabbit do that made Turtle gasp? Continue with other questions about the events and details in the paragraph. What did Rabbit do next? How is Rabbit racing?

☑ **MONITOR PROGRESS** Read aloud the first two paragraphs on Teacher Page T230. Ask: Why is Rabbit at home when Turtle reaches the road?

IF... students cannot explain that Rabbit is running back and forth, THEN... refer students to the following details in the first paragraph on Teacher Page T230: "Rabbit ran back" and "ran to the road again, and again, and again." Have students visualize Rabbit running back and forth, and then pose the question again.

Lesson 40 | Retell Stories

REMIND
STUDENTS
THAT...

- they can identify the characters in a story.
- they can describe where and when a story takes place.
- they can remember the main things that happen in a story.

PRACTICE 3: Retell a Story Ask: What happened at the beginning and in the middle of "A Steady Pace"? After students respond, display or distribute Student Page S234 and read it aloud.

> Turtle began to walk toward the road at a steady pace. When Turtle got to the road, Rabbit was way back at home.
>
> Rabbit came hopping up, out of breath. "I won," Turtle said. "As I tell you every time, 'slow and steady wins the race.'"
>
> "I know," smiled Rabbit. "I can count on you to say that."

Ask: What happens at the very end of the story? After students respond, ask: Is this the way the friends always race? (yes) Have students explain how they know. (Turtle says he tells Rabbit the same thing "every time," and Rabbit says she "can count on" Turtle to say the same thing. This shows that Rabbit and Turtle race this way often.)

☑ **INDEPENDENT PRACTICE** On the board, write the headings *Beginning, Middle, End.* Have individual students retell various parts of "A Steady Pace," indicating whether the event they are recounting occurs in the beginning, middle, or end of the story. Provide corrective feedback as needed, and place a checkmark next to the appropriate segment of the story.

IF... students struggle to retell events in sequence,
THEN... work with them to create a numbered list of events in chronological order.

A Steady Pace

Turtle and Rabbit were best friends, even though they were unalike. Rabbit loved trying new things — new foods, new dances, new vacation spots.

Turtle loved keeping everything the same — same foods, same dances, same vacation spots. Turtle felt happiest with things he knew all about. Turtle knew all about Rabbit.

So when Rabbit shouted, "Let's race to the road!" Turtle just said, "Fine, fine."

So when Rabbit shouted, "Let's race to the road!"
Turtle just said, "Fine, fine." Turtle gasped when
Rabbit jumped right over him to get ahead.

But Turtle was unsurprised when Rabbit ran back
and said, "Come on! Come on!" Rabbit ran to the
road again, and again, and again.

So when Rabbit shouted, "Let's race to the road!" Turtle just said, "Fine, fine." Turtle gasped when Rabbit jumped right over him to get ahead.

But Turtle was unsurprised when Rabbit ran back and said, "Come on! Come on!" Rabbit ran to the road again, and again, and again, and again.

Turtle began to walk toward the road at a steady pace. When Turtle got to the road, Rabbit was way back at home.

Rabbit came hopping up, out of breath. "I won," Turtle said. "As I tell you every time, 'slow and steady wins the race.'"

"I know," smiled Rabbit. "I can count on you to say that."

ASSESSMENT
LESSONS 39–40

Reading Literature

ASSESS MASTERY Use this Checkpoint to assess students' mastery of the Level A Reading standards listed here.

ADMINISTER THE TEST Administer the Checkpoint orally to each student. Distribute copies of the following page. Read aloud the story as students follow along. Then read aloud questions 1–4 below and have students respond. Check their answers using the Scoring chart.

1. What problem does Zip think he can solve? What part of the story answers this question?
2. The word *contain* means "to hold in." What does the author mean by saying the young mice "could barely contain their excitement"?
3. Who is the oldest character in the story? How do you know?
4. Tell three major events of this story in order.

SCORING

SKILL/LESSON	STANDARD	ANSWER	SCORING
1. Ask and Answer Questions (Lesson 39)	**RL.K.1**	Zip thinks he can solve the problem of having to run from the cat. Students should recognize that paragraph 2 answers the question.	_____ / 2
2. Ask and Answer Questions (Lesson 39)	**RL.K.4**	The young mice could not keep their feelings inside.	_____ / 1
3. Retell Stories (Lesson 40)	**RL.K.3**	Geezer is the oldest character. He was "the grumpiest of the old mice."	_____ / 2
4. Retell Stories (Lesson 40)	**RL.K.2** **RL.K.3**	Summaries will vary, but should feature three major story events in order.	_____ / 3

RL.K.1 With prompting and support, ask and answer questions about key details in a text.

RL.K.2 With prompting and support, retell familiar stories, including key details.

RL.K.3 With prompting and support, identify characters, settings, and major events in a story.

RL.K.4 Ask and answer questions about unknown words in a text.

An overall score of 80% is typically considered mastery. Use your judgment and your individual students' needs as well to determine skill mastery.

IF… you determine that students have not demonstrated sufficient mastery of one or more skills,
THEN… review needed skills, going back to the lessons to reteach and scaffold as needed.

Reading Literature

If Only the Cat Would Warn Us!

The young mice all complained. "We are so tired of running away from the cat!" One young mouse, Zip, knew what to do.

"We can hang a bell from the cat's neck," said Zip. "Then we will hear the cat coming."

"What a great plan!" the young mice cheered.

"What's all this noise?" grumbled the grumpiest of the old mice, Geezer.

The young mice told Geezer about Zip's idea. The mice could barely contain their excitement.

Geezer sighed. "Which one of you will be hanging the bell on the cat?" he asked. No one volunteered.

"Well, at least no one's foolish enough to climb onto a cat!" Geezer said. "There is a lesson you should learn from this," he said. "A plan is only good if you can get it to work."

Lesson 41 | **Recognize Types of Texts**

DIRECTIONS Follow along as your teacher reads aloud "Pinocchio's Good Deed" and "Wishing." Look at the picture.

Pinocchio's Good Deed

There once was an old woodcarver named Geppetto. He made puppets. One puppet was named Pinocchio. Pinocchio wished above all else to be a real boy.

A fairy visited Geppetto and Pinocchio. She said she would bring Pinocchio to life. However, he would not be a real boy yet. To become a real boy, he would have to do a good deed.

Pinocchio had many adventures. He wandered far and wide. One day, he visited his old home. There he found Geppetto, weak with sickness. Pinocchio made some soup for Geppetto and helped him drink it. Geppetto got better.

That night, Pinocchio dreamed of the fairy. When he woke up, he felt funny. Geppetto looked at Pinocchio and said, "You are a real boy!" Pinocchio remembered the fairy's words. Caring for Geppetto was the deed that made him real.

Lesson 41 | **Recognize Types of Texts**

Wishing

The boy wished for a drum set.
He wished and wished all day.
His mother said, "You'll get one
As soon as you can pay."

The boy asked for some money,
And then he begged and cried,
But still he had no dollars;
His wishes were denied.

One day he took a bus ride
And gave his seat away
To one sad man on crutches
Who thanked him in this way:

"I used to be a drummer,
But now I cannot play.
If you would take my drum set,
I'd thank you every day."

Lesson 41 | Recognize Types of Texts

INTRODUCE Tell students that they will hear and read many kinds of texts. Say: Two kinds of texts you will hear and read are stories and poems.

MODEL Display and read aloud Student Page S239.

Pinocchio's Good Deed

character names

There once was an old woodcarver named Geppetto. He made puppets. One puppet was named Pinocchio. Pinocchio wished above all else to be a real boy.

TEACH Say: This is the beginning of a story. A story has characters, a setting, and events. This story has characters named Geppetto and Pinocchio. **Draw students' attention to the character names in the text.** There is also a fairy. The picture shows the three characters. **Point out the three characters in the illustration.**

Next, read aloud the first stanza of "Wishing." Say: This is the beginning of a poem. Did you hear the words that rhyme, *day* and *pay*? When you listen to the poem, you can also hear its rhythm, or the way it sounds. **As you read the stanza aloud again, emphasize the rhyming words.**

Reread the story excerpt for students. Ask: Did you hear a rhythm or rhyming words? (no) **Point to the text and the illustration.** This is a story with a picture. It could be from a storybook. Stories tell about characters, settings, and events. Poems can also tell a story or describe someone or something. Poems often rhyme. Stories usually do not rhyme.

RL.K.5 Recognize common types of texts (e.g., storybooks, poems).

See also **L.K.4.b**

OBJECTIVES:
- Recognize stories and poetry.
- Distinguish between a story and a poem.

BUILD VOCABULARY

Use Suffixes
Write on the board the word *wished* from the first stanza of "Wishing."

Erase the suffix *-ed*. Say: To *wish* means "to want something now." *I wish I had a dog* means I want a dog at this time.

Restore the *-ed* to *wish*. *Wished* means that I wanted something before, but not now. *I wished I had a dog* means that I wanted a dog in the past, but I don't want one now.

Have students use the same strategy to distinguish the past-tense meaning of *asked* in the second stanza from that of the present-tense *ask*.

Lesson 41 | Recognize Types of Texts

REMIND STUDENTS THAT...

- they will hear and read both stories and poems.
- stories have characters, settings, and events.
- stories are organized by beginning, middle, and end.

PRACTICE 1: Identify Stories Have students tell you about a storybook they have seen. Have them describe what it looks like—its cover, pages, words, and illustrations. Then elicit a description of one story that includes its characters, its setting, and its key events. Say: That sounds like a story to me. It doesn't sound like a poem or a song.

Display or distribute copies of Student Page S240. Read the text aloud.

A fairy visited Geppetto and Pinocchio. She said she would bring Pinocchio to life. However, he would not be a real boy yet. To become a real boy, he would have to do a good deed.

Pinocchio had many adventures. He wandered far and wide. One day, he visited his old home. There he found Geppetto, weak with sickness. Pinocchio made some soup for Geppetto and helped him drink it. Geppetto got better.

Point to each character in the illustration and ask: Who is this? Have students explain what the illustration shows. Then reread the second paragraph of the above excerpt, pausing after each sentence. These sentences tell more about what happens in the story. They tell events in order, from beginning to end. What do they say? As they retell the paragraph, prompt students as needed with the question What happens next?

☑ **MONITOR PROGRESS** Read aloud the first paragraph from "Pinocchio's Good Deed" on Teacher Page T237 and pause after each sentence. Have students tell you how they know this is part of a story.

IF... students cannot explain that this is a story because it has characters and events told in order,
THEN... remind them about the key parts of a story—characters, setting, and events—and have students find examples of characters and events in the paragraph.

Lesson 41	Recognize Types of Texts

PRACTICE 2: Identify Poems Ask students to tell you the words of a familiar song, such as one they learned early in their childhoods. Poems are like songs. They often have words that rhyme. They have a rhythm that helps you remember the words.

Read aloud the first two stanzas of "Wishing" from Teacher Page T238. Say: This is the beginning of a poem. Then reread the stanzas as you clap the rhythm.

Read aloud the first stanza a third time and have students clap its rhythm with you. Then reread the second stanza, this time asking students to clap the rhythm with you and listen for rhymes. Ask: Which words rhyme in those lines? (*cried* and *denied*)

REMIND STUDENTS THAT...

- they will hear and read both stories and poems.
- poems can tell a story or describe something.
- poems often have rhyme and rhythm.

☑ **MONITOR PROGRESS** Display the following stanza of "Wishing" on Student Page S241. Read it aloud.

> One day he took a bus ride
> And gave his seat away
> To one sad man on crutches
> Who thanked him in this way:

Ask students to clap the rhythm as you read the stanza aloud a second time. Then have students identify the rhyming words. (*away, way*) Ask: How do you know that these lines are part of a poem? (They have rhythm and rhyming words.)

IF... students cannot recognize rhythm or rhyme in the poem,
THEN... guide them to clap the rhythm of a familiar song or nursery rhyme, and review with them the phonological awareness lessons on rhyme (Lessons 5 and 6).

Lesson 41   Recognize Types of Texts

REMIND
STUDENTS
THAT...

- stories have characters, settings, and events. They have a beginning, middle, and end.

- poems can tell a story or describe something. They often have rhythm and rhyme.

PRACTICE 3: Distinguish Between Stories and Poems Say: Stories and poems may be about the same things. For example, both stories and poems may be about a wish. Both stories and poems may tell about characters and events. But stories and poems do these things in different ways.

Display or distribute Student Page S242. Read each excerpt aloud.

Pinocchio's Good Deed

There he found Geppetto, weak with sickness.
Pinocchio made some soup for Geppetto and helped him drink it. Geppetto got better.
    That night, Pinocchio dreamed of the fairy.

Wishing

One day he took a bus ride
And gave his seat away
To one sad man on crutches
Who thanked him in this way:

Ask students how the ideas in the texts are similar. (The main character helps someone else and his wish comes true as a result.) Ask: What are the differences between the story and the poem? Help students contrast them. They should recognize that the story contains more detailed descriptions of events than the poem does. They should also recognize that the poem uses rhythm and rhyme to describe events, which the story does not.

☑ **INDEPENDENT PRACTICE** Read aloud the last paragraph of "Pinocchio's Good Deed" on Teacher Page T237 and the last stanza of "Wishing" on Teacher Page T238. Have individual students explain how the two texts are similar and different.

IF... students cannot explain how the story differs from the poem,
THEN... review the Practice page for each type of text before returning to the Independent Practice.

Pinocchio's Good Deed

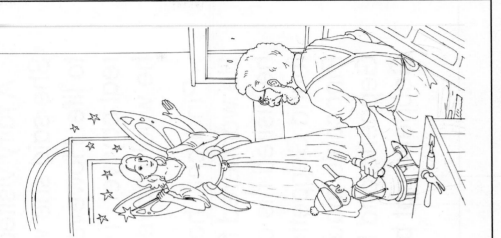

There once was an old
woodcarver named Geppetto.
He made puppets. One
puppet was named Pinocchio.
Pinocchio wished above all else
to be a real boy.

Pinocchio's Good Deed

A fairy visited Geppetto and Pinocchio. She said she would bring Pinocchio to life. However, he would not be a real boy yet. To become a real boy, he would have to do a good deed.

Pinocchio had many adventures. He wandered far and wide. One day, he visited his old home. There he found Geppetto, weak with sickness. Pinocchio made some soup for Geppetto and helped him drink it. Geppetto got better.

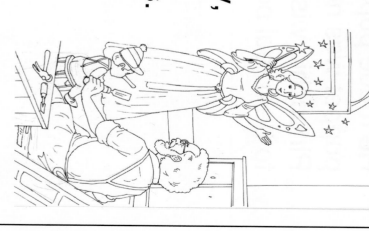

Recognize Types of Texts

Wishing

One day he took a bus ride
And gave his seat away
To one sad man on crutches
Who thanked him in this way:

Pinocchio's Good Deed

There he found Geppetto, weak with sickness.
Pinocchio made some soup for Geppetto and helped
him drink it. Geppetto got better.
That night, Pinocchio dreamed of the fairy.

Wishing

One day he took a bus ride
And gave his seat away
To one sad man on crutches
Who thanked him in this way:

Lesson 42 | Identify the Role of Storytellers

DIRECTIONS Follow along as your teacher reads aloud the story title, author, and illustrator. Then follow along as your teacher reads aloud the story. Look at the pictures.

Vacation Time
by Karla Beech
illustrated by Ariel Adams

"Hey, Eldin!" shouted Selver.

"Hey, Selver!" shouted Eldin.

Their parents started unpacking the campers. The boys high-fived and knocked shoulders and kicked at bits of gravel. It was how they greeted each other every July, when their families met in Arizona.

Selver and Eldin knew the daily plan. Every morning they would canoe with their parents. After lunch and a nap, if they were lucky, everyone would go on a hike. They would eat dinner around the campfire, roast marshmallows, and sing songs before bed.

The boys were sure that they knew every inch of the place. Selver said they could hike by themselves. So one afternoon, as their parents napped, "Bye!" they whispered, and off they ran into the trees.

Time flew by. Selver clambered up a big rock. Eldin climbed up, too. Then they slid down. Over and over, up and down they went.

Lesson 42 | **Identify the Role of Storytellers**

Vacation Time, *continued*

By 3:30 or so, Selver and Eldin were far across the meadow from the campsite.

"I'm feeling hungry," Eldin said. A little puff of wind tossed his blond hair.

"We forgot our snacks!" Selver exclaimed. "We'll have to remember them next time." A medium puff of wind tossed Selver's brown hair.

"Let's head back," Eldin said wisely. A big puff of wind blew his bangs off his forehead. The boys started walking across the meadow. Suddenly, the sky grew dark. A steady whoosh of wind started blowing behind them. Then, *CRA-A-A-A-CK!*

"What's that?" gasped Eldin.

"Lightning!" cried Selver.

"Run!" they yelled together.

Rain poured down. By the time they got to the campsite, the boys were dripping wet. Eldin's father stood just outside a camper door, wearing a plastic poncho and holding some towels underneath it.

"Thunderstorms come up pretty quickly here," he said. "You two look miserable! Have some towels." As the boys wrapped themselves up, Eldin's father asked, "Did you learn a lesson today?"

"Don't forget the snacks!" Selver said, shivering.

"Don't listen to Selver!" Eldin said.

Lesson 42 | Identify the Role of Storytellers

INTRODUCE Provide students with a simple explanation of authors and illustrators. Say: *An author writes the words of a story. When a story has pictures, they can be called illustrations. An illustrator draws the illustrations. Sometimes authors draw their own illustrations.*

MODEL Display and read aloud Student Page S245.

> ### Vacation Time
> author · · · · · · · · · · · · · ·
> *by Karla Beech*
> *illustrated by Ariel Adams* · · · · · illustrator
>
> "Hey, Eldin!" shouted Selver.
> "Hey, Selver!" shouted Eldin.
> Their parents started unpacking the campers. The boys high-fived and knocked shoulders and kicked at bits of gravel. It was how they greeted each other every July, when their families met in Arizona.

TEACH Point to the names under the title. Say: *Every story has an author. You can usually find the person's name right after the title of the story.* **Point to the author's byline and read it aloud.** *A story with pictures has an illustrator. If the illustrator is not the same person as the author, you can usually find the illustrator's name after the author's name.* **Point to the illustrator's byline and read it aloud.**

Ask: *Which part of the story did the author, Karla Beech, make? Tell me or point to it.* **Pause for responses.** *Yes, the author made the words. Which part of the story did the illustrator, Ariel Adams, make? Tell me or point to it.* **Pause for responses.** *Yes, the illustrator made the pictures.*

RL.K.6 With prompting and support, name the author and illustrator of a story and define the role of each in telling the story.

See also **L.K.5.a**

OBJECTIVES:
- Identify a story's author and illustrator.
- Explain how an author tells a story.
- Explain how an illustrator tells a story.

BUILD VOCABULARY

Word Categories
Point out the words *lunch* and *dinner* in the fourth paragraph.

Ask: When do you eat lunch? When do you eat dinner? Do both lunch and dinner have to do with eating food?

Even though you eat lunch and dinner at different times of the day, they are both meals, or groups of foods you eat at one time. So lunch and dinner can go into one group, or category: meals.

Help students use the same strategy to sort *wind, lightning,* and *rain* (in paragraphs 10, 12, and 14, respectively) into the category *weather.*

| Lesson 42 | Identify the Role of Storytellers |

REMIND
STUDENTS
THAT…

- most stories have words.
- many stories have pictures.

PRACTICE 1: Identify Authors and Illustrators Write the words *author* and *illustrator* on the board. Say: An author writes words. An illustrator makes pictures. Sometimes the same person does both things. Often, different people do these jobs.

Have students look at "Vacation Time" on Teacher Pages T243–T244. Point to the title and read it aloud. Say: This is the title of the story. Under the title you can see two names. Read aloud the author's byline. The story is by Karla Beech. Write the author's name on the board. What did Karla Beech do? (write the story) Read aloud the illustrator's byline. The illustrator is Ariel Adams. Write the illustrator's name on the board. What did Ariel Adams do? (draw the pictures)

☑ **MONITOR PROGRESS** Display or distribute Student Page S246 and read it aloud.

> The boys were sure that they knew every inch of the place. Selver said they could hike by themselves. So one afternoon, as their parents napped, "Bye!" they whispered, and off they ran into the trees.
>
> Time flew by. Selver clambered up a big rock. Eldin climbed up, too. Then they slid down. Over and over, up and down they went.

Have students tell you the part of the story created by Karla Beech (the words) and the part created by Ariel Adams (the picture).

IF… students cannot name the author and the illustrator,
THEN… review the bylines and have students repeat the following sentences with you: *The author is Karla Beech. The illustrator is Ariel Adams.*

Lesson 42	Identify the Role of Storytellers

PRACTICE 2: Explain How Authors Tell Stories Ask students to tell you the key events of one of their favorite stories. Then ask: Do you know who made up that story? If students know who originated the story or an author's name, have them give it. Otherwise, say: You may not always know the name of an author. However, you do know that an author is the person who makes up a story.

☑ **MONITOR PROGRESS** Display or distribute Student Page S247. Read the excerpt aloud.

> "Let's head back," Eldin said wisely. A big puff of wind blew his bangs off his forehead. The boys started walking across the meadow. Suddenly, the sky grew dark. A steady whoosh of wind started blowing behind them. Then, *CRA-A-A-A-CK!*
> "What's that?" gasped Eldin.
> "Lightning!" cried Selver.
> "Run!" they yelled together.

Ask: What do the author's words tell in this part of the story? Elicit details about the characters and events in the excerpt.

IF... students cannot describe the author's contribution to the story,
THEN... point to the illustration and ask: Where are these boys? How do you know? Point out that the author wrote the details that answer these questions.

Lesson 42 | Identify the Role of Storytellers

REMIND
STUDENTS
THAT...

• many stories have pictures.

• an illustrator makes the pictures for a story.

PRACTICE 3: Explain How Illustrators Tell Stories Read aloud Student Page S248 as students follow along. Emphasize the words *blond* and *brown*.

> "I'm feeling hungry," Eldin said. A little puff of wind tossed his blond hair.
> "We forgot our snacks!" Selver exclaimed. "We'll have to remember them next time." A medium puff of wind tossed Selver's brown hair.

Point to one of the illustrations on Teacher Pages T243–T244 and ask: Which boy is Eldin? (the light-haired boy) Which boy is Selver? (the dark-haired boy) How do you know? Pause for responses. The illustrator drew the picture to match the words in the story.

☑ **INDEPENDENT PRACTICE** Display or distribute Teacher Page T244. Read paragraphs 4 through 7 aloud and have students look at the picture.

"Let's head back," Eldin said wisely. A big puff of wind blew his bangs off his forehead. The boys started walking across the meadow. Suddenly, the sky grew dark. A steady whoosh of wind started blowing behind them. Then, CRA-A-A-A-CK!
"What's that?" gasped Eldin.
"Lightning!" cried Selver.
"Run!" they yelled together.

Ask: How does the picture help tell this part of the story? Have individual students identify the setting, the characters, and the event portrayed in the illustration. Who made the illustration? (Ariel Adams)

IF... students cannot describe the illustrator's contribution to the story, THEN... cover the text in the excerpt and have students use the illustration alone to describe what is happening. Point out that the illustration tells this part of the story without words.

Vacation Time

by Karla Beech

illustrated by Ariel Adams

"Hey, Eldin!" shouted Selver.

"Hey, Selver!" shouted Eldin.

Their parents started unpacking the campers. The boys high-fived and knocked shoulders and kicked at bits of gravel. It was how they greeted each other every July, when their families met in Arizona.

The boys were sure that they knew every inch of the place. Selver said they could hike by themselves. So one afternoon, as their parents napped, "Bye!" they whispered, and off they ran into the trees.

Time flew by. Selver clambered up a big rock. Eldin climbed up, too. Then they slid down. Over and over, up and down they went.

Lesson 42 Identify the Role of Storytellers

"Let's head back," Eldin said wisely. A big puff of wind blew his bangs off his forehead. The boys started walking across the meadow. Suddenly, the sky grew dark. A steady whoosh of wind started blowing behind them. Then, *CRA-A-A-A-CK!*

"What's that?" gasped Eldin.

"Lightning!" cried Selver.

"Run!" they yelled together.

Lesson 42   Identify the Role of Storytellers

"I'm feeling hungry," Eldin said. A little puff of wind tossed his blond hair.

"We forgot our snacks!" Selver exclaimed. "We'll have to remember them next time." A medium puff of wind tossed Selver's brown hair.

Lesson 43 | **Understand Illustrations in a Story**

DIRECTIONS Follow along as your teacher reads aloud the title and the story, "Clever Little Bug." Look at the pictures.

Clever Little Bug

"Dah dee dah, deedley dah, dah dah dah HAH!" sang the clever little bug. "It's a lovely day, and I'm on my way to play in the hay!" The clever little bug skipped along.

She felt a drop. "Is it going to rain?" she asked herself. Soon more drops fell. "Oops!" said the bug, and she sat down. Soon she felt quite wet. "A-ha!" she laughed. "I am sitting in a puddle!"

A cloud had stopped right above the clever little bug. The cloud was enjoying itself. It kept right on raining on the laughing little bug.

The laughing, clever little bug began to wonder. "What if my wings get wet? Will I be dry in time to fly home for the night?"

Clever Little Bug,
continued

"Think hard!" she told herself. "I don't want my wings to get too wet. Maybe I should get out of my puddle and hop."

The cloud sent more and more drops plopping into the puddle. However, the clever little bug was gone.

"Dah dee dah, deedley dah, dah dah dah HAH!" sang the clever little bug. "It's a rainy day, so I never got to play in the hay," she continued as she hopped up and down, safe and dry beneath a leaf. Smiling, she quietly said, "My wings will get dry—my wings will get dry in time to fly. Ha ha, cloud! Ha ha, rain!"

And until the rain stopped and the cloud moved away, the clever little bug had a dry place to stay.

Lesson 43	Understand Illustrations in a Story

INTRODUCE Remind students that illustrations are pictures that go with a text. Say: *Illustrations show what places and characters look like. They can help you imagine what is happening in a story.*

MODEL Display Student Page S251, which features the two illustrations from "Clever Little Bug." Read the story aloud.

Clever Little Bug

TEACH Say: *The first illustration shows something that happens in the story. It shows the bug sitting in a puddle. The bug is talking. Can you tell me what the bug is saying?* After students respond, reread the following part of the story from Teacher Page T239: *Soon she felt quite wet. "A-ha!" she laughed. "I am sitting in a puddle!"* Ask: *What other part of the story does the picture show?* Pause, then read: *A cloud had stopped right above the clever little bug. The cloud was enjoying itself. It kept right on raining on the laughing little bug.*

Point to the second illustration. Ask students to describe the illustration to you in detail. When they are done, ask: *What part of the story does this picture show?* After students respond, reread the following part of the story from Teacher Page T240: *. . . she hopped up and down, safe and dry beneath a leaf. Smiling, she quietly said, "My wings will get dry—my wings will get dry in time to fly. Ha ha, cloud! Ha ha, rain!" And until the rain stopped and the cloud moved away, the clever little bug had a dry place to stay.*

RL.K.7 With prompting and support, describe the relationship between illustrations and the story in which they appear (e.g., what moment in a story an illustration depicts).

See also **L.K.5.c**

OBJECTIVES:

- Describe illustrations.
- Connect illustrations to the story.
- Use illustrations to clarify understanding of events.

BUILD VOCABULARY

Real-Life Connections

Point out the word *clever* in the title.

Say: *Someone who is clever is smart and learns things quickly. A character in a story may be described as clever.*

What clever story characters do you know? What makes them clever? Make sure responses accurately reflect the word's meaning.

Have students use the same strategy to define the word *lovely* in the first paragraph and describe things or experiences that they think are lovely.

| Lesson 43 | Understand Illustrations in a Story |

REMIND STUDENTS THAT...

- illustrations show characters, places, and events in a story.

PRACTICE 1: Describe Illustrations Show two familiar illustrated classroom storybooks. Say: Illustrations include many details from the story. They help you see and imagine what happens.

Open each book to an illustrated page. Say: Tell me what these illustrations show. As students respond, prompt them to give details about characters, settings, and events.

☑ **MONITOR PROGRESS** Display or distribute Student Page S252.

Ask: What does the bug look like? (Answers will vary but might include that the bug has a body and a head, antennae, wings, hands, shoes, and a face.) Draw students' attention to the first illustration. Where is the bug in this picture? (in a puddle) Then draw their attention to the second illustration. Where is the bug in this picture? (under a leaf) What is happening in both pictures? (It is raining; the bug is smiling or talking.)

IF... students cannot describe the illustrations in detail,
THEN... focus on the character and story events with a question such as *Who is the character in this picture, and what is she doing?*

Lesson 43 | Understand Illustrations in a Story

PRACTICE 2: Connect Illustrations to a Story Display or distribute Student Page S253. Read it aloud.

> "Dah dee dah, deedley dah, dah dah dah HAH!" sang the clever little bug. "It's a lovely day, and I'm on my way to play in the hay!" The clever little bug skipped along.
>
> She felt a drop. "Is it going to rain?" she asked herself. Soon more drops fell. "Oops!" said the bug, and she sat down. Soon she felt quite wet. "A-ha!" she laughed. "I am sitting in a puddle!"

Point out the illustration on Teacher Page T249 and give students a few moments to examine it. Guide them in understanding that the illustration depicts what is described in the second paragraph on Student Page S253. Ask: Why do you think the illustration shows this part of the story? (because it is an important event in the story)

☑ **MONITOR PROGRESS** Display or distribute Teacher Page T249. Ask: What part of the story does the picture show? (the bug sitting in a puddle under a rain cloud) How do the picture and the text work together to help you understand what is happening in the story?

IF... students cannot identify the moment in the story that is depicted by the illustration,
THEN... have them name each part of the illustration (cloud, drops, bug, grass, puddle) and help them identify the words *drops, bug, puddle,* and *cloud* in the story, either by using the printed page or by reading the passage aloud and having students raise their hands as they hear each word.

REMIND STUDENTS THAT...

- illustrations show characters, places, and events in a story.
- they can describe illustrations in detail.

| Lesson 43 | Understand Illustrations in a Story |

- illustrations show characters, places, and events in a story.
- they can describe illustrations in detail.

PRACTICE 3: Use Illustrations to Clarify Events Display or distribute Student Page S254 and read it aloud.

> "Think hard!" she told herself. "I don't want my wings to get too wet. Maybe I should get out of my puddle and hop."
> The cloud sent more and more drops plopping into the puddle. However, the clever little bug was gone.

Ask: Where did the bug go? How could you find out? (under a leaf, under a flower; read more, look at the illustration)

☑ **INDEPENDENT PRACTICE** Display or distribute copies of Teacher Page T250. Read aloud the following text and have students examine the illustration.

Smiling, she quietly said, "My wings will get dry—my wings will get dry in time to fly. Ha ha, cloud! Ha ha, rain!" And until the rain stopped and the cloud moved away, the clever little bug had a dry place to stay.

Ask individual students to use the illustration to describe the bug's "dry place to stay" in detail.

IF… students cannot clarify the setting using the illustration,
THEN… ask them how a flower can keep something dry, and lead them to explain that the bug is under a leaf.

Clever Little Bug

Understand Illustrations in a Story

"Dah dee dah, deedley dah, dah dah dah HAH!" sang the clever little bug. "It's a lovely day, and I'm on my way to play in the hay!" The clever little bug skipped along.

She felt a drop. "Is it going to rain?" she asked herself. Soon more drops fell. "Oops!" said the bug, and she sat down. Soon she felt quite wet. "A-ha!" she laughed. "I am sitting in a puddle!"

Lesson 43   Understand Illustrations in a Story

"Think hard!" she told herself. "I don't want my wings to get too wet. Maybe I should get out of my puddle and hop."

The cloud sent more and more drops plopping into the puddle. However, the clever little bug was gone.

ASSESSMENT
LESSONS 41–43

Reading Literature

ASSESS MASTERY Use this Checkpoint to assess students' mastery of the Level A Reading standards listed here.

ADMINISTER THE TEST Administer the Checkpoint orally to each student. Distribute copies of the following page. Read aloud the story as students follow along. Then read aloud questions 1–4 below and have students respond. Check their answers using the Scoring chart.

1. What type or types of texts are in "The Dull Damselfish"?
2. Which four words of the saying are clues to the type of text it is?
3. Who is the illustrator of the text?
4. Who does the illustration show? What moment in the story does the illustration show?

SCORING

SKILL/LESSON	STANDARD	ANSWER	SCORING
1. Recognize Types of Texts (Lesson 41)	**RL.K.5**	story and poem	_____ / 1
2. Recognize Types of Texts (Lesson 41)	**RL.K.5**	*damselfish, wish, in, fin*	_____ / 1
3. Identify the Role of Storytellers (Lesson 42)	**RL.K.6**	Mark Morgan	_____ / 1
4. Understand Illustrations in a Story (Lesson 43)	**RL.K.7**	It shows Debbie the damselfish. It shows Debbie before she got her wish.	_____ / 2

An overall score of 80% is typically considered mastery. Use your judgment and your individual students' needs as well to determine skill mastery.

IF… you determine that students have not demonstrated sufficient mastery of one or more skills,
THEN… review needed skills, going back to the lessons to reteach and scaffold as needed.

RL.K.5 Recognize common types of texts (e.g., storybooks, poems).

RL.K.6 With prompting and support, name the author and illustrator of a story and define the role of each in telling the story.

RL.K.7 With prompting and support, describe the relationship between illustrations and the story in which they appear (e.g., what moment in a story an illustration depicts).

Reading Literature

The Dull Damselfish
written and illustrated by Mark Morgan

In a cool, blue pond lived a big family of damselfish. Everyone in the family looked ordinary. They were all great swimmers.

All the fish in the family were happy except Debbie. She wanted so much to be different that she made up a hopeful saying about herself.

Debbie, the dull gray damselfish,
Has figured out her favorite wish:
Great swimmer of the pond she's in,
Please give her one big purple fin!

Every day, Debbie bubbled this saying from her lips as she swam. Then one day, a great purple kite landed on the surface of the pond. Debbie wrapped the kite string around her tail and off they went, the dull damselfish and her giant purple fin!

Lesson 44 | **Identify Main Topic and Key Details**

DIRECTIONS Follow along as your teacher reads aloud the title and the article, "Sandcastles." Look at the picture.

Sandcastles

At the beach or in a sandbox, building castles is fun! All you need is sand and water. Having additional tools can make your work more interesting. Here are some ideas:

bucket with a bottom
bucket without a bottom
cups of different sizes
shovel
spatula
spoon
knife
imagination

Lesson 44 | **Identify Main Topic and Key Details**

Sandcastles, *continued*

Begin with sand and water. Do tests to find out how much water you need. Too much water will make the sand wet. Too little water will keep the sand from sticking together.

Mix sand and water in the bucket with a bottom. Make a ball of the sand and water in your hand. Does your ball of sand stay in shape when you set it on the ground? Then you have the right amount! You are ready to begin.

Start by making your biggest shapes. Use your hands to pile the sand, or use the bucket without the bottom. Fill the bucket with wet sand, turn the bucket over, tap the sides, and push gently on the sand while you lift the bucket off. There is your first tower!

After that, make more towers with the bucket, or use cups of different sizes. Use a shovel to dig. Use a spatula to smooth corners or rough spots. A spoon and a knife can help you make more shapes and carve details.

Before you stop, make sure to use your imagination. Make a sandcastle like nobody else's. That's the most fun of all!

Lesson 44 | Identify Main Topic and Key Details

INTRODUCE Remind students that a *topic* is what a passage is mostly about. **Say:** An article, like the one about making sandcastles, has a topic. No matter how many details there are, there is only one main topic. Often, the title of an article gives a clue about the topic. Inside the article, you will read key details about the topic.

MODEL Display Student Page S259 and read the two excerpts aloud.

Sandcastles

At the beach or in a sandbox, building castles is fun! All you need is sand and water. Having additional tools can make your work more interesting.

. . .

Before you stop, make sure to use your imagination. Make a sandcastle like nobody else's. That's the most fun of all!

TEACH **Say:** The title of this article is a compound word. That is one word made up of two smaller ones. **Say** *sandcastles.* What two words do you hear in *sandcastles?* **Point to the highlighted words** *sand, castle,* and *sandcastle* **in the excerpts.** This article is not about sand. It is not about castles. The title and the part both use the word *sandcastles.* The article is about sandcastles.

Say: Articles have key details about the main topic. **Point to the second sentence and read it aloud:** *All you need is sand and water.* A key detail about sandcastles is that to make them, you need two things. What are those things? **(sand, water)** To retell the main topic and these key details, you would say that the article is about sandcastles, which are castles made out of sand and water.

RI.K.2 With prompting and support, identify the main topic and retell key details of a text.

See also **RI.K.1, L.K.4.a**

OBJECTIVES:

- Ask and answer questions about a main topic.
- Ask and answer questions about key details.
- Retell a main topic and key details.

BUILD VOCABULARY

Familiar Word Meanings

Point out *sand* in paragraph 1

Say: When I read the word *sand,* I think of something you find at the beach that is gritty and can feel scratchy. But *sand* has another meaning. As a verb, *sand* means "to polish" or "to smooth something by using sandpaper."

Read aloud the sentence with *sand.* "All you need is sand and water."

Have students explain how the meaning of the plural noun *tests* in paragraph 2 is different from that of the verb in *The teacher tests his students.*

| Lesson 44 | Identify Main Topic and Key Details |

REMIND STUDENTS THAT…

- a topic is what a text is mostly about.
- the title of an article may have a clue to its topic.

PRACTICE 1: Ask and Answer Questions About a Main Topic Say: You can often learn the main topic of a text from its title. Sometimes, other parts of the text tell you about the main topic.

Reread the story's title and draw attention to the illustration on Teacher Page T257. Say: Just from the picture, what do you think the topic of the text might be? Pause for responses. It might be about a family at the beach. Point to the title. From the title, you know the topic is sandcastles. You can use the picture to ask questions about the topic, such as *How big is a sandcastle?* What other questions can you ask based on the picture?

☑ **MONITOR PROGRESS** Display Student Page S260. Read it aloud.

> At the beach or in a sandbox, building castles is fun! All you need is sand and water. Having additional tools can make your work more interesting.

Ask: What is this paragraph about? (building sandcastles) Have students tell you a question they could ask about building sandcastles.

IF… students cannot pose a question about building sandcastles, THEN… let them study the illustration on Teacher Page T257, and prompt them to ask how the family made the structure shown.

Lesson 44 | Identify Main Topic and Key Details

PRACTICE 2: Ask and Answer Questions About Key Details Say: Texts have many details. Some are key details. Without them, the text would not make sense. Key details teach about the topic. Other details are interesting, but you could still understand the text without them.

Display or distribute Student Page S261, and read it aloud. Ask students to listen for key details.

REMIND STUDENTS THAT...
- a topic is what a text is mostly about.
- they can ask and answer questions about a topic.

> Begin with sand and water. Do tests to find out how much water you need. Too much water will make the sand wet. Too little water will keep the sand from sticking together.
> Mix sand and water in the bucket with a bottom. Make a ball of the sand and water in your hand. Does your ball of sand stay in shape when you set it on the ground? Then you have the right amount! You are ready to begin.

Ask: What are these paragraphs about? (using the right mix of sand and water) Which details in this text help you understand why you should test your mix? (the details about what goes wrong if there is too much or too little water)

☑ **MONITOR PROGRESS** Display and read aloud the same excerpt from Student Page S261. Ask: What does the detail about a ball of sand keeping its shape help you understand? (the right mixture of sand and water)

IF... students cannot interpret the detail about a ball of sand keeping its shape, THEN... invite them to act out the two paragraphs, and then pose the question again.

Lesson 44 | Identify Main Topic and Key Details

REMIND STUDENTS THAT...

- a topic is what a text is mostly about.
- they can ask and answer questions about a topic.
- key details help readers understand a text.
- they can ask and answer questions about key details.

PRACTICE 3: Retell the Main Topic and Key Details Have students follow along while you read aloud Student Page S262.

> Start by making your biggest shapes. Use your hands to pile the sand, or use the bucket without the bottom. Fill the bucket with wet sand, turn the bucket over, tap the sides, and push gently on the sand while you lift the bucket off. There is your first tower!
>
> After that, make more towers with the bucket, or use cups of different sizes. Use a shovel to dig. Use a spatula to smooth corners or rough spots. A spoon and a knife can help you make more shapes and carve details.

Ask: What is the main topic of these paragraphs? (how to build a sandcastle) What are the key details in these paragraphs that tell about how to build a sandcastle? (Sample response: The first paragraph tells how to make the first tower of the sandcastle with your hands or the bucket without the bottom. The second paragraph tells how to make more towers with the bucket or cups of different sizes. It also tells what to use the shovel, spatula, spoon, and knife for.)

☑ **INDEPENDENT PRACTICE** Reread Teacher Pages T257–T258 aloud as students follow along. Have students work independently to identify the main topic and key details of "Sandcastles." Then call on individual students to retell the main topic and key details of the article in their own words. Provide corrective feedback as needed.

IF... students struggle to retell the main topic and key details,
THEN... create a three-step sequence diagram and use it to help students describe testing the sand-water mix, making the first tower, and adding details to their sandcastles.

Lesson 44   Identify Main Topic and Key Details

Sandcastles

At the beach or in a sandbox, building castles is fun! All you need is sand and water. Having additional tools can make your work more interesting.

Before you stop, make sure to use your imagination. Make a sandcastle like nobody else's. That's the most fun of all!

Lesson 44   Identify Main Topic and Key Details

At the beach or in a sandbox, building castles is fun! All you need is sand and water. Having additional tools can make your work more interesting.

Lesson 44   Identify Main Topic and Key Details

Begin with sand and water. Do tests to find out how much water you need. Too much water will make the sand wet. Too little water will keep the sand from sticking together.

Mix sand and water in the bucket with a bottom. Make a ball of the sand and water in your hand. Does your ball of sand stay in shape when you set it on the ground? Then you have the right amount! You are ready to begin.

Start by making your biggest shapes. Use your hands to pile the sand, or use the bucket without the bottom. Fill the bucket with wet sand, turn the bucket over, tap the sides, and push gently on the sand while you lift the bucket off. There is your first tower!

After that, make more towers with the bucket, or use cups of different sizes. Use a shovel to dig. Use a spatula to smooth corners or rough spots. A spoon and a knife can help you make more shapes and carve details.

Lesson 45 | **Define Unfamiliar Words**

DIRECTIONS Follow along as your teacher reads aloud the title and article, "Underwater Fliers." Look at the picture.

Underwater Fliers

Adélie (uh DAY lee) penguins live in Antarctica, an area covered in ice. The water around Antarctica is ice cold. Adélie penguins spend hours or days flying through the icy water. They do this in order to get food for their babies, called chicks. Adélie parents come up to breathe every minute or so.

Adélie penguins eat small animals called krill. Krill look like tiny shrimp. Billions of tons of krill live in Antarctic waters. Every kind of penguin in Antarctica needs krill to survive.

Underwater Fliers, *continued*

To find food, Adélie parents dive in the icy water. They tuck their heads to stay streamlined. They hold their feet by their tails to steer. To fly underwater they use their wings, just like birds in the air do. Water is much heavier than air. Flying underwater is much harder than flying in air. Penguins have very strong chest and wing muscles. You could say they use their wings like flippers. When penguins fly, they swim.

Adélie penguins return to shore to feed their chicks. Where the land is rocky or icy, the penguins jump straight out of the water. They can sometimes jump more than 9 feet (3 meters) into the air! Their hungry chicks are happy to see them.

Lesson 45 | Define Unfamiliar Words

INTRODUCE Explain that people are always learning new words. Say: Sometimes a new word makes sense right away, but often you have to stop and find out what the new word means.

MODEL Distribute or display Student Page S265 and read it aloud.

Underwater Fliers

Adélie (uh DAY lee) penguins live in Antarctica, an area covered in ice. The water around Antarctica is ice cold. Adélie penguins spend hours or days flying through the icy water. They do this in order to get food for their babies, called chicks. Adélie parents come up to breathe every minute or so.

TEACH Read the first sentence aloud. Say: Antarctica is where the penguins live, so it must be a place. How could I find out more about it? Reference materials, such as dictionaries and encyclopedias, can be good ways to learn more.

Read the first sentence and point to *covered*. Say: I know that a *cover* can be a lid or something that goes on top of something else. I think *covered* means "on top of something." If the area is *covered* in ice, that means ice is on top of it. That makes sense. Later, I can check a dictionary or ask questions to make sure I know the correct meaning of *covered*.

Read the last sentence and point to *breathe*. Say: I know that breath comes out of my mouth. To *breathe* means to make air go in and out of my mouth. Tell students when they see an unfamiliar word, they can use what they know to guess what it means.

RI.K.4 With prompting and support, ask and answer questions about unknown words in a text.

L.K.4 Determine or clarify the meaning of unknown and multiple-meaning words and phrases based on *kindergarten reading and content.*

See also **L.K.4.b**

OBJECTIVES:
- Ask about unfamiliar words.
- Tell about unfamiliar words.
- Use strategies to define unfamiliar words.

BUILD VOCABULARY

Use Prefixes
Point out *return* in the last paragraph.

Say: *Return* begins with the prefix *re-.* This word part has the meaning "again."

Read aloud the sentence with *return.* "Adélie penguins return to shore to feed their chicks." The penguins *turn again,* or come back to, the shore.

Have students identify other *re-* words and explain how the prefix helps determine the meaning of those words.

Lesson 45 | Define Unfamiliar Words

REMIND
STUDENTS
THAT...

• people are always learning new words.

• there are many ways to find out the meaning of a new word.

PRACTICE 1: Ask About Unfamiliar Words Remind students that a question often begins with the word *who, what, when, where, why,* or *how.* Say: When you hear an unfamiliar word, you can ask questions to learn what it means. Some questions are: *What do I already know about this word? What other word does this word sound like? Where can I find out more about this word? Who can I ask about this word?*

Distribute or display Student Page S266 and read the paragraph aloud.

> Adélie penguins eat small animals called krill. Krill look like tiny shrimp. Billions of tons of krill live in Antarctic waters. Every kind of penguin in Antarctica needs krill to survive.

Say: You can ask questions to learn what the word *krill* means. I will help you get started. What is the paragraph mostly about? **(what the penguins eat)** What other questions could we ask? **Pause for responses.** Some questions could be *Does* krill *refer to what a penguin eats?* or *What is krill like?*

☑ **MONITOR PROGRESS** Display or distribute Student Page S266. Read the following sentences aloud several times.

> Water is much heavier than air. Flying underwater is much harder than flying in air. Penguins have very strong chest and wing muscles.

Have students articulate questions they could ask to learn the meaning of the word *muscles.*

IF... students struggle to pose questions about the word *muscles,*
THEN... point out that the sentences compare and contrast moving in air and in water. Help students see that muscles help penguins swim in water.

Lesson 45 | Define Unfamiliar Words

PRACTICE 2: Talk About Unfamiliar Words Say: When you have guessed or learned the meaning of an unfamiliar word, you can talk about it with others.

Display or distribute Student Page S267. Read it aloud.

> Adélie penguins eat small animals called krill. Krill look like tiny shrimp. Billions of tons of krill live in Antarctic waters. Every kind of penguin in Antarctica needs krill to survive.

Ask students to tell you what the word *survive* means by using details in the text. Ask: What do penguins do with krill? (eat them) How important are krill to penguins? (Krill are important. All penguins in Antarctica need them.) So if penguins need krill to survive, what do you think *survive* means? ("to live" or "to stay alive")

☑ **MONITOR PROGRESS** Display the same paragraph from Student Page S267 and read it aloud again. Ask: What do you think the word *billions* means? How do details about penguins and krill help you understand *billions*?

IF... students cannot infer that *billions* is a very high number,
THEN... refer back to the passage and point out that every kind of penguin eats krill. Krill are very small. For penguins to survive, they must eat a large amount of krill.

REMIND STUDENTS THAT...
- unfamiliar words may sound like words they already know.
- they can ask questions to learn about unfamiliar words.

Lesson 45 | Define Unfamiliar Words

- they can ask questions to learn about unfamiliar words.
- there are many ways to find out the meaning of a new word.

PRACTICE 3: Use Strategies to Identify Unfamiliar Words Remind students they can use references, ask questions, look for smaller words, and try substituting a definition to explore the meaning of an unfamiliar word. Display or distribute Student Page S268 and read the first excerpt aloud.

> To find food, Adélie parents dive in the icy water. They tuck their heads to stay streamlined. They hold their feet by their tails to steer.

Ask students to picture a penguin in their minds. Reread the sentences, and then ask: What does the word *streamlined* mean? Guide students to use the context and prior knowledge of the words *stream* and *line* to guess a meaning of *streamlined*. Demonstrate *streamlined* by tucking your head and making your body as tight as possible, like a diver, to give students a visual. Also show students how to confirm the definition in a dictionary.

☑ **INDEPENDENT PRACTICE** Display or distribute Student Page S268 and read the second excerpt aloud.

> Penguins have very strong chest and wing muscles. You could say they use their wings like flippers. When penguins fly, they swim.

Ask students to use strategies to determine a meaning of the word *flippers*.

IF... students struggle to suggest a meaning for the word *flippers*,
THEN... demonstrate a flying motion with your arms, ask how a swimmer might use the motion, then return to the sentences and help students infer that flippers push on or through water.

Underwater Fliers

Adélie (uh DAY lee) penguins live in Antarctica, an area covered in ice. The water around Antarctica is ice cold. Adélie penguins spend hours or days flying through the icy water. They do this in order to get food for their babies, called chicks. Adélie parents come up to breathe every minute or so.

Lesson 45 | Define Unfamiliar Words

Adélie penguins eat small animals called krill.
Krill look like tiny shrimp. Billions of tons of krill
live in Antarctic waters. Every kind of penguin
in Antarctica needs krill to survive.

Water is much heavier than air. Flying underwater
is much harder than flying in air. Penguins have
very strong chest and wing muscles.

Lesson 45 | **Define Unfamiliar Words**

Adélie penguins eat small animals called krill. Krill look like tiny shrimp. Billions of tons of krill live in Antarctic waters. Every kind of penguin in Antarctica needs krill to survive.

Lesson 45   Define Unfamiliar Words

To find food, Adélie parents dive in the icy water. They tuck their heads to stay streamlined. They hold their feet by their tails to steer.

Penguins have very strong chest and wing muscles. You could say they use their wings like flippers. When penguins fly, they swim.

ASSESSMENT
LESSONS 44–45

Reading Informational Text

ASSESS MASTERY Use this Checkpoint to assess students' mastery of the Level A Reading standards listed here.

ADMINISTER THE TEST Administer the Checkpoint orally to each student. Distribute copies of the following page. Read aloud the passage as students follow along. Then read aloud questions 1–4 below and have students respond. Check their answers using the Scoring chart.

1. What are two key instructions about the water for pet fish?
2. What is the main topic of "Your New Pet Fish"?
3. Which words give the best clue to the meaning of *regularly*: "every week," "Water gets dirty," or "things living in it"?
4. The word *steady* can have these meanings: "staying the same," "calm," or "regular." Which meaning makes the most sense in the passage?

SCORING

SKILL/LESSON	STANDARD	ANSWER	SCORING
1. Identify Main Topic and Key Details (Lesson 44)	**RI.K.1**	Keep the temperature steady at the beginning, and change some of the water every week.	_____ / 2
2. Identify Main Topic and Key Details (Lesson 44)	**RI.K.2**	how to take care of pet fish	_____ / 1
3. Define Unfamiliar Words (Lesson 45)	**RI.K.4**	"every week"	_____ / 1
4. Define Unfamiliar Words (Lesson 45)	**L.K.4**	"staying the same"	_____ / 1

An overall score of 80% is typically considered mastery. Use your judgment and your individual students' needs as well to determine skill mastery.

IF... you determine that students have not demonstrated sufficient mastery of one or more skills,
THEN... review needed skills, going back to the lessons to reteach and scaffold as needed.

RI.K.1 With prompting and support, ask and answer questions about key details in a text.

RI.K.2 With prompting and support, identify the main topic and retell key details of a text.

RI.K.4 With prompting and support, ask and answer questions about unknown words in a text.

L.K.4 Determine or clarify the meaning of unknown and multiple-meaning words and phrases based on *kindergarten reading and content*.

ASSESSMENT
LESSONS 44–45   **Reading Informational Text**

Your New Pet Fish
by Delia Clark

Congratulations! You have brought home your new pets. These healthy fish will be easy to take care of if you do just three things.

1. Keep the temperature steady. Leave your fish in their bags. Float the bags in your fish tank for half an hour. This makes the temperature in the bags the same as it is in the tank. Then, open the bags and let your fish swim out!

2. Do not feed the fish too much! Follow the instructions you got at the pet store.

3. Change some of their water every week. Water gets dirty with things living in it. Your fish need fresh water regularly.

If you really like taking care of your fish, think about moving them to a big tank. Then you can control the water temperature and make sure their water is clean all the time.

Lesson 46	Examine the Presentation of Information

DIRECTIONS Follow along as your teacher reads aloud the title and the passage, "Sedan or Sports Car?" Look at the pictures.

Sedan or Sports Car?
by Jenna Burns

Today, people have many choices of cars. Cars come in many different types and sizes. People who like the outdoors often drive a kind of car called an SUV. Police have cruisers. Families have vans.

At one time, there were not that many different kinds of cars. Drivers used to have one main choice: sedan or sports car?

A sedan has a hard top and either two or four doors. A sedan can seat four or more people. A sedan can be plain or fancy. Long ago, sedans looked like the one in the picture. People drove these cars for fun. Of course, they also used them to get from one place to another. Sedans are great for families.

Lesson 46 | **Examine the Presentation of Information**

Sedan or Sports Car?
continued

Sports cars are for fun. Some sports cars used to look like the one in the picture. Does it look fun to you? 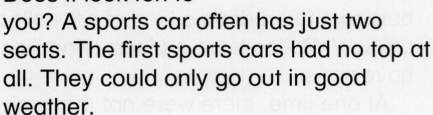 A sports car often has just two seats. The first sports cars had no top at all. They could only go out in good weather.

Sports cars are great for one or two people, but they are not so great for families. Most sports cars do not have backseats. Their trunks are tiny. Sports cars are light and fast.

What kind of car would you like to have? Which one is best for you? Would you like a sedan? You could take it to school or go on vacation. Or would you like a sports car? It would be fun to drive. You could also take it to school like a sedan. However, for a family vacation, it might be too small!

Lesson 46 | Examine the Presentation of Information

INTRODUCE Say: *Authors write words. When you write a letter or a story or a report, you are its author.*

MODEL Display or distribute Student Page S273 and read it aloud.

Sedan or Sports Car? ·········· title
by Jenna Burns ················ author

Today, people have many choices of cars. Cars come in many different types and sizes. People who like the outdoors often drive a kind of car called an SUV. Police have cruisers. Families have vans.

At one time, there were not that many different kinds of cars. Drivers used to have one main choice: sedan or sports car? ············· topic

---

TEACH Point to the byline. Say: *The author's name is Jenna Burns. The title gives a clue to her topic.* **Point to the last line of the excerpt.** *The author says people had to choose whether to drive a sedan or a sports car. I will look in the text for the points she makes and the reasons she gives for her points.*

Read aloud the following sentences from "Sedan or Sports Car?": *Sedans are great for families.* and *Sports cars are great for one or two people, but they are not so great for families.* Say: *The author has two key points: sedans are good for families, but sports cars are great for one or two people. What reasons support these points?* **Pause for student responses.** *The author writes, "A sedan has a hard top and either two or four doors. A sedan can seat four or more people." That sounds like a good reason for a family to have a sedan. She also writes, "Most sports cars do not have backseats. Their trunks are tiny." That is a reason sports cars would not be good for a family.*

RI.K.6 Name the author and illustrator of a text and define the role of each in presenting the ideas or information in a text.

RI.K.8 With prompting and support, identify the reasons an author gives to support points in a text.

See also **L.K.4.b**

OBJECTIVES:
- Identify an author and the author's role.
- Identify the author's key points.
- Identify reasons that support each point.

BUILD VOCABULARY

Word Parts as Clues to Meaning
Point out plural nouns in the first paragraph. (*choices, cars, types, sizes, cruisers, vans*)

Say: *When I see a word that ends in -s or -es, I have a clue that the word might be a plural noun. I know that both those spellings show that a word means "more than one."*

Have students look through classroom books to find words that end with *-ing*. Have them use the above strategy to explain how that word part gives a clue to a word's part of speech (usually a verb) and its meaning.

Lesson 46 | Examine the Presentation of Information

- all texts have at least one author.
- a text may have an author and an illustrator.

PRACTICE 1: Identify the Author's Role Hold up a dictionary or other nonfiction text. Ask: Did someone write this book? Help students acknowledge that someone wrote it. When you read words on pages, you know that an author wrote them. You may not always know the name of an author. Sometimes, books have more than one author. However, we do always know that an author is the person who presents ideas and information in a text.

Display or distribute Student Page S274. Point to each line as you read the page aloud.

Sedan or Sports Car?
by Jenna Burns

Today, people have many choices of cars.

Point to the byline. Say: This line tells me who the author is. The author of this passage is Jenna Burns. She wrote the article we just read. That article has the title "Sedan or Sports Car?"

☑ **MONITOR PROGRESS** Have students choose a book from a classroom library or a textbook. Ask students to point to the author's name and explain what the person has done.

IF... students cannot identify the author and define the author's role,
THEN... share several fiction and nonfiction texts in the classroom and discuss who provided the words in each text.

Lesson 46 | Examine the Presentation of Information

PRACTICE 2: Identify the Author's Key Points Display or distribute Student Page S275. Read the paragraph aloud. Encourage students to listen for the author's key point.

> A sedan has a hard top and either two or four doors. A sedan can seat four or more people. A sedan can be plain or fancy. Long ago, sedans looked like the one in the picture. People drove these cars for fun. Of course, they also used them to get from one place to another. Sedans are great for families.

Ask: What information does the author include about a sedan? **Encourage students to give details that describe a sedan.** It has a hard top, it can seat four or more people, and it can be plain or fancy.

Explain that the author uses pieces of information to make a point. Say: The information about the sedan tells me that the author's point in this paragraph is that sedans are great for families.

☑ **MONITOR PROGRESS** Read aloud the following paragraph from Teacher Page T272.

Sports cars are for fun. Some sports cars used to look like the one in the picture. Does it look fun to you? A sports car often has just two seats. The first sports cars had no top at all. They could only go out in good weather.

Ask: In this paragraph, what is the author's key point about sports cars?

IF... students do not recognize the key point that sports cars are for fun, THEN... tell students to pay special attention to the first sentence and the last sentence, and then reread the paragraph for students.

| **Lesson 46** | **Examine the Presentation of Information** |

REMIND
STUDENTS
THAT...

• an author provides
information and ideas
in a text.

• in informational texts,
authors make key
points.

PRACTICE 3: Identify Reasons that Support the Author's Points Say: If I say,
"vanilla is the best flavor of ice cream," do you know why I think that? Pause for
responses. No, you probably do not know my reason. You would need to hear
my reason. In the same way, an author has to tell you his or her reasons for the
key points in a text.

Display or distribute Student Page S276, and read the first paragraph aloud.

> A sedan has a hard top and either two or four
> doors. A sedan can seat four or more people. A
> sedan can be plain or fancy. Long ago, sedans
> looked like the one in the picture. People drove
> these cars for fun. Of course, they also used
> them to get from one place to another. Sedans
> are great for families.

Say: Imagine there are five people in your family. Why would a sedan be good
for your family? (A sedan can seat four or more people.) This is one reason
that supports the author's point that a sedan would be great for families.

☑ **INDEPENDENT PRACTICE** Distribute Student Page 276. Read the second
paragraph aloud as students follow along.

> Sports cars are great for one or two people,
> but they are not so great for families. Most
> sports cars do not have backseats. Their trunks
> are tiny. Sports cars are light and fast.

Have students work independently to identify the author's point and two
reasons that support that point. Call on volunteers to share their responses
aloud. Provide corrective feedback as needed.

IF… students have difficulty identifying reasons that support the author's point
that sports cars are "not so great for families,"
THEN… ask guiding questions, such as Do sports cars have backseats? Do they
have big trunks? How would these features affect a family going on a car trip?

Sedan or Sports Car?

by Jenna Burns

Today, people have many choices of cars. Cars come in many different types and sizes. People who like the outdoors often drive a kind of car called an SUV. Police have cruisers. Families have vans.

At one time, there were not that many different kinds of cars. Drivers used to have one main choice: sedan or sports car?

Sedan or Sports Car?
by Jenna Burns

Today, people have many choices of cars.

Lesson 46   **Examine the Presentation of Information**

A sedan has a hard top and either two or four doors. A sedan can seat four or more people. A sedan can be plain or fancy. Long ago, sedans looked like the one in the picture. People drove these cars for fun. Of course, they also used them to get from one place to another. Sedans are great for families.

A sedan has a hard top and either two or four doors. A sedan can seat four or more people. A sedan can be plain or fancy. Long ago, sedans looked like the one in the picture. People drove these cars for fun. Of course, they also used them to get from one place to another. Sedans are great for families.

Sports cars are great for one or two people, but they are not so great for families. Most sports cars do not have backseats. Their trunks are tiny. Sports cars are light and fast.

Lesson 47   Understand Illustrations in a Text

DIRECTIONS Follow along as your teacher reads aloud the title and passage, "Living in the Desert." Look at the illustrations.

Living in the Desert

Deserts are very dry places. The Sonoran Desert in the United States can get very hot during the day. But it can become very cold at night.

Deserts are very hard places to live. Water is hard to find. Some plants such as cactuses can store water, or hold it to use later. Animals get water from their food. For example, kangaroo rats never need to drink water. They get all the water they need from the seeds they find on the desert floor.

Kangaroo rats and pocket mice build homes underground. This helps keep them cool during the hot days. It also protects them from snakes. At night, these little animals come out of their homes to look for food.

Lesson 47 | **Understand Illustrations in a Text**

Living in the Desert, *continued*

The diamondback rattlesnake spends much of the day resting. It lives under rocks or other places to get out of the sun. Sometimes it even steals the underground nests of other animals! The rattlesnake will eat a mouse if it catches one.

Rattlesnakes can also sense the heat of other animals. This helps the snakes find food. It also helps them slither away from animals that want to attack them.

The gray fox is another animal that lives in the desert. Like other desert animals, the gray fox does most of its hunting at night.

Lesson 47 | Understand Illustrations in a Text

INTRODUCE Say: You know that authors write words. Many texts you see also have pictures. Sometimes, the author makes the pictures. Other times, an illustrator draws pictures to go with the author's text.

MODEL Display or distribute Student Page S279. Have students study the illustration as you read aloud the text.

Kangaroo rats and pocket mice build homes underground. This helps keep them cool during the hot days. It also protects them from snakes. At night, these little animals come out of their homes to look for food.

TEACH Ask: What do you see in this picture? Encourage students to point out every detail, including the texture of the earth, the background, and the appearance of the animals. Where is the mouse? Point to the words *homes underground* and say: You can see that the illustration shows the mouse's underground home. Point to the words *mice* and *snakes* as you read each one. Where do you see snakes in the picture? Point out that the illustration shows animals mentioned in the text.

Say: The text says the underground home protects mice from snakes. What details in the illustration help show you that the mouse's home helps protect it from snakes? Guide students to suggest that the snakes might be looking for a mouse to eat, but the mouse is hidden in its underground home. The picture helps you understand that a snake hunts other animals for food, so the mouse needs a home that hides and protects it.

RI.K.7 With prompting and support, describe the relationship between illustrations and the text in which they appear (e.g., what person, place, thing, or idea in the text an illustration depicts).

See also **L.K.5.b**

OBJECTIVES:

- Describe illustrations.
- Link illustrations to a text.
- Explain how illustrations clarify a text.

BUILD VOCABULARY

Use Antonyms

Say: Words that mean the opposite of each other are antonyms. What is the antonym of *up*? (*down*)

Direct students to look at the first paragraph. Read aloud sentences containing antonyms. "The Sonoran Desert in the United States can get very hot during the day. But it can become very cold at night." What pair of antonyms do you hear? (*hot, cold*)

Have students discuss antonym pairs that they know or find antonyms for words in the passage.

Lesson 47 | Understand Illustrations in a Text

REMIND STUDENTS THAT...

- sometimes an author prepares text and illustrations at the same time.

- sometimes a separate person draws pictures to go with a text.

PRACTICE 1: Describe Illustrations Display or distribute Student Page S280. Read the text aloud.

The diamondback rattlesnake spends much of the day resting. It lives under rocks or other places to get out of the sun.

Ask students to describe the snakes in the picture. What do they look like? Where are they? What are they doing? Help them note key details such as the diamonds on the left-hand snake's back and the rattle at the end of its tail.

☑ **MONITOR PROGRESS** Have students study the same illustration on Student Page S280 as you read the following sentence about the diamondback rattlesnake from Teacher Page T278: *Sometimes it even steals the underground nests of other animals!*

Say: Describe the nest in the illustration. Use your own words and also words from the passage.

IF... students do not use relevant words to explain that the nest is an underground home of a desert rat or mouse,
THEN... direct students to look only at the bottom right corner of the illustration and have them examine it more closely.

Lesson 47 | Understand Illustrations in a Text

PRACTICE 2: Link Illustrations to Text Display or distribute Student
Page S281. Read aloud the sentence about plants. Have students point to the
plants in the illustration.

Some plants such as cactuses can store
water, or hold it to use later.

The gray fox is another animal that lives in
the desert.

Ask: What information do you learn about the plants from the text? What
information do you learn from the illustration?

☑ **MONITOR PROGRESS** Display or distribute Student Page S281. Read
aloud the sentence about the fox. Ask: How does the illustration connect to
this sentence?

IF… students cannot recognize the fox in the illustration,
THEN… remind them that a fox is an animal, and guide them to find the only
animal in the illustration.

Lesson 47	Understand Illustrations in a Text

PRACTICE 3: Explain How Illustrations Clarify Text Explain that usually an illustration matches what an author writes. Therefore, an illustration can help make the text clear.

Direct students to look closely at the illustration on Teacher Page T278. Read this sentence aloud, emphasizing the word *most*: *Like other desert animals, the gray fox does most of its hunting at night.*

Ask: Does *most* mean *all*? **(no)** Does the fox do some of its hunting during the day? **(yes)** What part of the illustration makes this clear? **(the sun)**

☑ **INDEPENDENT PRACTICE** Display or distribute Student Page S282. Read the sentence aloud. Have students examine the illustration independently Say: Look at the snake on the right. How does the illustration help you understand what it means to "slither away"?

It also helps them slither away from animals that want to attack them.

IF… students cannot explain how the illustration of the snake relates to the verb *slither,*
THEN… guide students to connect prior knowledge about how snakes move with what is shown in the illustration, using the phrase *slither away.*

Lesson 47 Understand Illustrations in a Text

Kangaroo rats and pocket mice build homes underground. This helps keep them cool during the hot days. It also protects them from snakes. At night, these little animals come out of their homes to look for food.

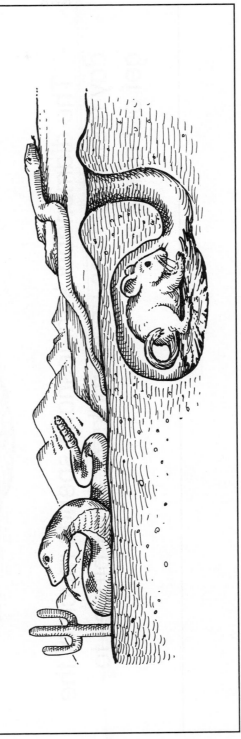

Lesson 47 | Understand Illustrations in a Text

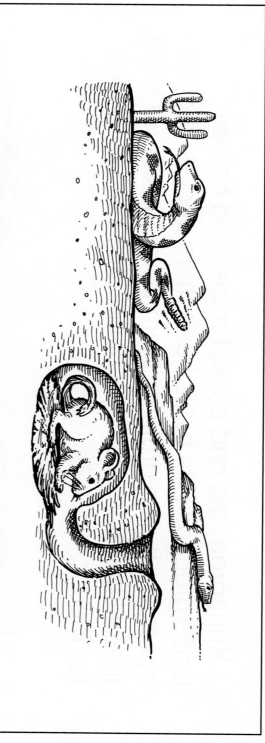

The diamondback rattlesnake spends much of the day resting. It lives under rocks or other places to get out of the sun.

Some plants such as cactuses can store water, or hold it to use later.

The gray fox is another animal that lives in the desert.

Lesson 47 | **Understand Illustrations in a Text**

It also helps them slither away from animals that
want to attack them.

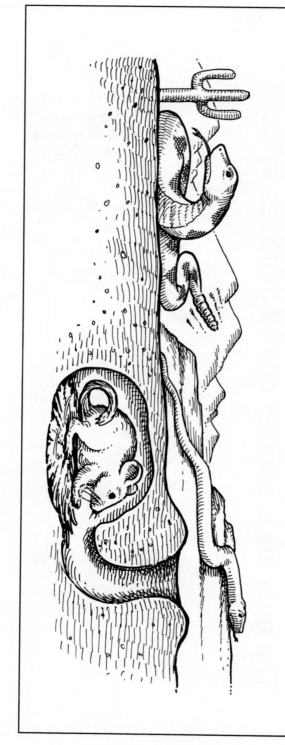

Lesson 48 | **Compare Texts**

DIRECTIONS Look at the titles and illustrations. Follow along as your teacher reads aloud "New York Is the Place for Pizza!," "Chicago Is the Place for Pizza!," and "The Absolute Best Place for Pizza!"

New York Is the Place for Pizza!

New York-style pizza is the most delicate, delicious dining you'll ever have. Its crust is so thin that you can fold it like paper. Its toppings are so gooey that you can almost drink them. Grab a slice. Have a bite, and then have another. You'll love New York pizza!

Chicago Is the Place for Pizza!

Nothing, *nothing,* satisfies your hunger like a deep-dish Chicago-style pizza. Imagine a slice of pie so thick you need a knife and fork to eat it. The filling is cheesy rich. It is tomato tasty. Mmmmmm . . . dive in to a Chicago pizza today!

Lesson 48 | **Compare Texts**

The Absolute Best Place for Pizza!

Paragon Pizza is *the* place to eat. We have stores from New York to Alaska. Our chefs are food geniuses. Whether you want a New York-style slice to hold in your hand or a Chicago deep-dish pie in a pan, Paragon Pizza will amaze you. You'll soon be back for more!

Lesson 48 | Compare Texts

INTRODUCE Say: A text's topic is what the text is about. You can hear or read more than one text about the same topic. When you think about different texts about the same topic, you can figure out how they are alike and different.

MODEL Display or pass out Student Page S285. Read aloud the following sentences from the texts.

topics

New York-style pizza is the most delicate, delicious dining you'll ever have.

Nothing, *nothing,* satisfies your hunger like a deep-dish Chicago-style pizza.

Paragon Pizza is *the* place to eat.

what the author wants reader to believe

TEACH If you wish, use a three-cell Venn diagram to record responses to the following questions. Ask: What topic do all three of these sentences have in common? (pizza) Point to the highlighted claims as you read each sentence aloud. What do all the authors want you to believe? (that their pizza is the best) Point to the highlighted topics. What does each author believe is the best? (a different pizza) Reiterate that the texts have the same topic and similar attitudes toward the topic. The texts are different, too. One author loves New York-style pizza. Another author loves Chicago-style pizza. The third author loves a restaurant that serves both kinds of pizza.

RI.K.9 With prompting and support, identify basic similarities in and differences between two texts on the same topic (e.g., in illustrations, descriptions, or procedures).

See also **L.K.5.d**

OBJECTIVES:
• Identify texts with the same topic.
• Describe text similarities.
• Describe text differences.

BUILD VOCABULARY

Shades of Meaning
Point out the word *grab* in "New York Is the Place for Pizza!"

Ask: What does *grab* mean? What are some other words that mean something similar? How are the other words different from *grab*? Students should suggest words such as *take, yank, hold,* and *snatch.*

Use a pencil or other object to act out the difference between *picking up* and *grabbing.*

Have students use the same strategy to demonstrate shades of meaning for other related words, such as *smile* and *grin* or *giggle* and *laugh.*

| Lesson 48 | Compare Texts |

- a topic is what a text is mostly about.
- they may hear or read more than one text about a topic.

PRACTICE 1: Identify Texts with the Same Topic With students, reread the three texts on Teacher Pages T283–T284. Display or distribute Student Page S286.

New York-style	Chicago-style

Guide students to use the graphic organizer to identify texts that address the topics. Ask: Which two texts have New York-style pizza as a topic? ("New York Is the Place for Pizza!" and "The Absolute Best Place for Pizza!") What key phrase tells you that the topic is New York-style pizza? (New York-style pizza) What does each text say about New York-style pizza? Review the descriptions of the pizza and reread the texts as necessary to help students respond.

☑ **MONITOR PROGRESS** Review Student Page S286. Then ask: Which two texts mention Chicago-style pizza? ("Chicago Is the Place for Pizza!" and "The Absolute Best Place for Pizza!") What words and phrases in each passage tell about the topic of Chicago-style pizza? Reread the texts as necessary to help students respond. (Sample answer: They both include "Chicago-style pizza." One text refers to a slice of pie so thick you need a knife and fork to eat it, with a filling that is "cheesy rich" and "tomato tasty." The Paragon text calls Chicago pizza a "deep-dish pie in a pan.")

IF… students cannot locate details about Chicago-style pizza in two texts, THEN… ask students to look or listen for the key phrase *Chicago-style pizza* and imagine how the pizza looks, smells, and tastes as they listen to you reread the texts, and then repeat the question.

Lesson 48 | Compare Texts

PRACTICE 2: Identify Text Similarities Display or distribute Student Pages S287 and S288. Read them aloud.

New York Is the Place for Pizza!

New York-style pizza is the most delicate, delicious dining you'll ever have. Its crust is so thin that you can fold it like paper. Its toppings are so gooey that you can almost drink them. Grab a slice. Have a bite, and then have another. You'll love New York pizza!

Chicago Is the Place for Pizza!

Nothing, *nothing,* satisfies your hunger like a deep-dish Chicago-style pizza. Imagine a slice of pie so thick you need a knife and fork to eat it. The filling is cheesy rich. It is tomato tasty. Mmmmmm . . . dive in to a Chicago pizza today!

Ask: What do these texts have in common? (They describe a kind of pizza in an appetizing way.) How do both authors try to make you hungry for their kind of pizza? Guide students to recognize that both authors describe what it will feel like to eat a slice of their pizza. If you are using a Venn diagram, add quotations to the New York and Chicago cells. These authors like different kinds of pizza, but they use a similar writing style to describe them.

☑ **MONITOR PROGRESS** Reread Student Pages S287 and S288 with students. Then ask: How are the two texts alike?

IF... students do not recognize that each text uses detailed sensory descriptions,
THEN... have them act out each description of eating, and then ask what is similar about their responses to two experiences.

Lesson 48 | Compare Texts

REMIND STUDENTS THAT…

• they will hear and read more than one text about a topic.

• two texts on the same topic will be different in some ways.

PRACTICE 3: Identify Text Differences Display or distribute Student Pages S287 and S288. Reread the texts aloud for students.

New York Is the Place for Pizza!

New York-style pizza is the most delicate, delicious dining you'll ever have. Its crust is so thin that you can fold it like paper. Its toppings are so gooey that you can almost drink them. Grab a slice. Have a bite, and then have another. You'll love New York pizza!

Chicago Is the Place for Pizza!

Nothing, *nothing,* satisfies your hunger like a deep-dish Chicago-style pizza. Imagine a slice of pie so thick you need a knife and fork to eat it. The filling is cheesy rich. It is tomato tasty. Mmmmmm . . . dive in to a Chicago pizza today!

Say: These texts are both about pizza. What is different about these two texts? Have students focus on the final sentence in each text, and guide them to state that one text persuades readers to eat New York-style pizza and the other persuades readers to eat Chicago-style pizza. If you are using a Venn diagram, quote the final sentences in the New York and Chicago cells.

☑ **INDEPENDENT PRACTICE** Reread Teacher Pages T283–T284 aloud. Have individual students answer these questions to identify differences between the three texts: *Which text talks about both New York- and Chicago-style pizza? Which one only talks about a [thin/thick] slice of pizza? What does it say about the [thin/thick] slice of pizza?*

IF… students have difficulty answering the questions,
THEN… reread the texts and help them identify key details that are unique to each text.

Lesson 48 | **Compare Texts**

New York-style pizza is the most delicate, delicious dining you'll ever have.

Nothing, *nothing*, satisfies your hunger like a deep-dish Chicago-style pizza.

Paragon Pizza is *the* place to eat.

T-Chart

New York-style	Chicago-style

New York Is the Place for Pizza!

New York-style pizza is the most delicate, delicious dining you'll ever have. Its crust is so thin that you can fold it like paper. Its toppings are so gooey that you can almost drink them. Grab a slice. Have a bite, and then have another. You'll love New York pizza!

Chicago Is the Place for Pizza!

Nothing, *nothing*, satisfies your hunger like a deep-dish Chicago-style pizza. Imagine a slice of pie so thick you need a knife and fork to eat it. The filling is cheesy rich. It is tomato tasty. Mmmmmm . . . dive in to a Chicago pizza today!

ASSESSMENT
LESSONS 46–48

Reading Informational Text

ASSESS MASTERY Use this Checkpoint to assess students' mastery of the Level A Reading standards listed here.

ADMINISTER THE TEST Administer the Checkpoint orally to each student. Distribute copies of the following page. Read aloud the passages as students follow along. Then read aloud questions 1–4 below and have students respond. Check their answers using the Scoring chart.

1. Who is the author of the text about tomatoes? What reason does the author give for starting tomato plants indoors?
2. Which text does the illustration go with? How can you tell?
3. Which topic is in both texts: planting seeds, beans, or tomatoes?
4. What is different about the planting time in the two texts?

SCORING

SKILL/LESSON	STANDARD	ANSWER	SCORING
1. Examine the Presentation of Information (Lesson 46)	**RI.K.6, RI.K.8**	Indra Seth; In spring, it is still too cold for gardening outdoors.	_____ / 2
2. Understand Illustrations (Lesson 47)	**RI.K.7**	the text about beans; it shows plants in rows of soil outdoors	_____ / 2
3. Compare Two Texts (Lesson 48)	**RI.K.9**	planting seeds	_____ / 1
4. Compare Two Texts (Lesson 48)	**RI.K.9**	In the bean text, the planting time is when the ground is warm. In the tomato text, the planting time is when the ground is still too cold for a garden.	_____ / 1

An overall score of 80% is typically considered mastery. Use your judgment and your individual students' needs as well to determine skill mastery.

IF... you determine that students have not demonstrated sufficient mastery of one or more skills,
THEN... review needed skills, going back to the lessons to reteach and scaffold as needed.

RI.K.6 Name the author and illustrator of a text and define the role of each in presenting the ideas or information in a text.

RI.K.7 With prompting and support, describe the relationship between illustrations and the text in which they appear (e.g., what person, place, thing, or idea in the text an illustration depicts).

RI.K.8 With prompting and support, identify the reasons an author gives to support points in a text.

RI.K.9 With prompting and support, identify basic similarities in and differences between two texts on the same topic (e.g., in illustrations, descriptions, or procedures).

Reading Informational Text

Planting Beans
by Rob Gould

Have you ever opened a green bean and seen the seeds? You can plant those seeds outside. In about eight weeks, you will have beans to eat. Make sure the ground is warm before you plant. That way, your beans will grow quickly and be strong.

Starting Tomatoes Indoors
by Indra Seth

It is spring, but the ground is too cold for a garden. So begin your garden indoors! Plant some tiny tomato seeds in a sunny spot. The seeds will begin to sprout.

When the weather is warm, move the plants to the soil. Start by putting the plants outside for a few hours a day. Increase the time outdoors a bit each day for a week. Finally, add the plants to your garden. Soon you will have bright red tomatoes to add to your salads. Yum!

Lesson 49 | Ask and Answer Questions About a Prompt

INTRODUCE Explain to students that people often write about a topic to show that they know something about that topic. Say: In school, you will have assignments to draw or write about a topic.

MODEL Distribute Student Page S291 for students. Read aloud the prompt and complete the chart together.

Prompt: Give information about an animal you know about. Draw and describe the animal.

What is the topic?	What kind of writing is it?	What details do I include?
animal I know about	Does it give an opinion? no	details that describe the animal (words and pictures)
	Does it give information? yes	
	Does it tell a story? no	

TEACH Say: When you get an assignment, you must figure out exactly what you have to do. Asking and answering questions about the assignment will help you figure it out. First, find the topic. Read the prompt again. What are you supposed to draw and describe? Pause for responses. The topic in this assignment is an animal you know about. Write *animal I know about* in the left column.

Say: Sometimes an assignment will tell you the kind of writing you are supposed to do. You might give an opinion, give information or explain how something works, or tell a story. Reread the prompt and have students answer the questions in the middle column of the chart to determine the kind of writing.

Circle *describe* in the prompt. Say: This word tells you how to give information. Circle *Draw*. You can draw to help describe the animal. These words tell you how to give information. Explain that in the right column, students can state that they must describe, or tell about, the animal through both drawing pictures and writing words.

W.K.1 Use a combination of drawing, dictating, and writing to compose opinion pieces in which they tell a reader the topic or the name of the book they are writing about and state an opinion or preference about the topic or book (e.g., *My favorite book is . . .*).

W.K.2 Use a combination of drawing, dictating, and writing to compose informative/explanatory texts in which they name what they are writing about and supply some information about the topic.

W.K.3 Use a combination of drawing, dictating, and writing to narrate a single event or several loosely linked events, tell about the events in the order in which they occurred, and provide a reaction to what happened.

OBJECTIVES:

• Ask questions to identify the topic in a prompt.

• Ask questions to understand the type of writing requested in a prompt.

• Use a chart to record all aspects of a writing prompt.

Writing T • 291

| Lesson 49 | Ask and Answer Questions About a Prompt |

PRACTICE 1: Opinion Writing Say: Some assignments may ask you for your opinion. An opinion is what you think about a topic. For example, an assignment might ask you to answer a question, such as *Which juice do you think is best?* The topic of the assignment is "the best juice." You have to decide what you think about it and why you have that opinion. **Help students understand that an opinion is not right or wrong, but it can be supported by reasons.**

Distribute or display Student Page S292. Read the prompt aloud for students.

Opinion Writing

Prompt: Draw and write an opinion about which art supplies are the best for coloring: colored pencils, crayons, paints, or markers.

What is the topic?	What kind of writing is it?	What details do I include?

Say: To find the topic, you can ask *What is this assignment about?* **Guide students to identify the topic of the prompt as "art supplies for coloring."**

Say: You can ask *What is the assignment asking me to do?* to find out what kind of writing you need to do. **Make sure students understand that the assignment asks students to give an opinion.** What other details must your drawing and writing include? (the choice of pencils, crayons, paints, or markers)

Finally, reread the prompt aloud, emphasizing the word *best*. **Conclude by asking:** Which art supply do you think is the best?

☑ **MONITOR PROGRESS** Using the prompt above, have students tell you what should go in each column of the chart on Student Page S292. Encourage them to pay extra attention to the *What kind of writing is it?* column.

IF... students cannot identify the topic,
THEN... rephrase the prompt as a question and ask students what they would draw in response.

Lesson 49 | Ask and Answer Questions About a Prompt

PRACTICE 2: Informative/Explanatory Writing Say: When you know the basic topic of an assignment, ask questions to learn more about what you are supposed to do. The assignment may have details about the kind of writing as well as the topic. Pay close attention when an assignment says "be sure to" or "include." Those words are clues to details.

Distribute or display Student Page S293 and read it aloud.

Ask: What is the topic? (weather) What questions does the assignment want you to answer about the topic? (*What is the weather like where I live? How is the weather here different during different times of the year?*)

Read the prompt aloud again. Ask: What kind of writing should you do? (describe the weather) Is this an opinion, an explanation or information, or a story? (information)

☑ **MONITOR PROGRESS** Using the prompt above, have students tell you what should go in each column of the chart on Student Page S293. Encourage them to pay extra attention to the *What details do I include?* column.

IF... students misunderstand the prompt,
THEN... read the prompt several times, posing questions about several words at a time (*Draw and describe, what the weather is like, where you live*, etc.) to make sure students understand each component of the prompt.

REMIND STUDENTS THAT. . .
- they can figure out the topic of an assignment.
- they can ask and answer questions to figure out the kind of writing an assignment is asking them to do.
- they can use a chart to make sure they understand every part of an assignment.

Lesson 49 | Ask and Answer Questions About a Prompt

REMIND STUDENTS THAT. . .

- they can figure out the topic of an assignment.

- they can ask and answer questions to figure out the kind of writing an assignment is asking them to do.

- they can use a chart to make sure they understand every part of an assignment.

PRACTICE 3: Narrative Writing Say: Assignments usually list some details about what you must do or include. Point out that in narrative writing, students should include details about their characters, the action or events, and the place where the action happens. Distribute or display Student Page S294 and read it aloud.

Narrative Writing

Prompt: Draw and tell a story about an unexpected hero who saves the school. The hero can be any person, animal, or creature.

What is the topic?	What kind of writing is it?	What details do I include?

Explain that a *narrative* tells a story. Say: The topic of this assignment is a hero. What kind of hero? Read the prompt aloud again if necessary. Make sure students understand what *unexpected* means. Use questions to help them give you as many details about the hero as they can. What is the hero supposed to do? (save the school) What kind of writing does the assignment ask you to do? (tell a story) What are the other details in the assignment? (The hero can be a person, animal, or creature.)

☑ **INDEPENDENT PRACTICE** Using the prompt above, have students tell you what should go in each column of the chart on Student Page S294. Encourage them to pay extra attention to the *What is the topic?* and *What details do I include?* columns.

IF... students cannot separate details from the basic topic,
THEN... help them generate questions they should or could ask about the topic of a hero, such as these: *What kind of hero is in my story? When does my hero save the school? Where does my hero live? What can my hero do?*

Lesson 49   Ask and Answer Questions About a Prompt

Prompt: Give information about an animal you know about. Draw and describe the animal.

What is the topic?	What kind of writing is it?	What details do I include?
	Does it give an opinion?	
	Does it give information?	
	Does it tell a story?	

Lesson 49   Ask and Answer Questions About a Prompt

Opinion Writing

Prompt: Draw and write an opinion about which art supplies are the best for coloring: colored pencils, crayons, paints, or markers.

What is the topic?	What kind of writing is it?	What details do I include?

Lesson 49

Informative/Explanatory Writing

Prompt: Draw and describe what the weather is like where you live. Be sure to include descriptions about how the weather is different during different times of the year.

What is the topic?	What kind of writing is it?	What details do I include?

| Lesson 49 | Ask and Answer Questions About a Prompt |

Narrative Writing

Prompt: Draw and tell a story about an unexpected hero who saves the school. The hero can be any person, animal, or creature.

What is the topic?	What kind of writing is it?	What details do I include?

Lesson 50 | Use a Topic to Recall and Gather Information

INTRODUCE Explain that often writing assignments ask for students to draw on information they already know or gather information before they start drawing or writing their responses. Say: *Your experiences and what you already know can help you complete an assignment. Knowing where to find information can also help you.* Point out that students can use the topic of a writing assignment or prompt to help them complete this step.

MODEL Distribute or display Student Page S295 and read it aloud.

Informative/Explanatory Writing

Prompt: Give information about an animal you know about. Draw and describe the animal.

TEACH Point out that an important step in writing is to remember or gather information about a topic. Ask: *What is the topic of this assignment?* (an animal I know about) *What are you supposed to do?* (draw and describe it) *The assignment asks you to describe an animal you already know about. If you already know about it, you can use your knowledge to give a good description and draw a good picture.*

Point out that some writing assignments will ask students to explain a topic that they do not already know about. As an example, ask: *What if the assignment said that you should describe an animal you wish you knew more about? Where could you find information?* Guide students to name several print or digital resources, such as books, magazines, or websites. Offer additional suggestions, such as asking an expert or visiting a zoo, pet store, farm, or museum.

W.K.8 With guidance and support from adults, recall information from experiences or gather information from provided sources to answer a question.

OBJECTIVES:
- Recall relevant information to respond to a prompt.
- Gather information from sources to respond to a prompt.

Lesson 50 | Use a Topic to Recall and Gather Information

REMIND STUDENTS THAT. . .

- they know how to figure out the topic of an assignment.
- they may have had experiences that will help them answer questions.
- sources may contain information they can use to answer a question.

PRACTICE 1: Opinion Writing Remind students that an opinion is what they think about a topic. Explain that writers have to use information about a topic to support their opinion about that topic. Distribute or display Student Page S296 and read it aloud.

Opinion Writing

Prompt: Draw and write an opinion about which art supplies are the best for coloring: colored pencils, crayons, paints, or markers.

Ask: What is this assignment asking you to do? Make sure students understand the topic, what an opinion is, and their choices. Tell me about your experiences with each kind of art supply. Draw out details of how easy or difficult each art supply is to use, asking questions such as: What other materials do you need to use with this supply? For example, you might need a sharpener to use colored pencils. Are there enough colors, or too few or too many? Can you mix the colors?

Ask: Which kind of supply is your favorite for coloring? As students respond, ask: Why? Have them provide details from the discussion to support their opinions.

☑ **MONITOR PROGRESS** Display or distribute Student Page S296 and reread it aloud. Provide and read aloud the following sentence frames: *In my opinion, _____ are the best for coloring. This is because _____.*

Help students complete the frames. Ask: What would you draw to show this opinion?

IF... students cannot choose which medium is best, THEN... review with them the reasons they said they liked one of the materials the most. Point out that this is information from their experiences. Then help students use that information to complete the sentence frames.

Lesson 50 — Use a Topic to Recall and Gather Information

PRACTICE 2: Informative/Explanatory Writing Point out that in informational writing, an assignment will ask for students to explain information about a topic. Make available several books about weather or pictures of the local area along with a recent weather page from a website or a newspaper. Display or distribute Student Page S297 and read the prompt aloud.

Informative/Explanatory Writing

Prompt: Draw and describe what the weather is like where you live. Be sure to include descriptions about how the weather is different during different times of the year.

REMIND STUDENTS THAT. . .

- they know how to figure out the topic of an assignment.
- they may have had experiences that will help them answer questions.
- sources may contain information they can use to answer a question.

Ask: What is the topic of this assignment? (weather where I live) What do you already know about this topic? **Pause for responses.** You can use what you know to complete the assignment.

Then say: You can also use information from sources. Look at these sources. Discuss each source with students, asking questions such as: Which picture looks like good weather? What does that weather feel like? What does the website or the newspaper tell about weather? What other kind of weather happens here? Then reread the prompt and have students explain how they might use information from the sources in their responses.

☑ **MONITOR PROGRESS** Display or distribute Student Page S297. Reread the prompt, and then read aloud the following sentence frames for student responses:

In January, the weather where I live is _____.
In May, the weather is _____.
In October, the weather is _____.

IF... students cannot find useful information in the sources,
THEN... guide them to describe the pictures you have provided and ask them to describe how it would feel to be in the weather shown.

Lesson 50 | Use a Topic to Recall and Gather Information

PRACTICE 3: Narrative Writing Explain to students that many writers use information to help them write stories, even if those stories are fictional or not about real-life events. Say: When you get a narrative or story assignment, think about the information you already have about the topic. You can use your experiences as part of that information.

Distribute or display Student Page S298 and read the prompt aloud.

Narrative Writing

Prompt: Draw and tell a story about an unexpected hero who saves the school. The hero can be any person, animal, or creature.

Say: Think of what you already know about heroes. Use questions to guide student responses, such as: What stories have you already heard about heroes? What person, animal, or creature would be an *unexpected* hero? Why might the school need to be saved? How could your unexpected hero save the school? Point out that experiences students have had in school or books that they remember will help them make up a story. Give examples of nonviolent situations, such as starting a fundraiser to keep a school open.

☑ **INDEPENDENT PRACTICE** Display or distribute Student Page S298. Reread the prompt, and then read aloud the following sentence frames for student responses:

My unexpected hero will be _____.
The school will need to be saved from _____.
The hero will save the school by _____.

IF... students struggle to think of a plot,
THEN... provide a sample unexpected hero and a problem for the hero to solve, such as a saving a dog in a dangerous storm. Guide students to use what they know about dogs and storms in drawing a picture and completing the sentence frames.

Lesson 50 Use a Topic to Recall and Gather Information

Informative/Explanatory Writing

Prompt: Give information about an animal you know about. Draw and describe the animal.

Lesson 50 | Use a Topic to Recall and Gather Information

Opinion Writing

Prompt: Draw and write an opinion about which art supplies are the best for coloring: colored pencils, crayons, paints, or markers.

Informative/Explanatory Writing

Prompt: Draw and describe what the weather is like where you live. Be sure to include descriptions about how the weather is different during different times of the year.

In January, the weather where I live is _____.

In May, the weather is _____.

In October, the weather is _____.

Narrative Writing

Prompt: Draw and tell a story about an unexpected hero who saves the school. The hero can be any person, animal, or creature.

My unexpected hero will be _____.

The school will need to be saved from _____.

The hero will save the school by _____
_____
_____.

Lesson 51 | Add Details to Writing

INTRODUCE Show students an illustration in a picture book. Say: Tell me everything you see in this picture. Point to various parts of the picture as you encourage students to identify every detail in the illustration. You have just told me all of the details you see in this picture. You can add details to your drawings and writing to make them stronger.

MODEL Display Student Page S299 and read it aloud.

W.K.5 With guidance and support from adults, respond to questions and suggestions from peers and add details to strengthen writing as needed.

OBJECTIVES:

• Answer questions about a draft.

• Add details to strengthen a draft.

Informative/Explanatory Writing

Prompt: Give information about an animal you know about. Draw and describe the animal.

Draft: *My cat is brown. It has green eyes.*

TEACH Ask: What was the assignment? Reread the prompt if necessary. Then read the draft response. Do you think the writer knows a lot about the cat? Has the writer told everything he or she knows? After students reply, ask: What questions could we ask the writer to find out more about the cat? Guide students to mention questions about the cat's name, age, and behavior.

Say: Imagine asking the writer those questions. What other details could the writer add to the draft? After students respond, say: When you do an assignment, other people can ask you questions about it. Answering their questions will help you add details to make your work stronger. You can help others, too. Ask them questions to learn more details about their topic.

Lesson 51 | Add Details to Writing

- they can ask questions about other students' drawings and writing.

- answering questions will help them think of details to add to their own drafts.

PRACTICE 1: Opinion Writing Display and read aloud the prompt and first draft on Student Page S300.

Opinion Writing

Prompt: Draw and write an opinion about which art supplies are the best for coloring: colored pencils, crayons, paints, or markers.

Draft: Colored pencils are best for coloring.

Ask students if they think the draft response is interesting. Point out that the writer hasn't given a reason for his or her opinion. Ask: What questions could you ask the writer to make this answer better and more interesting? Guide students to ask questions such as these: *Why are colored pencils best? Why are colored pencils better than crayons, paints, and markers? Why do you like to use colored pencils?*

☑ **MONITOR PROGRESS** Display or distribute Student Page S300. Reread the prompt, and then read aloud the second draft.

Draft: I think markers are the best for coloring. I like them best.

Say: Imagine that this is your draft. So that you can add details, I will ask: What makes you like markers better than crayons? After students respond, ask how they would add that detail to their draft and drawing.

IF... students do not understand how details strengthen a draft,
THEN... reread the sample draft and ask: Would this make you want to try markers? What details would make you want to try markers?

Lesson 51 | Add Details to Writing

PRACTICE 2: Informative/Explanatory Writing Display Student Page S301.
Read the prompt and first draft aloud.

Informative/Explanatory Writing

Prompt: Draw and describe what the weather
is like where you live. Be sure to include
descriptions about how the weather is different
during different times of the year.

Draft: Where I live the weather is nice. We can wear shorts
and t-shirts all year. Sometimes it rains.

Ask: What do you think the writer means by "the weather is nice"? What
questions could you ask the writer to find out? **Help students form either-or
questions such as these:** *Is it warm or hot? Is it sunny or cloudy?*

☑ **MONITOR PROGRESS** Display or distribute Student Page S301. Reread the
prompt, and then read aloud the second draft.

Draft: Spring is rainy here. It snows sometimes in winter.

Ask: What details would make these descriptions stronger? What questions
can you ask to find out?

IF... students cannot think of details to add,
THEN... ask them to use their senses—sight, hearing, smell, taste, and
feeling—to think of questions to ask about the draft.

REMIND
STUDENTS
THAT. . .

• they can ask
  questions about
  other students'
  drawings and writing.

• answering questions
  will help them think
  of details to add to
  their own drafts.

Lesson 51 | Add Details to Writing

REMIND
STUDENTS
THAT. . .

- they can ask questions about other students' drawings and writing.
- answering questions will help them think of details to add to their own drafts.

PRACTICE 3: Narrative Writing Display and read aloud the prompt and first draft on Student Page S302.

Narrative Writing

Prompt: Draw and tell a story about an unexpected hero who saves the school. The hero can be any person, animal, or creature.

Draft: One day a storm came. I was at school. A dog saved everyone.

Ask: What else could this writer tell you that would make the story better? On the board, write *who, what, when, where, why,* and *how*. Point to each word and say: Think of a [who] question to ask about the story. Have students offer answers to the questions they pose. Finally, ask: How could you use those answers to make the story and drawing stronger?

☑ **INDEPENDENT PRACTICE** Display or distribute Student Page S302. Reread the prompt, and then read aloud the second draft.

Draft: It rained really hard. The school basement filled with water. A dog saved the school.

Ask: What details would make this story better? Pose questions to help students agree on three details to add, such as where the dog was, what the dog did, and how the problem was solved.

IF... students struggle to imagine an unexpected hero,
THEN... have students explain how an adult would solve the problem, and then have them change the adult in the story to an animal. Ask them to retell the story using the animal hero.

Lesson 51 | **Add Details to Writing**

Informative/Explanatory Writing

Prompt: Give information about an animal you know about. Draw and describe the animal.

Draft: My cat is brown. It has green eyes.

Opinion Writing

Prompt: Draw and write an opinion about which art supplies are the best for coloring: colored pencils, crayons, paints, or markers.

Draft: Colored pencils are best for coloring.

Draft: I think markers are the best for coloring. I like them best.

Informative/Explanatory Writing

Prompt: Draw and describe what the weather is like where you live. Be sure to include descriptions about how the weather is different during different times of the year.

Draft: Where I live the weather is nice. We can wear shorts and t-shirts all year. Sometimes it rains.

Draft: Spring is rainy here. It snows sometimes in winter.

Narrative Writing

Prompt: Draw and tell a story about an unexpected hero who saves the school. The hero can be any person, animal, or creature.

Draft: One day a storm came. I was at school. A dog saved

Draft: It rained really hard. The school basement filled with water. A dog saved the school.

ASSESSMENT
LESSONS 49–51

Writing

ASSESS MASTERY Use this Checkpoint to assess students' mastery of the Level A Writing standards listed here.

ADMINISTER THE TEST Administer the Checkpoint orally to each student.

1. Read aloud the prompt on the following page.
2. Read questions 1–3, reread the relevant text as necessary, and have students respond. Check their answers using the Scoring chart.

SCORING

SKILL/LESSON	STANDARD	ANSWER	SCORING
1. Ask and Answer Questions about a Prompt (Lesson 49)	**W.K.1** **W.K.2** **W.K.3**	Topic: a place in my home town or city that I know well Kind of Writing: informative Details: how it is used, the people who visit or work there	_____ / 3
2. Use a Topic to Recall and Gather Information (Lesson 50)	**W.K.8**	Responses will vary; students should complete all the sentence frames.	_____ / 4
3. Add Details to Writing (Lesson 51)	**W.K.5**	Responses will vary; students should complete all the questions.	_____ / 3

An overall score of 80% is typically considered mastery. Use your judgment and your individual students' needs as well to determine skill mastery.

IF... you determine that students have not demonstrated sufficient mastery of one or more skills,
THEN... review needed skills, going back to the lessons to reteach and scaffold as needed.

W.K.1 Use a combination of drawing, dictating, and writing to compose opinion pieces in which they tell a reader the topic or the name of the book they are writing about and state an opinion or preference about the topic or book (e.g., *My favorite book is ...*).

W.K.2 Use a combination of drawing, dictating, and writing to compose informative/ explanatory texts in which they name what they are writing about and supply some information about the topic.

W.K.3 Use a combination of drawing, dictating, and writing to narrate a single event or several loosely linked events, tell about the events in the order in which they occurred, and provide a reaction to what happened.

W.K.5 With guidance and support from adults, respond to questions and suggestions from peers and add details to strengthen writing as needed.

W.K.8 With guidance and support from adults, recall information from experiences or gather information from provided sources to answer a question.

ASSESSMENT **Writing**
LESSONS 49–51

> **Prompt:** Draw and describe a place in your home town or city that you know well. Be sure to include information about how the place is used and information about the people who visit or work there.

1. What should go in each column of this chart?

What is the topic?	What kind of writing is it?	What details do I include?

2. Complete the following sentence frames:

_____ is a place I know well. The place is used _____. The people there _____. My experiences there include _____.

3. Listen to the following draft:

The ice rink is a place I know well. It is open all year. People go there to skate.

What questions could help the writer add details to strengthen the draft?

Who _____?

What happens _____?

How does the ice rink _____?

Lesson 52 | Understand Nouns, Verbs, and Prepositions

INTRODUCE Say: When you talk, you use different kinds of words. **Point to a desk and ask:** What is this? **(a desk)** The word *desk* is a noun. A noun is one kind of word. It names a person, place, or thing. Today you will learn about nouns and other kinds of words called verbs and prepositions.

MODEL Display or distribute Student Page S305.

Henrik hid under the desk.

Drake built a boat.

The boy sees six concerts.

TEACH Read the first sentence aloud. **Say:** There are two nouns in this sentence. One of them is *desk*. The other noun is the name of a person. Can you tell me that noun? *(Henrik)*

Next, ask: What did Henrik do? **(He hid under the desk.)** The word *hid* is a verb. Verbs are also called action words. Verbs tell what happens. **Reread the sentence.** The word *under* is a preposition. Prepositions show how words are related. *Under* tells where Henrik is in relation to the desk.

Read aloud the second sentence. **Say:** This sentence has two nouns and a verb. What are the two nouns? *(Drake, boat)* What is the verb? *(built)*

Read aloud the third sentence. **Say:** The words *boy* and *concerts* are nouns. There is more than one concert, so the word has an s on the end: *concerts*. Adding s to a noun makes it mean "more than one." The word *sees* is a verb; it tells what is happening.

L.K.1 Demonstrate command of the conventions of standard English grammar and usage when writing or speaking.

L.K.1.b Use frequently occurring nouns and verbs.

L.K.1.c Form regular plural nouns orally by adding /s/ or /es/ (e.g., *dog, dogs; wish, wishes*).

L.K.1.e Use the most frequently occurring prepositions (e.g., *to, from, in, out, on, off, for, of, by, with*).

OBJECTIVES:

- Use common nouns, verbs, and prepositions.
- Form regular plural nouns.

Lesson 52 | Understand Nouns, Verbs, and Prepositions

L.K.1.b Use frequently occurring nouns and verbs.

See also **L.K.1**

REMIND STUDENTS THAT. . .

• nouns are words that name people, places, and things.

• verbs are action words; they tell what happens.

PRACTICE 1: Use Common Nouns and Verbs Explain that a sentence always has a noun and a verb. Say: *Rosa sits* is a sentence. The noun in this sentence is *Rosa.* It names the person doing the action. The verb is *sits.* It tells the action.

Clap your hands and say the sentence *The people clap.* Ask: What is the noun? (*people*) What is the verb, or the action word? (*clap*) Repeat with the sentences *Dogs bark, Planes fly,* and *Doors open.*

Extend the activity by having students tell you several two-word sentences of their own. Ask students to identify the noun and verb in each sentence. Offer the following sentence frames from Student Page S306, if needed.

Fish _____. _____ walk.

Cars _____. _____ run.

☑ **MONITOR PROGRESS** Display or distribute Student Page S306 and read each column aloud. Have students make sentences by combining a noun on the left and a verb on the right.

Children   sing.
Cats   play.
Birds   jump.

IF... students cannot distinguish nouns and verbs,
THEN... act out the three verbs above and have students imitate you.
Emphasize that verbs tell about actions or about what happens.

Lesson 52 | Understand Nouns, Verbs, and Prepositions

PRACTICE 2: Form Regular Plural Nouns Say: To make most nouns mean "more than one," add *s* or *es* to the end of the noun. For example, if I want to say that I have more than one hat, I add *s* to *hat*. I have many *hats*.

Display or distribute Student Page S307.

> Bill has one <u>shirt</u>. Jim has two <u>shirts</u>. shirts, *s*
> Leah has nine <u>boxes</u>. Kim has one <u>box</u>. boxes, *es*
> The family has one <u>car</u>. The police department has ten <u>cars</u>. cars, *s*
> Tuesday is one <u>day</u>. A week has seven <u>days</u>. days, *s*

Reread aloud the first pair of sentences. Have students clap when they hear a noun that means "more than one." (They should clap for *shirts*.) *Shirts* means more than one shirt. Notice that an *s* was added to the end of the noun *shirt* to make it *shirts*.

Repeat the activity with the remaining sentence pairs. Have students clap when they hear the noun that means "more than one." Have them say what the plural noun is and whether an *s* or *es* was added to the noun to make it plural.

☑ **MONITOR PROGRESS** Display or distribute Student Page S307. Read each word aloud and ask: How can you change the noun so it means "more than one" of this item?

desk desks	**bus** buses	**dish** dishes
window windows	**pen** pens	**wall** walls

IF... students cannot form these regular plural nouns,
THEN... place two desks together, draw two buses, and hold up two pens. In each case, have students tell you what they see.

L.K.1.c Form regular plural nouns orally by adding /s/ or /es/ (e.g., *dog, dogs; wish, wishes*).

***See also* L.K.1**

REMIND STUDENTS THAT. . .

- nouns are words that name people, places, and things.

- verbs are action words; they tell what happens.

- adding *s* or *es* to a noun makes it mean "more than one."

Lesson 52 | Understand Nouns, Verbs, and Prepositions

L.K.1.e Use the most frequently occurring prepositions (e.g., *to, from, in, out, on, off, for, of, by, with*).

See also **L.K.1**

REMIND STUDENTS THAT...

• nouns are words that name people, places, and things.

• prepositions show how nouns are related.

PRACTICE 3: Use Common Prepositions Remind students that prepositions show how nouns are related. Then ask students to explain what they do when they walk from the classroom to outside the school building. As they respond, point out any common prepositions that they use. For example, if they say "The children walk to the door," point out that *to* tells where the noun *children* goes in relation to the noun *door*.

Display or distribute Student Page S308 and read the words aloud.

in	into	under	over
on	to	before	after
with	off	from	for

Say: I am going to choose a preposition and then use it in a sentence. **Point to** *over*. I know *over* means "across something." I can make a sentence with *over*, such as *I jumped over the puddle.*

Define any unfamiliar words for students. Then encourage them to choose two prepositions and use those prepositions in short sentences. If needed, offer sentence frames, such as *I ate _____ the party* or *Casey is _____ Tennessee.*

☑ **INDEPENDENT PRACTICE** Display or distribute Student Page S308, and read aloud the following sentence frames for students. Then have them choose a preposition to complete each sentence. Answers may vary, but make sure students use appropriate prepositions.

Some children go _____ the playground.
The kitten jumped _____ the couch.
I eat breakfast _____ my family _____ I leave the house.

IF... students cannot choose an appropriate preposition,
THEN... review the list on Student Page S308 and have students practice making a sentence for each preposition.

Lesson 52   **Understand Nouns, Verbs, and Prepositions**

Henrik hid under the desk.

Drake built a boat.

The boy sees six concerts.

Lesson 52   Understand Nouns, Verbs, and Prepositions

Fish _____ walk.

Cars _____ run.

Children   sing.

Cats   play.

Birds   jump.

Lesson 52 | **Understand Nouns, Verbs, and Prepositions**

Bill has one shirt. Jim has two shirts.

Leah has nine boxes. Kim has one box.

The family has one car. The police department has ten cars.

Tuesday is one day. A week has seven days.

desk _____   bus _____   dish _____

window _____   pen _____   wall _____

Lesson 52   Understand Nouns, Verbs, and Prepositions

in	into	under	over
on	to	before	after
with	off	from	for

Some children go ———— the playground.

The kitten jumped ———— the couch.

I eat breakfast ———— my family ———— I leave the house.

Lesson 53 Capitalize and Punctuate Sentences

INTRODUCE Remind students that a noun is a word that names a person, place, or thing, and that a verb is an action word. Say: *A sentence usually has a noun (or pronoun) and a verb. So a sentence tells about an action and a person, place, or thing. A sentence always starts with a capital letter and ends with a punctuation mark.*

MODEL Display or distribute Student Page S309. You may wish to point out that the art includes Spanish punctuation marks (the inverted question mark and inverted exclamation point) that are placed in front of sentences in Spanish. In English, sentence punctuation appears only at the end of sentences. Read aloud each sentence for students.

L.K.1.d Understand and use question words (interrogatives) (e.g., *who, what, where, when, why, how*).

L.K.2.a Capitalize the first word in a sentence and the pronoun *I*.

L.K.2.b Recognize and name end punctuation.

See also **L.K.1, L.K.2**

OBJECTIVES:
- Recognize sentences.
- Begin a sentence with a capital letter.
- End a sentence with a punctuation mark.
- Capitalize the pronoun *I*.

Whales swim.   Birds fly.   Bugs crawl.
Dogs eat food.   Where is Kat?   Now I will eat.

TEACH Reread the top row of sentences for students. Each of these groups of words is a sentence. Each sentence has a noun: *Whales, Birds, Bugs.* Each sentence has a verb: *swim, fly, crawl.* These sentences are two words long. The first word starts with a capital letter. Write *W* and *B* on the board. There is a period at the end of each sentence. Make a dot on the board.

Next, read aloud the sentence *Dogs eat food.* This is also a sentence. It has more than one noun. Write *Dogs* and *food* on the board. This sentence has at least one noun and one verb (*eat*). Read aloud *Where is Kat?* This sentence is a question. It ends with a question mark, not a period. Write a question mark on the board. Read aloud and write *Now I will eat.* This sentence has a capital letter for the first word, *Now,* as well as a capital *I. I* is a word for a person. It is always capitalized. When you write about yourself, capitalize the word *I.*

Lesson 53 | Capitalize and Punctuate Sentences

L.K.2.a Capitalize the first word in a sentence and the pronoun *I*.

See also **L.K.2**

REMIND STUDENTS THAT…

• a sentence begins with a capital letter and ends with a punctuation mark.

• the word *I* is always capitalized.

PRACTICE 1: Capitalization in Sentences Remind students that a sentence tells about an action and a person, place, or thing. Then say: A sentence always begins with a capital letter. Some words inside a sentence can also have a capital letter. The word *I* is always capitalized.

Next, display or distribute Student Page S310.

> You have rice.
> I have noodles.
> What game can I play?

Read the first sentence aloud and ask: Which word has a capital letter? (*You*) Next, read the second sentence aloud and ask: Which word has a capital letter? (*I*) Say: In this sentence, *I* is the first word so it is capitalized, but remember that the word *I* is always capitalized. Finally, read the third sentence aloud and ask: How many words should be capitalized in this sentence? (two) Which word or words should be capitalized? (*What* and *I*)

☑ **MONITOR PROGRESS** Display Student Page S310 and read the sentences aloud.

> lions roar.
> yet i am not afraid.
> are you afraid?

Have students identify which letters should be capitals in the sentence and the question. (the *l* in *lions,* the *y* in *yet,* the word *I,* and the *a* in *are*)

IF… students do not correctly name the capital letters,
THEN… review the definition of a sentence and capitalization of the word *I*.

Lesson 53 | Capitalize and Punctuate Sentences

PRACTICE 2: Identify and Use End Punctuation Say: A sentence always ends with punctuation, or a mark that tells you the sentence has ended. These sentences show three different punctuation marks.

Display or distribute Student Page S311.

> Our power is out.
> This is an emergency!
> Who can we call to get it fixed?

Reread the first sentence and circle the period. One mark is the period. It tells you that you have come to the end of a thought. Read aloud the second sentence and circle the exclamation mark. Another type of mark is the exclamation mark. It tells you that the sentence says something loudly or with strong feeling. Finally, read aloud the third sentence and circle the question mark. The question mark tells you that the sentence asks a question. Explain that punctuation helps readers understand the meaning of a sentence.

Extend the activity by writing *Have a good day* on the board. Write a period and then say: This sentence is a simple thought. Erase the period and write an exclamation mark. Now this sentence shows excitement. Erase the exclamation point and write a question mark. Now this sentence is asking a question. Explain that by changing the mark, writers can make the same words either a statement, an exclamation, or a question. You may want to point out, though, that usually a question has several different words or a different order of words than a statement does. "Have a good day" as a question would probably be asked, "Will you have a good day?"

☑ **MONITOR PROGRESS** On the board, draw a question mark, an exclamation mark, and a period. Have students make up a sentence for each of the marks.

IF... students confuse the exclamation mark and the period,
THEN... explain that exclamation marks are only for sentences that have a lot of feeling or excitement, and have students give a new sample exclamation.

L.K.2.b Recognize and name end punctuation.

See also **L.K.2**

REMIND STUDENTS THAT...

- a sentence begins with a capital letter, and the word *I* is always capitalized.
- a sentence ends with punctuation.
- a question ends with a question mark.

Lesson 53 | Capitalize and Punctuate Sentences

L.K.1.d Understand and use question words (interrogatives) (e.g., *who, what, where, when, why, how*).

L.K.2.b Recognize and name end punctuation.

See also **L.K.1, L.K.2**

REMIND STUDENTS THAT…

- a sentence begins with a capital letter, and the word *I* is always capitalized.

- a sentence ends with a punctuation mark.

- a period shows the end of a thought, an exclamation point shows loudness or a strong feeling, and a question mark shows that the writer is asking a question.

PRACTICE 3: Form and Punctuate Questions Say: People ask questions all the time, such as *Which book is the best?* or *May I have some water, please?* You know how to ask questions, too. Questions begin with a capital letter and end with a question mark.

Display Student Page S312 and read aloud the first two sentences.

Who wants a cheese sandwich?
Where can I buy some cheese?
I wish I knew why we are out of bread.

 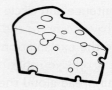

Have students identify the capital letters in each question. Ask: What punctuation mark always comes at the end of a question? (question mark) Read aloud the third sentence. How can you turn this sentence into a question? Guide students to form the question. Say: If I remove the first four words and move the word *are*, then I create the question *Why are we out of bread?*

Extend the activity by helping students form questions using statements such as *I want to know what your name is* or *I want to know if you have any brothers or sisters.*

☑ **INDEPENDENT PRACTICE** Display Student Page S312. Read each line aloud.

when will we get home
i'd like to know which sport you want to play

Ask: Which letters should be capitalized? What mark should be at the end of each line? How could you change the second line into a question?

IF… students cannot form a question from a statement,
THEN… explain that to turn a statement into a question, some words are moved and removed. Suggest that students listen for a word that begins with the /w/ sound and use it to begin the question.

Lesson 53 **Capitalize and Punctuate Sentences**

Whales swim.

Birds fly.

Bugs crawl.

Dogs eat food.

Where is Kat?

Now I will eat.

You have rice.

I have noodles.

What game can I play?

lions roar.

yet i am not afraid.

are you afraid?

Lesson 53   **Capitalize and Punctuate Sentences**

Our power is out.

This is an emergency!

Who can we call to get it fixed?

Who wants a cheese sandwich?

Where can I buy some cheese?

I wish I knew why we are out of bread.

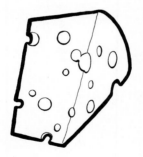

when will we get home

i'd like to know which sport you want to play

Lesson 54 Sort Words into Categories

INTRODUCE Say: You know that people can be related yet different. The same is true for words. Some words fit into the same groups. Some are opposites. That means that they are the complete other thing. They are as different from each other as they can possibly be. Some words are similar yet also different in ways you can recognize.

MODEL Display or distribute Student Page S313.

Colors: red, orange, yellow, green, blue
Opposites: cold/hot, strong/weak, win/lose, arrive/leave

Similar yet different: walk, stomp, march, hike, stride

TEACH Read aloud the first category, *Colors*. Say: You can put some words together in groups. For example, these words all stand for colors.

Say: Other words are opposites. **Point to the illustrations.** For example, *cold* and *hot* are opposites. **Read aloud the second category, *Opposites*.**

Next, say: Some words describe similar actions that are a bit different. **Read aloud the third category, *Similar yet different*.** For example, *walk* and *hike* are two words about using one's legs, but walking and hiking are different in some ways.

Explain that students can sort words into groups. Say: If I say *cereal, salad, jacket,* and *socks,* you would put *cereal* and *salad* in a group called "food." You would put *jacket* and *socks* in a group called "clothes." You can recognize opposites. If I say *asleep, juggling,* and *awake,* you would probably say that *awake* and *asleep* are opposites. You can also describe the differences between similar words. If I say *sleep, snooze,* and *nap,* you can tell me how the words are alike and different.

L.K.5.a Sort common objects into categories (e.g., shapes, foods) to gain a sense of the concepts the categories represent.

L.K.5.b Demonstrate understanding of frequently occurring verbs and adjectives by relating them to their opposites (antonyms).

L.K.5.d Distinguish shades of meaning among verbs describing the same general action (e.g., *walk, march, strut, prance*) by acting out the meanings.

See also **L.K.5**

OBJECTIVES:

• Recognize related words.

• Recognize antonyms.

• Understand shades of meaning among verbs.

Lesson 54 | Sort Words into Categories

L.K.5.a Sort common objects into categories (e.g., shapes, foods) to gain a sense of the concepts the categories represent.

See also **L.K.5**

REMIND STUDENTS THAT...

- they can recognize related words.
- they can sort words into groups.

PRACTICE 1: Sort Words into Categories Say: You can put words with related meanings into groups. This is called sorting. Groups can be anything—words about temperatures, foods, ways to travel from place to place, shapes, colors, times, feelings, and more. What are some groups you can think of? After students respond, choose one of the groups they suggested and ask: What are some words you can put into this group?

Then display or distribute Student Page S314. Point to and read the three headings. Ask students to suggest words, such as those that appear below, to go under each heading.

Pets	**Games**	**Family**
dog	tag	uncle
fish	hide and seek	aunt
lizard	video games	grandparent
hamster	board games	sister

☑ **MONITOR PROGRESS** Display or distribute Student Page S314. Read aloud the following words. Have students tell you the group to which each word belongs: *pets, family,* or *games.*

gerbil	**cousin**	**grandmother**
pets	family	family
soccer	**mother**	**turtle**
games	family	pets
cat	**baseball**	**brother**
pets	games	family

IF... students struggle to place related words into categories,
THEN... discuss the meaning of each category with students, read aloud a word that goes in each, and have students try sorting again.

Lesson 54 | Sort Words into Categories

PRACTICE 2: Identify Opposites Review the concept of verbs. Verbs are action words. They tell about what happens. Some actions are opposites of each other. That is, they are as different from each other as they can possibly be. For example, *fall asleep* and *wake up* are opposites. Then briefly introduce the concept of adjectives, or words that describe. Words can describe things that are the same and things that are opposites. For example, you can describe a person as *sleepy* or *wide awake*. Those are opposites.

Then display or distribute Student Page S315.

neat	messy	tiny	huge
true	false	rise	fall
close	open	lose	find

Read aloud the six words and define unfamiliar words as needed. Then reread the word *neat* and ask: What word has the opposite meaning from *neat*? Elicit that *messy* would be a word with the opposite meaning, and write *messy* beside *neat*. You may want to point out that some words have more than one opposite if the opposites are very close in meaning. For example, *sloppy* is also the opposite of *neat*. Continue with the other words, guiding students to offer the word that completes each pair of opposites.

Extend the activity by listing pairs of words, such as *hot/cold, clean/neat, night/day,* and *small/tiny*. Define unfamiliar words. Then have students tell you which pairs are opposites.

☑ **MONITOR PROGRESS** Display or distribute Student Page S315. Read aloud the following sets of words, and then have students identify the opposites in each set.

safe, loose, unsafe	safe, unsafe
top, outside, bottom	top, bottom
take, give, miss	take, give

IF... students cannot identify the opposites,
THEN... work through the meanings of one set of words and help students rule out the unrelated word; repeat as necessary.

L.K.5.b Demonstrate understanding of frequently occurring verbs and adjectives by relating them to their opposites (antonyms).

See also **L.K.5**

REMIND STUDENTS THAT...

- they can recognize related words.
- they can sort words into groups.

Lesson 54 | Sort Words into Categories

L.K.5.d Distinguish shades of meaning among verbs describing the same general action (e.g., *walk, march, strut, prance*) by acting out the meanings.

See also **L.K.5**

REMIND STUDENTS THAT...

• they can recognize related words.

• they can sort words into groups.

• some words have opposite meanings.

PRACTICE 3: Identify Shades of Meaning in Verbs Write *Hello* on the board and read the word aloud. Have students say the word with you in a whisper, then in a normal speaking voice, and then in a shout. Say: We just whispered, talked, and shouted. These words all refer to ways of speaking, but the meanings of the words are different. You can act out the different meanings.

Display or distribute Student Page S316.

touch	press	push
stare	look	peek
hold	hug	squeeze

Explain that you will read words about things a person can do. Read aloud each set of three words in a row and have students act out each word in the set. Help students with meanings as necessary. After each set, say: Now you know the differences among these words. They are close in meaning but not the same.

☑ **INDEPENDENT PRACTICE** Display or distribute Student Page S316. Read aloud each set of three words in a row, and then have students act out the words in each set.

cry	whimper	sob
giggle	chuckle	laugh

IF... students cannot identify shades of meaning in the verbs,
THEN... act out one set of words with students, and then have them act out the other set.

Lesson 54   **Sort Words into Categories**

Colors: red, orange, yellow, green, blue

Opposites: cold/hot, strong/weak, win/lose, arrive/leave

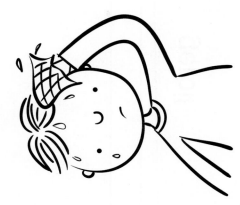

Similar yet different: walk, stomp, march, hike, stride

Pets	Games	Family

gerbil   cousin   grandmother

soccer   mother   turtle

cat   baseball   brother

Lesson 54   **Sort Words into Categories**

neat _____   tiny _____

true _____   rise _____

close _____   lose _____

safe, loose, unsafe

top, outside, bottom

take, give, miss

Lesson 54 | **Sort Words into Categories**

touch	press	push
stare	look	peek
hold	hug	squeeze

cry	whimper	sob
giggle	chuckle	laugh

ASSESSMENT Language
LESSONS 52–54

ASSESS MASTERY Use this Checkpoint to assess students' mastery of the Level A Language standards listed here.

ADMINISTER THE TEST Administer the Checkpoint orally to each student.

1. Read aloud the passage on the following page.
2. Read questions 1–6, reread the relevant text as necessary, and have students respond. Check their answers using the Scoring chart.

SCORING

SKILL/LESSON	STANDARD	ANSWER	SCORING
1. Understand Nouns, Verbs, and Prepositions (Lesson 52)	**L.K.1**	Nouns: dog, cat Verb: ran Preposition: after	_____ / 4
2. Capitalize and Punctuate Sentences (Lesson 53)	**L.K.2**	Why did it do that?	_____ / 1
3. Capitalize and Punctuate Sentences (Lesson 53)	**L.K.2**	the first letter	_____ / 1
4. Sort Words into Categories (Lesson 54)	**L.K.5**	*ran, chasing, run*	_____ / 3
5. Sort Words into Categories (Lesson 54)	**L.K.5**	*happy*	_____ / 1
6. Sort Words into Categories (Lesson 54)	**L.K.5**	A snoozing dog is asleep; a sleepy dog wants to be asleep.	_____ / 2

An overall score of 80% is typically considered mastery. Use your judgment and your individual students' needs as well to determine skill mastery.

IF… you determine that students have not demonstrated sufficient mastery of one or more skills,
THEN… review needed skills, going back to the lessons to reteach and scaffold as needed.

L.K.1 Demonstrate command of the conventions of standard English grammar and usage when writing or speaking.

L.K.2 Demonstrate command of the conventions of standard English capitalization, punctuation, and spelling when writing.

L.K.5 With guidance and support from adults, explore word relationships and nuances in word meanings.

See also **L.K.1.b, L.K.1.c, L.K.1.d, L.K.1.e, L.K.2.a, L.K.2.b, L.K.5.a, L.K.5.b, L.K.5.d**

ASSESSMENT
LESSONS 52–54

Language

A Good Game
by Becky Garcia

The dog ran after the cat. Why did it do that? The happy cat had scratched the snoozing dog's nose. The sleepy dog was mad! However, chasing was a good game. The animals had a fun run.

1. In the first sentence, what are the nouns? What is the verb? What is the preposition?

2. Which sentence in the story ends with a question mark?

3. Which letter is capitalized in each sentence?

4. Which words in the story are about moving fast?

5. Which word is the opposite of *mad: happy, sleepy,* or *fun*?

6. What is the difference between a snoozing dog and a sleepy dog?